GenderQueer

Voices From Beyond the Sexual Binary

Edited by Joan Nestle, Clare Howell, and Riki Wilchins

alyson books
los angeles | new york

MANUFACTURED IN THE UNITED STATES OF AMERICA.

THIS TRADE PAPERBACK ORIGINAL IS PUBLISHED BY ALYSON BOOKS,
P.O.. BOX 4371, LOS ANGELES, CALIFORNIA 90078-4371.
DISTRIBUTION IN THE UNITED KINGDOM BY TURNAROUND PUBLISHER SERVICES LTD.,
UNIT 3, OLYMPIA TRADING ESTATE, COBURG ROAD, WOOD GREEN,
LONDON N22 6TZ ENGLAND.

FIRST EDITION: AUGUST 2002

05 06 07 08 09 **a** 10 9 8 7 6 5 4 3

ISBN 1-55583-730-1
ISBN-13 978-1-55583-730-3

CREDITS

CHERYL CHASE'S "AFFRONTING REASON" ORIGINALLY APPEARED IN *LOOKING QUEER,* EDITED BY
 DAWN ATKINS (HARRINGTON PARK PRESS, 1998). REPRINTED BY PERMISSION OF THE HAWORTH
 PRESS, INC.
C. JACOB HALE'S "WHOSE BODY IS IT ANYWAY?" ORIGINALLY APPEARED IN *THE MONARCH READER,*
 45 (1997).
COVER DESIGN BY MATT SAMS.
COVER PHOTOGRAPHY BY PHOTODISC.

Contents

Epilogue

Introductions: Three Voices

Genders on My Mind

Joan Nestle

One of the stories I performed in my 12-year-old fantasies when I lived in the Bayside section of Queens, N.Y., in 1952 was the story of Pat Ward, the call-girl mistress of the oleomargarine king, Mickey Jelke. He was a round, untidy heir to a fortune, and she was the always demure-looking, Peter Pan collar–wearing "woman of sin" who had seduced him. This was the social picture that was presented on the covers of the tabloids of the time. Ward was undergoing severe questioning in the courtroom, and the papers were filled with her image; the photographers delighted in showing the face and form of a prostitute who looked like someone's sister. On my own after school, it was my job to clean the three-room apartment I shared with my working mother. I see it all so clearly, looking back after almost 50 years. To give myself company as I tucked the sheets in and swept the floors, I became Pat Ward and her accusers, but the part I liked playing the most was the male lawyer who defended her.

The sensationalized story of Pat Ward captured my attention and my heart because caught up in the black-and-white images of the *New York Post* was the mix of gender, sex, rebellion, and exile that delineated the 1950s for me, that time so often touted as the golden age of conformity. Because I was on my own so much and because my mother neglected to school me in gender expectations, I was more an untidy street ruffian than a 12-year-old girl. Others tried to intercede and teach me gender

3

manners. Once my fourth-grade teacher, Mr. Olsen, stopped me in the school yard and bent down to tuck my blouse inside my skirt, "You have to dress more ladylike," he said. Over and over again, surrogate parents tried to normalize my appearance, but I saw myself as an adventurer, not a little girl. Gender expectations seemed to me to be formal middle-class rituals that did not fit into the realities of my life, much like the school's expectation that we would all go to the dentist every year.

As I entered my teens, my mother did have some warning words for me: "If you do not wear a girdle, your ass will be like the side of a barn" or "Why don't you put on some lipstick? You look like a ghost." When these decrees came from my mother, they felt more about sex than gender. I soon became girlhood lovers with Roz, the kosher butcher's daughter. Never having known my father, I loved to please the large, round man who came home to his wife and daughter in his blood-stained apron. To Moishe, I was Hershey (his play on Nestle), the tomboy friend of his very feminine daughter. The gender role he defined for me in his family was made very clear one afternoon in the 1950s when he took Roz and me to a YMHA swimming pool. To encourage her to learn to swim, he suddenly picked me up and threw me in the pool. As I floundered around, I could hear his voice above the churning water: "See, Hershey is not afraid." I felt very proud, even though I knew I was being used to seduce his little girl into less lethargic behavior. Gender, even in the 1950s, with its seemingly ironclad prescriptions, had its underbelly, its slippages where small transgressions could become lifelong remembrances of other possibilities. More than anything, I wanted Max's appreciation, and if I had to be the "boy" in my adopted family, I could do that easily. The economic and familial realities of my life made me a changeling in many ways, and I suspect that this is true for many others. When we talk about the magnetic pull of gender—its huge tidal wave of expectations—we should also keep in mind that we have, as well, a lifelong reservoir of small transgressions.

One thing I know for sure: I will never give up drag even at 50, if for no other reason than it upsets the neighbors…the future of the homosexual lies in some kind of unity. We don't seem able to band together. We could start by stopping to hate the types we are not comfortable with.
—from an interview with "Miss Destiny" in One: The Homosexual Viewpoint, September 1964

One night in 1955, I was riding home on a Bayside bus after a day of shopping with Roz. I was wearing a gray blazer and gray slacks; I had my usual short hair. Sitting in an aisle seat, I half-watched the passengers climbing on as the bus stopped at the subway station to pick up returning workers from Manhattan. I did not realize until she had walked by me that my mother was one of those tired people. I turned to her and shouted, "Hey, Mom, it's me." My mother turned and then went as gray as my blazer before she disappeared in the onrush of the other boarding passengers. When we were reunited at our stop, she pulled me to a halt as soon as the bus pulled away and said, "You must never dress like that again in public. Do you hear me? Never again!" There was terror in her voice and disgust on her face. At that moment my mother had recognized that I was, in the parlance of the 1950s, a freak, and "freak" then became my self-image, a word synonymous with gender nonconformity. The discussions we now have of gender play and drama, of deconstruction and reconstruction, are for me always anchored in that word. Because at 61, I am even more aware of my legacies, one of the reasons I wanted to be part of this book lies in that look my mother gave me on a darkened street in Queens so many years ago, when I had just thought I was out adventuring with my girlfriend, yet I had unwittingly fallen off the map for what was considered gender-human in the 1950s.

I am a transsexual—a person who has changed her physical sex (female to male). I have become increasingly disturbed by the wall being erected between transsexuals and lesbians...
—Karl Ericsen, *The Ladder*, April-May, 1970

I reflect several things as one of the editors of this collection: the 1950s, the pre-Stonewall femme tradition, the archivist, the lesbian feminist, the sex radical. I know that for at least 40 years, the second wave of the feminist movement has discussed, researched, debated, and acted on the gender oppression of women. The whole field of women's studies, a pioneering movement of scholars and activists, of the academy and of communities, was constructed around understanding and contesting the regional and international dimensions of the social, cultural, and economic predicaments of women. I owe the feminist movement my life as a woman, which means, in some ways, my life as a femme. By the '60s, I knew how to live as a freak, but I did not know how to live as a woman. Even though at times I have been labeled a traitor to the cause of feminism, I have always known that the deeper exploration of my femme passion was made possible by the gender dignity I was finding in the new world of lesbian feminism.

But there were tensions from the beginning. Whether it was Janice Raymond railing on about the transsexual conspiracy in her book *The Transsexual Empire* (1979), or the tight strictures about who could come to a feminist conference or be given a meeting place or be welcomed at a women's festival, it became clear that some gender and sexual issues were far from being clearly understood. Too often we talked and made judgments about the offending persons in their absence—for example, conferences about prostitution without a sex worker present. As Gayle Rubin has pointed out, we often thought we were speaking about sex and gender when we were only speaking about gender, and a certain restricted concept of gender at that. ("Thinking Sex: Notes for a Radical Theory of the Politics of Sexuality," in *Pleasure and Danger: Exploring Female Sexuality*, ed. Carole Vance, 1984.)

These tensions burst out in the "sex wars" of the early 1980s when one of the targets of the women's movement's antipornography forces became other feminists, the new "freaks"—primarily S/M and femme/butch lesbians, passing women, sex workers, and, at times, sexually hungry straight women.

In the years that followed, there was an explosion of public lesbian sexual discussion. As part of this outpouring of voices and ideas about sexuality, in 1992—it is hard to believe that this is almost 10 years ago— I edited *The Persistent Desire: A Femme-Butch Reader,* a collection of writings by fem and butch women, both past and present, that has a direct relationship to this present collection. In my earlier writings, one of the points I had been trying to make was that femme and butch allowed for a two-gendered sexual discussion within the single category of lesbian.

In *Persistent Desire,* I wanted to document as many voices from as many different cultural settings as I could—the excitement, price, and complexity of femme/butch desire. It was, I thought, my final contribution to the long, contentious debate over what kinds of desires were permissible in the lesbian-feminist world. As I was doing outreach for the collection in the year before its publication, I was sent in the mail an anonymous piece titled "Letter to a Fifties Femme from a Stone Butch," a piece that gave me all I wanted: the '50s historical setting, the grandeur of fem-butch courage in the face of so much state and social brutality, a depiction of the kind of love and support both butches and femmes needed to give each other to survive the world around them. I despaired about finding the author until one afternoon when I was speaking about femme/butch on a panel at the Gay Community Center in New York, Leslie Feinberg rose from the audience and read that letter, her letter, to the audience. The rest is history, genderqueer history.

Now is the time for more honesties. In *Persistent Desire*, I thought I was securing a historical position for the community that had given me so much, the fem-butch world of the 1950s and '60s. However, I was not as insightful as one of the contributors, Gayle Rubin, who, in the final section of the book, extended the boundaries to include all the expressions of lesbian masculinities: "Drag, cross-dressing, passing, transvestism, and transsexualism are all common in lesbian populations, particularly those not attempting to meet constricted standards of political virtue." (*Of Catamites and Kings: Reflections on Butch, Gender and Boundaries*, p. 468)

As the '90s went by, word kept getting back to me that many of the butch contributors to *Persistent Desire* were "transitioning"—in one of the many stages in the continuum of changing their gender from woman to man. These gender complexities all came home to me in 1998 when I was doing a mini book tour for my new book, *A Fragile Union* (Cleis Press), and reading in the women's bookstore in Oakland, Calif. For the first time, a large group of genderqueer men in different stages of transitioning were part of my audience. After the reading, one of the men stood up and thanked me profusely for "giving him permission" for his genderqueer journey. People applauded, and I felt like a fraud. I knew that in my first work, *A Restricted Country* (Firebrand Books, 1987), I had not extended my thinking about gender far enough. Indeed, I used one of the essays in *A Fragile Union* to critique an earlier essay of mine, "Esther's Story," for its assertion that Esther, while a passing woman, did not see herself as a man. As Rubin had so rightly said, in my defense of one besieged community, I had oversimplified another.

Later in the night, another incident occurred that has haunted me. A long line of readers filed past me, asking me to sign their books or just wanting to speak. Toward the end of the night, a very handsome butch woman appeared in front of me with *A Fragile Union* opened to the essay "My Fem Odyssey," in which I discuss my sense of sexual autonomy as a femme woman. In that small, quiet world that often is created between the author and the reader on a busy bookstore night, everything else seemed to fall away. Her first words to me were, "I feel I have failed you." I was stunned by her sadness. Pointing to my essay that included my declaration of femme independence and then to the transitioning people around her, she said, "I feel I am not good enough, that being butch is not good enough." My head and heart were spinning after that night.

Perhaps they still are. When Riki, whom I have known for more than 15 years, and Clare, whom I met when this project started about three years ago, asked if I would be part of *GenderQueer*, I protested that I was not a suitable third voice, since I was born a woman and remain a biological and gender-identified woman. In addition, as a femme, I have not been overly pleased with the proliferation and center-staging of lesbian masculinities, and I still think we are missing a huge chunk of the gender-sex-desire conversation. After much back and forth, we worked out that perhaps I could be a bridge between communities, communities that historically have been at odds with each other and still are, as evidenced in the continuing exclusion of genderqueer women and men from the grounds of the Michigan Womyn's Music Festival.

Every hour every day we encounter
something new
Electric this, Atomic that—a modern point
of view.
Now anything can happen and we shouldn't
think it strange,
If oysters smoke cigars
Or lobsters drive imported cars,
For we live in a time of change...
When the First Lady is a he—and the
President is me
It's a switch—it's a twist—it's a change.
Still these things would shock most people
But I really don't know why,
For the world is full of changes—who
knows this more
than I!

—from the stage act of Christine Jorgensen, 1954, *Christine Jorgensen: A Personal Autobiography*, with introduction by Susan Stryker, Cleis Books, 2000, original, 1967

What I have come to understand is that there are pluralistic gender histories, pluralistic challenges to the male/female, woman/man, lesbian, butch/femme constructions and identities as I had come to know them. I no longer strain to fit all the genderqueer ways of self under one transformative banner. Actually, the multiplicity of biological and constructed selves now is closer to the world I inhabited in the bars of the 1950s, when intersexed and passing people were part of the restricted and policed territory that were our public homes.

Writers like Louis Sullivan, Kate Bornstein, Judith Halberstam, Jay Prosser, Sandy Stone, Riki Wilchins, to name just a few, have ensured that the world of gender discussion will never be the same, not for feminists, not for anyone. They and so many others in living their lives are creating new gender histories: histories that will include the lives of men who spent many years living as lesbian feminists; women who started their biological lives as men and now live as lesbians; histories that will include the voices of people who live as both sexes when the medical world allows them; and histories of mourning for the gendered selves not allowed to survive. Every few years of my life, I think, *Now we should really be talking about...* and I fill in one of the hot issues of the early-'70s consciousness-raising groups like "class" or "mothers." This is such a time—now we can have much fuller, varied, challenging, and representative discussions about gender than we ever had before. Now we have the genderqueer voices in first person. Think of the richness of the conversation 50 years from now, if we survive the present world.

All of us have a choice: We can stand on old ground, protecting 40-year-old borders, or we can throw open the gates and see what lies ahead in new thinking, new organizing, new narratives, new intersections between political, cultural, economic, and gender-sex struggles. More than ever we have the tools for a deeper critique of gender both as a means of social control and as a promise of greater global freedom of gender and sexual expression.

Wherever they go, Swazi girls now will be expected to wear a bundle of bright traditional tassels signifying celibacy. In addition, long pants will be forbidden for the young girls. "You should look like a girl, not a boy," said a government official.
—"To Fight AIDS, Swaziland's King Orders Girls to Avoid Sex for Five Years," *The New York Times,* September 28, 2001

For me, gender is both a real, material reality embedded in the histories of all of us and an imagined place where my body can shape-change into hardness, into boyness, into the sheep drover Jim who makes love to his barmaid girlfriend Peg. This imagined place of gender freedom where desire and sexuality find whatever form they need has become even more important to me both as I age and as the world careens toward fundamentalist madness. War is a time of heightened masculinity when women disappear off the public stage except as victims or supporters of their men. War in some terrible way is the final victory of gender hierarchies. Just as they did in the 1950s, under the government-orchestrated fear of subversives, differences—imagined and lived—will now become even more suspect, more dangerous and endangered.

In a recent article on fertility ethics, a reporter for *The New York Times* wrote, "It is simple to see if the embryo is male, with an X and a Y chromosome, or a female, with two X chromosomes" (October 1, 2001). I think of the voices in this collection, of the long, complex journeys in thought, feeling, and body that are here, and shake my head—never simple, never simple, not in what societies have planned for their "women" and "men" and not in what we are asking, wanting for ourselves.

Note: I want to thank my lover, Dianne Otto, for her careful reading of this essay and for being the Peg of my life.

A Continuous Nonverbal Communication
Riki Wilchins

As I write this, it's been barely a month since the World Trade Center attack. In the interim, we've been flooded with video images from around the United States and around the world. Of all of them, perhaps none will stay with me longer than images of Afghan women, who inevitably appear on television as dark, human cocoons silently gliding across the screen.

It was telling that among the first acts of the new fundamentalist regime were demands that women cover themselves from head to toe and men wear full beards and masculine attire, and a reunderscoring of the illegality of homosexuality—all on threat of punishment or death. This instinct to control bodies, genders, and desires, may be as close as we have to a universal constant. It is common to cultures rich and poor, left-wing and right-wing, Eastern and Western.

And here I mean *gender* in its widest sense—including sexual orientation, because I take it as self-evident that the mainspring of homophobia is gender: the notion that gay men are insufficiently masculine or lesbian women somehow inadequately feminine. And I include sex, because I take it as obvious that what animates sexism and misogyny is gender, and our astonishing fear and loathing around issues of vulnerability or femininity.

In a society where femininity is feared and loathed, all women are genderqueer. In a culture where masculinity is defined by having sex with women and femininity by having sex with men, all gay people are genderqueer.

Fundamentalist regimes often begin with gender, because of all the things we have to say to each other, first and foremost among them is our gender. It's the reason we dress as we do every morning, style our hair specific ways, stand and walk and gesture and even inflect our voices the way we do. Gender is what attracts us to other people and how we hope to make ourselves attractive to them. In fact, throughout our entire waking lives we are carrying on a continuous nonverbal dialogue with the world, saying, "This is who I am, this is how I feel about myself, this is how I want *you* to see *me*."

Unfortunately, when we do so, many of us lose our childhoods, our jobs, and even our lives, because in this continuous nonverbal conversation, the world is talking back to us too, saying, "No, no—this is how we see you, this is how you should feel about it, this is who *you* can *be*."

"The body," Simone de Beauvoir told us, "is a situation." She might have said a *political* situation, one that enmeshes us from infancy in a web of expectations, rules, and demands concerning how we look, act, or dress, our sex and physical characteristics, what bodies we must desire and how we should desire them.

As we age, the web tightens. The gender transgressions of infancy are no longer as amusing or accepted in childhood; childhood's are increasingly unwelcome by puberty; and the gender experimentation of puberty must be abandoned by early adulthood, when all young men and women are expected to be…men and women.

And only men and women. This ostensibly "natural" progression, inexorably producing men from males and women from females, consumes an extraordinary investment of social resources. Others devote time and energy regulating our gender, and we spend an even greater amount learning, rehearsing, exploring, and perfecting our gender. By adulthood, our role is inhabited so completely that it feels inevitable. And should the experimentation of childhood inadvertently re-emerge, we find it awkward, embarrassing, and even threatening.

Threatening, but not departed. For although it looks like something we *are*, gender is always a *doing* rather than a being. In this sense, *all gender is drag*. And as with any drag, there's always the chance that we'll do something wrong, fall off the stage, do something unscripted outside the lines. So even a "real man"—all muscles, Clint Eastwood clenched teeth, and Sly Stallone dominance—might one day find himself crying during a movie, wondering what it feels like to wear a revealing dress, or feeling strange physical empathies with his pregnant wife.

In these moments of awkward embarrassment are also something like a kind of freedom, the hint of another kind of person we might have been if only we didn't inhabit a world where every one of 6 billion human beings must fit themselves into one of only two genders.

This is a secret that the youth of today already know. As you'll read in these narratives, gender is the new frontier: the place to rebel, to create new individuality and uniqueness, to defy old, tired, outdated social norms and, yes, occasionally drive their parents and sundry other authority figures crazy. More power to them. As one said to trans activist Dana Rivers, "I was too young for women's rights and gay rights. Gender is the civil rights movement of my time." Who could not be intrigued and stirred by such sentiments?

Yet the question still lingers: Why has it taken so long for gender's emergence as a civil rights issue?

Bang the Symbols Slowly

In the introduction to *Sexual Politics*, one of feminism's earliest manifestos, Kate Millett complained that analyzing patriarchy was so difficult because there was no alternative system to which it might be compared. Her comment could well apply to trying to analyze the gender system. The problem is not that we don't know the gender system well enough but that we know it all too well and can't envision any alternative. Thus, trying to understand gender sometimes feels like trying to take in the Empire State Building while standing only three inches away: It's at once so big, so overwhelming, and so close that we can't see it all at once or conceptualize it clearly.

Gender is like a lens through which we've not yet learned to see. Or, more accurately, like glasses worn from childhood, it's like a lens through which we've always seen and can't remember how the world looked before. And this lens is strictly bifocal. It strangely shows us only black and white in a Technicolor world so that, as this book's narratives clearly illustrate, there may certainly be more than two genders, but two genders is all we've named, all we know, and all we'll see. And as basic as gender is personhood; changing that will take a more radical political upheaval than we've yet seen from any recent human rights movement.

Initiating such political action is made more challenging by the fact that gender is not only a formal system like marriage, backed by readily accessible public policy, law, and institutions. Nor is gender only a set of extralegal social practices such as are contained in the sexist treatment of women or the racist codes of Jim Crow.

While it is certainly both of these, gender is primarily *a system of symbols and meanings—and the rules, privileges, and punishments pertaining to their use—for power and sexuality:* masculinity and femininity, strength and vulnerability, action and passivity, dominance and weakness. It's because gender is not just a system of laws and practices but also a way of thinking and seeing that it has taken so long to come to the fore as a political issue. Yet unlike the struggles against homophobia, racism, and sexism, the struggle against genderism will not only be about gaining rights for an oppressed class of men and women. It will be about gaining equality for all men and women. And paradoxically it will be about the rights of some of us to not be men or women.

No Matter Where You Go, There You Are

As a system of meanings in which we participate each day, gender also feels exquisitely personal. So when someone gender-bashes or gender-baits us, we think, *It's my own fault. If only I were more butch, if only I were more femme, if only I were taller, shorter, slimmer, heavier, had smaller breasts or larger muscles...if only I'd dressed or acted or felt differently, this never would have happened to me.* We blame ourselves, and so we try to change ourselves.

But feminism was right: The personal is political, and nowhere more so than with gender. The feelings of shame, humiliation, and fear are not the result of personal failings. Nor are they the inadvertent side effects of a benign system of gender norms. Such feelings are the gender system itself at work: enjoining us in policing ourselves, reminding us of our place, shaming us into submission, and making our gender appear natural, seamless, and voluntary.

Changing ourselves—becoming smaller, curvier, butcher, or thinner—will not change anything, because the gender system cannot be challenged or contested through individual effort. Genderism is an organizational and systemic oppression; it can be challenged only through an organized and systemic response.

If you come away from these writings with only one realization, I hope it will be that whatever feelings of shame or dread you've experienced around your own gender are not just private problems but political issues. And they are not yours alone but something all of us have shared.

A movement for gender equality will not only have to work the halls of justice and the halls of Congress but also engage with new and fuzzier sorts of political questions: How do we come to know our selves, how do we come to understand our bodies, and how have we come to be the "us" that we are? It will need to begin thinking out loud about the political tools to recover that small inner voice that once said, "This is who I am, this is how I see myself, this is how I want you to see me."

A tall task for any new movement.

You're Trapped in Whose Body?

Another facet of the delay in gender's political emergence is that while cultural sensitivity to gender has exploded in recent years, it has also been strangely limited and stunted. All that explosive force has been channeled into one area: transgenderism. So whenever gender is mentioned, it is inevitably written down—and too often written off—as only transgender, something only affecting a small, if embattled, minority.

Oh, to be sure, we must all bow before the gods of inclusion. We must ensure no "LGB" issues forth without its trailing "T." But you and I, *we* don't have problems with our gender. All the men we know are tops, and all the women high-heeled femmes. While it's hard not to cheer the emergence of transgender as an important queer cause, confining the dialogue on gender to one identity has had the curious side effect of relieving the rest of society—gay and straight—from examining its own history of transcending gender norms.

But genderqueerness will not stay put in any one community. It's an issue that transcends boundaries and identities, if only because the boundaries and identities at issue are themselves gender-based. Rethinking gender—a task of this book—will mean rethinking our politics.

This Book

It is this last issue—the equation of gender with transgender and even what transgender should mean—that has most clearly haunted the creation of this book and the tensions we've had to navigate as editors.

We began with three very different visions of what a gender anthology would look like. Along the way we've argued, struggled, and occasionally fought over how to combine then in the confines of single book.

For one of us, the conception of gender is a product of her experiences as a working-class lesbian femme in the 1950s and '60s. Gender was an elaborate, prescribed set of subcultural codes and rituals that communicated desire through clothing, posture, and stance. Part of her editorial challenge has been the fear that her bona fides will be questioned, that—as someone who does not necessarily favor changing bodies and has not changed her own—she will be told she does not have the standing to be part of a "transgender" struggle.

For another, openly transexual, gender is about the freedom of disengaging from the binary system of gender identity and the need to develop the pride and courage to survive the daily assaults that brings on. She has been drawn to offering those narratives that will best help others in similar circumstances whose most important challenge is developing the courage to face daily harassment. Part of her editorial challenge has been accepting a wider vision of gender, one that doesn't have a "hierarchy of queerness" in which some can be more oppressed or needy than others.

For me, well, I've long since renounced labels and categories of all kinds. Not that I don't think others should have them or they are always bad things—far from it. But I no longer find any that fit. For me, gender has moved from the personal firmly to the political, to a human rights movement in the process of being built. Part of my editorial challenge has been staying true to the vision of a gender equality movement for all, while accepting that coeditors and readers bring very specific and personal needs, some distinctly nonpolitical, to a book like this.

We have approached our task with a singular and sometimes frustrating tension. But over time, that tension has become central to this anthology. Among the three of us, we track a rough trajectory of the chronological path of gender in the public mind.

Gender originated as a feminist concern; men were the norm and women considered "the gendered sex." Rather than attacking the binary, feminism emphasized redistributing power more equitably between the two sides. As gay rights grew, the gender dialogue centered on roles, as illustrated through the flamboyant dress and behavior of butches and femmes, tops and bottoms, queens and (later) kings. As gayness retreated to sexual orientation, a transexual voice began to be heard that was new, militant, and vocal, shifting the dialogue to more radical transgressions that involved changing bodies and sexes.

And now other voices are coming forward, promoting gender equality as a political movement and the next civil rights cause. Within these strands are all the tensions that have informed this book and all the forces that have both delayed and promoted gender's emergence as a primary social issue. In that sense, this book is the result of three decades of omission: a whisper in the silence, a pent-up exhalation, an emancipation delayed.

We approach these chapters with a sense of wonder at how different these writers' lives must be, only to find that their voices are our voices, their stories ours, and that they are us. We have all had experiences like these, only few of us have spoken them. This is book for all of us. It's about the parts of us that have always been considered socially embarrassing, that every movement has left out and left behind because they were politically unacceptable, because they couldn't be "mainstreamed" without changing that mainstream forever.

Well, the time for changing that mainstream is now. Gender *is* the civil rights movement of our time, because gender rights are human rights. And I look forward to the day when they are universally recognized and respected as such.

Stories
Clare Howell

The power of stories is my calling to this book. I discovered that power when I was 13. Until then, reading had been a process of work for me, coping with school, with occasional classics like *Treasure Island, Tom Sawyer,* and *Huckleberry Finn* to give my imagination a ride. One summer—between the sixth and seventh grades—I came across *A Good Man Is Hard to Find,* a collection of short stories by Flannery O'Connor, and the world opened up.

For the first time, I encountered real people living lives I knew—exaggerated but recognizable. Intuitions and instincts I couldn't bring into focus, much less articulate, crystallized to understanding in a heartbeat as I read "The Artificial Nigger." In the haunted land where I grew up—rural south Georgia, late '50s, early '60s—the racial landscape factored into every breathing moment through an intricate dance of manner and custom set firmly in place by cultural law. It was not oppressive for me, being white and male, but I found myself bewildered, in the land of contradiction.

In 10 pages, Mr. Head and grandson Nelson showed me clearly what I needed to know but couldn't ask—how we grow up into a world that values some lives more than others. That story and others in that collection offered me a moral perspective, an insight into human nature that I had not possessed. They helped me make sense of the world.

Each of us has a story in which we play our part, making a life and defining ourselves in relation to others, our community. For most people, it's simple, if not easy. They look to their families, teachers, and peers, recognize the appropriate models, and get on with it, for better or worse. But for many gender-different young people, the models at hand are not sufficient. They are confused, buffeted between social pressure and fearful parents.

Even in this day of media saturation, there are countless gender suspects throughout this country who come into their wits wondering if they are the only one. They see no one like them. For many, the only support and affirmation they find is in stories—either true or true-to-life. Hence, this book. I want to make a book I needed 35 years ago. But this is ultimately a book for everyone who senses a genderqueer within, to whatever degree, whether they're living the dream or not.

These stories are about out-front genderqueers, people who express their gender in ways that defy societal norms and feel the weight of cultural pressure to conform, to "act their proper gender." There's a wide range of experience here—transgender, intersex, gay and lesbian, bisexual, and people who love them.

But beyond the gender these are real, everyday people who don't make headlines or lead glamorous lives. This is the face of genderqueer America, from sea to sea, young and old: from a nonracist skinhead transman who's into haiku and firearms to a butch lesbian who wants to be a mother; from a drag queen who helped ignite the gay liberation movement at the Stonewall uprising and still struggles for acceptance in the gay community to a fourth-grade drag king; from the mother of a transman letting go of a daughter and welcoming a son to an intersexed woman who survived horrific childhood abuse to build a 40-year lesbian relationship. Here, among the courage, pain, hilarity, grief, exasperation, and wonder, is resourcefulness and daring.

I joined this project because I admire my fellow editors—Joan, who is a beacon of integrity and a source of strength in the butch/femme community (besides being the sweetest person any of us will ever know), and Riki, who is the most dynamic gender activist-theorist working today.

I support Riki's efforts—and have from her days as a street radical to her mellowing as a Washington activist—because her work is vital in redefining the focus of activism. But frankly, I don't care about gender theory or a national movement for gender or transgender rights. I believe real change comes only from the bottom up, one heart and mind at a time. That's why my activism is simply going to work each day as a public librarian, greeting patrons at the reference desk as an obviously transgendered person, and meeting their questions and (sometimes) ridicule with openness, however they choose to approach me.

I say "obviously transgendered" because I make little effort to present either a feminine or masculine appearance. I lived half a lifetime creating the caricature of a man and have no interest in spending the other half doing "woman." So my example as the face of genderqueerness to hundreds of new faces every day in Brooklyn is my activism. Sometimes it's a struggle because I accrue no stability or continuity of identity in the public eye. Most of the people I see every day I've never seen before, so I'm continually called upon to declare my gender. When asked, I say "woman," but I do not correct anyone's assumption otherwise.

Bearing witness—day after day, week after week—through the mundane actions of everyday life is my contribution to the trans civil rights campaign. Riki has her political work, Joan her writing and editing. We bring different passions to the struggle for tolerance and understanding, but we're all headed in the same direction and we're all in it for the duration. This book has been a labor of love for all of us.

A Certain Kind of Freedom:
Power and the Truth of Bodies—
Four Essays on Gender

Riki Wilchins

It's Your Gender, Stupid!

Take Me to Your Gender

Gender. Everyone talks about it, but no one knows what it is or agrees on a definition. Gender *identity?* Gender *expression?* Gender *characteristics?* The gender *system?* A softer synonym for "sex"? *Gender* never stands alone, but always seems to need a noun to refer to.

So, it seems strange in a book devoted to gender that no writer takes the space to define what *gender* means. We assume that it's a common term of meaning, although it appears to be anything but. As with pornography, we may not be able to define it, but we know it when we see it.

The fact that *gender* is used in so many different but related contexts hints that we've touched on something very basic and pervasive in the human condition. So does the fact that we "know it when we see it." But I believe all the confusion surrounding gender means that perhaps just the opposite is the case: that gender is a set of meanings, and so like children learning to tell Daddy from Mommy and little boys from little girls, we see it once we know it.

Early Morning Do

The most popular conception of gender is as a sort of inner substance, an essence we all carry within us, that is always conveniently binary and, except in the case of transexuals, matched to our physical

23

sex. It is the "expression" of this gendered core that leads us to various gender behaviors: from wearing dresses or ties to displaying dominance or vulnerability during sex.

But according to theorist Judith Butler, gender refers not to something we *are* but to something we *do*, which, through extended repetition and because of the vigorous suppression of all exceptions, achieves the appearance of a sort of coherent psychic substance.

In this view, there is no doer behind the deed, no gendered identity behind the acts that we say result from it. The acts are all there is, and it is the strict regulation of these acts within the binary—females must produce feminine behaviors and males masculine—that produces the appearance of two coherent and universal genders.

Thus, I don't pull on certain clothes in the morning or style my hair a particular way because of something within me. I do these acts in a manner consistent with either masculine or feminine norms because to do otherwise would render me socially unintelligible. People wouldn't know what I was or how to treat me, and I would be the target of a great deal of hostility.

My achieving a consistent appearance and behavior is then offered as proof of a binary gender inside me.

If my gender is a doing that has to be redone each day just like I pull on those clothes each morning, that would help explain why sometimes my gender "fails": Even though I've felt like a man (and then later like a woman), people didn't always recognize me as such. Even I couldn't always recognize myself as such.

Better Dead Than Read

If I can "fail" accidentally, maybe there are ways I can fail on purpose that will create room for me to grow, to find new ways of expression that resonate more deeply. If gender is a doing and a reading of that doing, a call-and-response that must be continually done and redone, then it's also unstable, and there are ways I can disrupt it. Maybe universal and binary genders are not so inevitable after all.

This is an attractive line of thinking, especially for anyone who has found themselves transcending narrow, outdated, 20th-century gender norms. Which is to say, all the writers in this book and most of its readers.

But how do we square this with some of the facts? For instance, transexuality. It is undoubtedly true that some people (the author included) have, or do, feel a profound sense of discomfort at being confined to one sex and gender instead of another. If gender is a *doing*, does that imply that the transexual in distress is somehow reenacting his or her own pain each morning in a repeated series of gendered acts?

And transexuality aside, most people do report experiencing a stable, long-term sense of identification with either male or female, man or woman. That would seem to constitute pretty good evidence of gendered identities.

But then again, there are only two types of identities one can report experiencing. For instance, I said, "I feel like a woman trapped in a man's body," and my doctors understood and shipped me off to surgery. But if I'd worn my Intersex Society of North America HERMAPHRODITES WITH ATTITUDE T-shirt and told them, "I feel like a herm trapped in a man's body," they wouldn't have understood and would have shipped me off to a rubber room.

Moreover, paradoxical as it sounds, there is room to question whether any identification, however stable and long-term, actually constitutes *having* an identity. Identification is always an act, a repetition, a name we give to a collection of discrete traits, behaviors, urges, and empathies.

A System of Meanings

Let me repeat something from the introduction: Gender is a system of meanings and symbols—and the rules, privileges, and punishments pertaining to their use—for power and sexuality: masculinity and femininity, strength and vulnerability, action and passivity, dominance and weakness.

To gender something simply means investing it with one of two meanings. So anything and everything can be gendered, for example: ships, clothing, sexual positions, pens, bowls, hand positions, head tilts, vocal inflections, body hair, and different sports. Indeed, in many romance languages, every object is given a gender (*vive la difference*, Le Monde, *la dolce vita, el toro, el Riki*).

Because being gay itself is a transgression of the rules of gender, because those rules heavily disfavor femininity, gay and feminist (and lately transgendered) critics have tended to focus on gender's many repressive aspects.

The punishments we exact for using the "wrong" words cross from the mundane to the fatal, including hostile stares in the women's room, being humiliated after gym class for being a "sissy" or a "dyke," unfair termination for being a "ball-buster," assault for being a "faggot," arrest for "impersonating a woman," rape for being "too sexy," forced psychiatric treatment for gender identity disorder, genital mutilation for intersexed infants, and, of course, murder.

But like any language, gender's primary effect is not repressive but productive: It produces meanings. These are created through a vast and visible top-down structure: binary birth certificates, restrooms, adoption policies, immigration laws, passports, and marriage laws. But they are also produced and maintained from the bottom up, through thousands of small, everyday acts—interactions that create and destroy gendered meanings in every moment. These microexchanges of meaning—in an elevator, over a meal, while buying a newspaper, when answering the phone—stamp us with our gender, bind us to it, and require us to answer to it in order to interact with other people.

Thus not only does gender restrain us as individuals, but it is through the language of gender that we become who we are, that we come to recognize ourselves—and be recognized by others—as men and women, and only as men and women.

As an academic concept, gender has been remarkably productive. Every year witnesses a new crop of articles, books, and theory about gender. Yet as a civil rights cause, gender is just beginning.

One can see in it the outlines of something that links misogyny, homophobia, transphobia, and the restricted way we raise our youth. Indeed, a widespread understanding of gender would have enormous potential to transform society and remove inequity and violence.

A Sex by Any Other Name Would Still Smell as Sweet

If gender is a system of meanings, then what are we to make of the recent and remarkable degree to which "gender" is replacing "sex" to refer not only to men and women but also male and female? Perhaps this is only a way to avoid saying the overloaded word "sex," which also means intercourse, in public speech.

Yet it also seems to contradict the widely accepted notion that sex is a natural, physical property of bodies, while gender is something culturally derived from sex. In Butler's formulation, sex (male/female) is to "raw" as gender (man/women) is to "cooked." Sex is there "on the far side of language," while gender is something added on afterward.

The increasing use of gender to replace sex may be an acknowledgment, if only unconsciously, that once you start looking there is nothing, or at least very little, on the far side of language. As an experiment, I recently asked a large group of very hip queer youths to list on a blackboard all the attributes that made up a "real man" and "real woman." Interestingly, on the list beneath "real man" was "has a penis"; the list beneath "real woman" included doesn't have a penis." Not one person in the entire group thought to list "doesn't have a vagina" or even "has a vagina" as an identifying trait of bodies. I take from this that although the body's moving parts may all be "over there" on the far side of language, nearly everything we make of them to render them meaningful to us is right here, in our laps.

I'd Like to Buy a Women's Dictionary

Gender as a language is at once terribly simple, because it has only two meanings, and terribly complex, because it touches us across the entire plane of contact between our bodies and society. In most languages, words can be used by anyone who can master them. But gender is a language that creates and sustains binary difference. To achieve this, gendered signs must be highly regulated so they don't fall into the wrong hands, as if certain dictionary words were colored blue for boys and pink for girls. Wearing a skirt, smoking a pipe, crying in public, moaning during sex, scratching your crotch, describing anything (but God) as divine: These are some of the signs that may be given by only one half of the population or the other.

20/20 Hind-Cite

If gender is a system of meanings, then, in a book of the same name, what is meant by "genderqueer"? For one thing, it brings back together those two things that have been wrongly separated: gender and gayness.

For Butler, "successful" genders are those that cite other earlier examples. Thus we learn to become men and women and to be recognized as such by copying other examples. In popular thought, men and women are considered examples of "real" genders, and drag, transexuals, and butch/femme couples are considered copies. Thus drag is to copy as woman is to real. Drag imitates real life.

But if Butler is right, if gender is always an artifice that copies something else, then all gender is a reuse of familiar stereotypes according to the rules for their use. All gender is drag. And those that fail, that are read as "queer," are simply those that break the rules. Thus neither a Streisand drag queen doing "Barbra" nor Barbra herself doing "woman" is any more or less real. There is no real gender to which they might be compared. Both use common symbols to achieve a visual meaning. The drag queen appears "false" because we don't grant her access to those symbols.

Considering gender as a language, I would approach queerness somewhat differently. What did I mean when I told my doctors that I felt "like a woman?" How was it possible for me to feel like anything other than myself? Perhaps I only meant that I was feminine. But although one can be seen as feminine, feel feminine feelings, or to express femininity through our clothing, hairstyle, and posture, can anyone really *be* feminine?

Achieving femininity sounds like a lot of work: how I feel, how I express myself to others, and how they perceive me. It's one thing to feel consistently male or feminine or like a boy, but keeping all that feeling/expressing/being-perceived continuously intact must take a lot of concentration. Having any gender at all is really a sort of accomplishment, a sustained effort.

Genderqueers are people for whom some link in the feeling/expressing/being-perceived fails. For example, a stone butch may feel masculine and embody—in his own mind and behavior—masculinity. Yet because of his sex (the pronoun strains here), she might still be read as womanly, like a girl trying on her boyfriend's clothes, especially if she is large-breasted and large-hipped.

If genderqueer bodies are those that fail because they don't follow the rules, the grammar of gender-as-language, then what are the boundaries of such a term and what are its exclusions? Is a lesbian femme harassed for her miniskirt and fuck-me pumps genderqueer? Is a 3-year-old who tries on his sister's dress or a 40-year-old who loses a promotion because her boss believes women should be seen but not promoted? What about a football captain who's humiliated by his coach because he wept after a tough loss?

If genderqueerness is not something we do but an identity we are, then none of these people would seem to be candidates. So one of the problems is that a narrow definition will exclude the millions of people

28

who rub up against gender norms but don't step all the way out.

Some feminist theorists have questioned the queerness and radicalness of any sort of gender that doesn't do just that: leave norms behind. They consider transexuals, butch/femmes, and drag queens as not only not genderqueer but actually gender-conforming, because they partake of binary stereotypes. For them, the only "radical" choice is adopting more androgynous genders that fall totally off the binary map.

But how are we to tell someone who faces discrimination or violence that they aren't really queer? Surely their attackers think they are.

Using queerness itself as a category of analysis seems to invite a new round of debate devoted to who is "really queer." A voice that originated from one set of margins begins to create its own marginalized voices. These twin problems of identities—boundaries and hierarchies—emerge whenever we try to base politics on identity.

It's Not Me, I'm Just on Loan

If gender is always a bending of self toward prevailing norms, then gender is always a kind of displacement, from which not even genderqueers are immune.

For instance, Clare Howell recently said to me, "I know I sound like a man." This kind of displacement repositions her voice as coming from somewhere else. This is like the cross-dresser who declares, "I like wearing *women's* clothes." It's safe to say that no cross-dresser ever wore "women's clothes." If the bill came to him, they're his clothes, he bought them: They're obviously *men's clothes*. The displacement in naming them "women's clothes" prevents us from getting outside the terms of the language, from getting to something new that might redefine skirts or dresses or femininity as being about men.

Many cross-dressers would reply that the point of dressing for them is that these *are* women's clothes. It is the otherness of the clothing, the fact that they are "women's," that is precisely what allows them to feel feminine. But once again, we can't get to someplace new, where femininity might be something about men that is not anchored in Woman (or vice versa).

(I remember telling my therapist one day in what felt like a breakthrough: If I'm a woman and I haven't had surgery, then this must be a woman's penis. Wet dreams must be part of women's experience. However, I would be slow to make this argument at the next feminist conference.)

I don't mean to fall into the familiar trap of criticizing those who want to eat their cake but not have it. Some genderqueers, including cross-dressers, are not interested in that "something new." They will always enjoy appropriation *as* appropriation for its own sake. These strategic displacements renounce ownership and participation. They announce that "this part of my gender isn't me, it belongs to someone else, and I only appropriate/approximate it." They announce an acceptance of a particular gender's rules of access, who "owns" which words and who is allowed to use them. For instance, it's not possible for Clare to declare, "I sound like other men with breasts" or "I sound like other women trapped in male impersonators' bodies" or "I sound like a Clare," because those are not legitimate categories of description. By definition Clare must sound like something else, because her own body is not among the available choices.

Jenell, one of my favorite cross-dressers, always reminds me that hir enjoyment *is* transgression itself. If microminiskirts ever become fashionable for men, she'll have to decamp and find something else that is queer. In this sense, we are working somewhat at cross purposes. We both want to end the intolerable discrimination suffered by those who transcend gender stereotypes. But while I want to empty out those margins and bring queerness into the mainstream, she'd rather keep transgression in place, where s/he can enjoy it, but end its stigmatization. In retrospect, I think we both are right.

You Make Me Feel Like a Natural Woman Impersonator

Why do most genderqueers perceive themselves as falling within a long succession of binaries: female/male, butch/femme, top/bottom, boy/girl? Just as when we were children, we all learned to distinguish binary mommy from binary daddy, brother from sister, and little girls from little boys, it seems that like everyone else, genderqueers see in twos.

It is popular to explain genderqueerness as resulting from a "spectrum of gender" along which all individuals—queer and nonqueer—fall. This is presented as a more enlightened and inclusive approach to bodies. Yet when you look closer, every spectrum turns out to be anchored by the same familiar two poles—male/female, man/woman, gay/straight. The rest of us are just strung out between them, like damp clothes drying on the line. The spectrum of gender turns out to be a spectrum of heterosexual norms, only slightly less oppressive but not less binary than its predecessors. Maybe the problem is that gender is a way of seeing: black-and-white glasses through which we view a Technicolor world. Wherever we look, no matter what is "out there," we see only black and white.

✳ There is an apocryphal story of an American anthropologist who visited a remote island where natives had 17 genders. Upon his return, he reported to the anthropological society that, "like all others we've studied, this culture also has only men and women."

We Are Men With Breasts. We Come in Peace.

I recently spent a week at a large queer activist conference in the Midwest. I was dressed in my best Banana Republic menswear and looking, if I may say, pretty phat for a woman trapped in a six-foot male impersonator's body. I went across the street to a sports bar to get some change, and when I entered the whole room just seemed to stop: woman *and* men turned from the immense TV screen showing the Sunday NFL game to watch me. It was intimidating. I got suddenly very nervous and self-conscious. I knew, for these people, I might just as well have landed from Mars. Before I knew it I was raising my voice, feminizing my stance, and trying to blend in a little.

I try to remind myself that if we can hold our course, it is at precisely such moments that we create a certain kind of freedom. It's a hard thing to keep in mind when you're afraid, that at these times we are doing the best and the most anonymous kind of activism.

What, I always wonder, did those people see? I asked my lover on one such occasion what she thought people were seeing and she replied, "Well, you do look like a man with breasts." Which, fortunately, was exactly the gender I was trying to do that day. As if that were possible. I only wish that option were available. Mostly I think people just try to figure out *what* in the world I am.

Don't Fuck With Mother Nature

But there are lots of things about bodies and genders that don't fit the binary model into which we try to force them, even that most unassailable of binaries: biological sex. Biological sex is considered to be the most basic and natural product of bodies. All creatures reproduce, and to reproduce—unless you're an amoeba—requires two sexes. But consider the lowly seahorse, a creature that is said to "switch sexes." (No, not with the help of a little aquatic seahorse surgeon.) We say it changes "from male to female" because what else could it change from or to?

And the "female" hyena, which not only dominates its species like a male but also has what any decent biologist would admit is a penis. Yet it must be a female, because it bears young. Or the male garter snake, which often morphs into a female after birth to attract male snakes to keep it warm. Something I might try during the next snowstorm.

But what if reproduction doesn't have to include two sexes? Or what if there are other sexes, and they can reproduce as well? But that's not possible, is it? Because any creatures that can reproduce must be either male and female—*by definition*. Hence surgeons' frantic search to locate the "real" sex of intersexed infants before their genitals are cut up to resemble "normal" male or female. The infant's "real sex," *by definition,* cannot be intersex, cannot be whatever it is. Any sex but binary male or female is pathology, unnatural, and unreal, to be discarded and corrected with the knife. We say two sexes is "nature's way." But Man produces this feminine version of Mother Nature—passive, pure, and reserved—when we need her, and then pushes Her aside when the facts don't fit His needs.

The debate over the naturalness of binary sex is circular: Whatever reproduces must be one of two sexes because there are only two sexes to be. Thus it is gender as a system of meaning that produces the "natural" Mother Nature, male and female sexes, and the gender binary that establishes what is genderqueer.

Queerer Bodies

When I Was in Gender and You Were the Main Drag

Somewhere inside yourself, you just know.
—nontransgendered lesbian explaining how she knows she's a woman

Inside, I just know.
—transgendered lesbian explaining how she knows she's a woman

Nothing in man—not even his body—is sufficiently stable to serve as the basis for self-recognition, or for understanding other men.
—Michel Foucault, presumably explaining how he doesn't know if he's a man or a woman, *Language, Counter-Memory, and Practice*, 1977

When it comes to gender, each of us, in our own private way, is an implicit philosopher. For instance, you probably believe that your body is male or female, that you are gay or straight (or bi), that feminism is distinct from gay rights, that physical sex is genetic but gender learned, and that sexual orientation is distinct from other kinds of gendered behavior. These beliefs probably feel to you like "just common sense." But that is only because philosophical beliefs, aged in the keg, and widely enough accepted, are promoted to common sense. None of these concepts is just "out there." We think them because we think about bodies and the world in very particular ways. If you spoke about these thoughts a lot, people would call you a theorist, and if you spoke about really big thoughts, people would call you a bigamist.

In this section, I want to encourage you to think those big thoughts. This is an anthology of personal narratives written by some very exceptional people, often living very painful lives, and I hope it's accessible to readers on an emotional level. But that's not all. While the exceptionalism and the pain are important, for me, they are not the point of this book. The real importance lies in how these writers' lives show that the ways we think about bodies is broken, is frequently oppressive, and needs to be changed.

And I don't just mean changed in the sense of being more tolerant and inclusive, although that is important. Nor do I mean better ways of thinking about gender, although that's important too. I mean changed in the largest sense: revising how we think about things like language and meaning, truth and difference, knowledge and power. Especially the political effects of these things on people, when they suppress individual experience, discourage difference, and prevent new forms of knowledge from emerging.

These are big themes. But of all the things we know in the world, the most fundamental is our bodies. If the ways we have of knowing don't work there, I can see only two conclusions: Either these are bodies that have "failed" or the ways we have of knowing about them have failed—and, by extension, the ways we have of knowing about all bodies and many other things have failed as well.

These stories point the way to a new kind of freedom. Not an ultimate freedom, because I doubt that exists, but a different kind of freedom nonetheless. Whatever we are, whatever that fuzzy thing called "self" may be, I think these stories point to the way toward being more of that self in a deeper and fuller sort of way.

Every model of reality has margins where it begins to run out of explanatory steam, where we can see its problems and limitations. This anthology is about the people at those margins and thus about those who have found their bodies the target of discrimination because they transcended narrow stereotypes, because they were perceived as too old, young, black, short, fat, disabled, deaf, hairy, ill, butch, flamboyant, or any of a thousand other things. In short, this is about all of us.

We're not the ones who are broken. It's the model that's broken. The model of Western thought about bodies itself, and much more besides. So, welcome to my breakdown.

A Fluid Analogy

What is knowledge? Consider something simple and familiar: bodily fluids. We'll check someplace objective and scientific, perhaps several medical textbooks.

We begin with menstrual blood. "Menstruation entails the discharge from the body of a couple of teaspoons of lukewarm fluid. This discharge occurs about once a month for a number of years, and women's bodies lose perhaps 500 gametes slowly over about 40 years."

As a bodily fluid, menstrual blood is a loser. It symbolizes—there's no kind way to say this—waste, weakness, loss, passivity—all the general ills associated with a feminine disposition. Young girls are often properly appalled to learn this, spending hours staring in shamed silence at their bodies, imagining all the little potential human beings leaking out, perhaps even at that very moment.

We move on to ejaculation. "Ejaculation entails the discharge from the body of a couple of teaspoons of lukewarm fluid. This discharge occurs— oh, up to five times a day it seems—for a number of years. Men's bodies lose perhaps two gazillion (the number is imprecise here) gametes each time: potential little human beings sprayed onto the carpet, handkerchiefs, rolled pieces of liver, and hollowed-out pumpkins."

As a bodily fluid, semen is the Man. It symbolizes—there's no unkind way to say this—dominance, strength, activity, vitality, potency—all the general benefits associated with a masculine disposition. Young boys are often properly proud to learn this, spending hours in rapt contemplation of their own pubescent, potent crotches.

"With a Capital P / And That Rhymes with T / And That Stands For..."

Bodies bear an enormous weight of cultural meaning. While acknowledging that bodies are "really there," one can reasonably question the meanings we give them. Anything but the barest facts—weight, mass, height—seems to go well beyond knowledge into the politics of meaning. I don't mean politics here with a capital P, as in civil rights and political parties. I mean "small p" politics: the power to say and track and even control different things about bodies.

For instance, when I shaved my legs and put on my first dress, everyone wondered what it meant. When I yearned for surgery, everyone thought it meant I was crazy. I thought it meant I really wanted to wear a dress and have a more feminine body. There wasn't anything else to know, any more than there was something to know about my inexhaustible craving for chocolate.

While my wearing dresses has resulted in my being diagnosed with a mental illness (gender identity disorder), it never occurred to anyone to ask whether my choco-cravings constituted a mental disorder, because we don't regulate or politicize attraction to chocolate. If we did, no doubt the nation's therapy couches would be filled with "cross-chocolaters," disgorging their deepest, darkest, semisweet secrets. ("And you were how old when *your mother* gave you your first piece of chocolate? Well! First, let's try something we call 'behavioral therapy.' Just put your foot in this warm clamp here, hold on to this electrode while I plug in your chair, and we'll watch some *nice* pictures of chocolate together.")

Cashing in on Knowledge in a Different Register

Maybe that seems silly. But not as silly when you consider that while our taste for specific foods passes without comment, our taste in specific bodies and pleasures seldom does. People immediately start asking what it means.

Why do men want to wear women's clothes? Why would a femme, who could have a "real man," instead want a wife-beater tank-top, strap-it-on butch? Why do some men want to become women? The only reason to track such things about bodies as their sex, genders, and desires is because we want to *do* something with them. Knowledge about bodies does not stand passively by, awaiting discovery by an objective and dispassionate Science.

Beyond measurable facts, knowledge about bodies is something we create. We go looking for it, and we fashion it in ways that respond to cultural needs and aims. We create the idea of binary genders because it marks something we want to track and control about bodies' appearance and behavior. We create gender identity disorders (GIDs) because we want to control sex and discourage the desire to change the body's sexual characteristics. We create the knowledge of sexual orientation and study it exhaustively because we want to know and control the individual's capacity to contribute to reproduction. There is no bright-line separation here between knowledge and politics. Knowledge marches to the beat of power. Specific kinds of knowledge *about* bodies enable us to exercise specific kinds of power *over* them. Such knowledge is not "disinterested." It is *very* interested, it is purposeful, it has aims.

For instance, when I went in for a nose job, the doctors were agreeable, quick, and friendly. But when I went in for that groin job, my whole life went to hell. Everything came under fire: my upbringing (probably failed), my mother (probably overbearing), my father (probably distant), and the demands of modern manhood (obviously threatening). I'm really a man (I'm still Arnold), finally a woman (but I look like Brooke), basically homo (news to my girlfriend), and actually a transvestite (news to my tailor).

Luckily for me, here come the professionals. Doctors, lawyers, psychiatrists on one hand and theorists, academics, and writers on the other. Not to mention gender's Holy Trinity: Sally, Jerry, and Oprah.

The fact that many of us prefer different bodies, genders, or pleasures is clearly knowledge in the same register as the meaning of those bodies, genders and pleasures. In fact, I would go a step further. The propagation of norms for things like pleasure and gender, and the pursuit and categorization of divergence from such norms, are also knowledge in a different register. And the realm in which that knowledge lives is not Science but Politics.

If You're Not Part of the Problem, You're Not Part of the Solution

Prefer what is positive and multiple: difference over uniformity, flows over unities, mobile arrangements over systems. Believe that what is productive is not sedentary but nomadic.
—Michel Foucault, *Language, Counter-Memory, and Practice*, 1977

There is a huge and ongoing current critique of Western knowledge—sometimes called "postmodernism"—that is questioning what we know, how we know it, and what effect it has on those we know it about. And of all the things we know, indeed feel we *must* know, none is more fundamental than our own bodies. If that knowledge is showing cracks, then what else might be faulty as well? It is this nexus—the models of how we think and the problems posed by bodies that don't fit the model—that has led to the explosion of interest in genderqueerness and "gender studies."

Whenever·I wanted to feel feminine, I couldn't because I was a boy, too tall, too wide-shouldered, not "real." Later, when I sometimes wanted to feel masculine, I couldn't because I had breasts, I was too curvy, I was no longer a "real" man. And when I wanted to feel something that was neither—well, that was impossible. It doesn't matter that some of these were things other people said about me and others things I said silently to myself. What matters is that the way in which we think—and especially the way we "think the body"—has too often become an off-the-rack, one-size-fits-all approach. One that favors that which is universal, known, stable, and similar. But my experience of my body and my place in the world was exactly the opposite: mobile, private, small, often unique, and usually unknown. These are places familiar to many people on knowledge's margins where many of us wish to go. And these stories, standing just beyond the sexual binary, point a way.

Truth Corrupts, Absolute Truth Corrupts Absolutely

"Let's assume you're right…"
"No, let's not assume I'm right. Let's assume there are lots of different 'rights' out there and this is just one of them."

—exchange in a gender seminar

The philosophical tradition, at least from Plato on, has always favored the concept of the same; i.e., the aim of philosophical thought has been to reveal the essential characteristics that two things hold in common.
—Newton Garver, *Wittgenstein and Derrida*, 1994

Why are we so frightened of difference and multiplicity? Perhaps it is the Western belief in the One True God? Strength, goodness, and truth are properties of our God's oneness. And all those tribes with multiple gods, tribes that were slaughtered by the ancient Hebrews, must have been weak, false, evil, and duplicitous.

Probably we fear that the alternative to the universal is not plurality but an endless abyss, a chaos where no person's knowing is any more (or less) right than any other's. And if all this reminds you of the revolt against queer bodies as well as the "threat" of multiculturalism, then go to the front of the class.

Some cultures accommodate, even exalt, difference. Yet in the West we pursue unity, we believe in singularity, we worship not only our God but final Truths. If it's not true somewhere, then it's not really true. There is no room for what is private or unique. To seek the Truth—always capital T—is to seek what is universal and perfect.

Unfortunately, such an approach is a kind of intellectual fascism that squeezes out individual truths. As the exchange quoted above illustrates, valuing of difference can cause real confusion in my presentations.

Good modernists that they are, my students assume that there is a (single) right answer about things like gender and the meaning of bodies. Our job is arguing over the right one. It's a winner-take-all approach to knowledge. But where gender and meaning is concerned, there are lots of little truths. The way you understand your hips, your chest, your hair. How you feel when your lover holds you, gets on top, makes you come. The rush when you dress up, dress down, put on silk or leather. These are immensely small and private experiences. They are among our most intimate experiences of ourselves in the world. And they are precisely what is lost when we propound and pursue singular and monolithic Truths about bodies, gender, and desire.

We have "centered" all such knowledge over a binary of masculine/feminine. Body hair must mean masculine. Breasts must be feminine and passive. Hips are maternal, muscles masculine. An erect clitoris is vulnerable, an erect penis is commanding and strong. We need to de-center knowledge about the body. We need to allow other kinds of meanings to emerge, and other experiences of the body. We need room to find truths—always small t—that resonate with ourselves. To do this, many of us will need to transcend and transgress the kinds of knowledge that are out there. But that is how things change. That's why if you're not part of the problem, you're not part of the solution.

One Truth With No Trimmings, Please

Counseling, NOT Cutting! Get Your Scalpels Off Our Bodies!
　　　　　　　　—Hermaphrodites With Attitude poster

Knowledge is not made for understanding; it is made for cutting.
—Michel Foucault, *Language, Counter-Memory, and Practice*, 1977

*There is nothing abstract about the power that sciences and theories
have to act materially and actually upon our bodies and our minds...*
 —Monique Wittig, *The Straight Mind*, 1992

If multiplicity is a pinging under the hood, a "noise" in the system waiting to be found and fixed, then there's no louder *ping* than one that disrupts two perfect and complimentary opposite sexes. Male and female are Nature's way, our highest physical Truth. But what if Nature doesn't oblige? What if She exasperates us by producing bodies that aren't "natural?" What if that pinging under the hood is the sound of genderqueer bodies that just...don't...fit?

I am speaking, of course, of intersexed infants. Such children, who are not clearly male or female, occur in about one in every 2,000 births. Because anything that is not male or female is not a true sex, we pronounce them "abnormal," fit them legally into male or female, and fit them physically into boy or girl by cutting them up at the rate of about five every day. Thus are "natural" males and females maintained. In the aphorism of the Intersex Society's Cheryl Chase, intersex is the sex that can't exist. Because by definition, every child must be male or female. Inside every intersex infant is a real boy or girl just waiting to come out.

For instance, in one segment of *Primetime,* a pediatrician showed color slides of intersex genitals while Diane Sawyer tried to guess their "real sex": That surreal change went something like this:

DS: That's a male, right?
Doctor: Nope. A female. And this one?
DS: A female.
Doctor: No. A male.
DS: Now, this is surely a male. That looks like a penis.
Doctor: Sorry, another female. This one?
DS: Female?
Doctor: Male.
DS: Shee-it!

The surgeon's job is figuring out which sex the child really is "underneath" whatever sex they "appear" and to surgically restore them to what Nature intended. If Nature produces some kids that aren't "natural," well, even Nature stops now and then to down a brewski. Such doctors are not malicious or destructive. In fact, they are anything but. They are usually dedicated physicians and surgeons who are doing what they see as compassionate surgery for little, if any, fee.

But it is part of the peculiar tyranny of our taste for perfect and singular Truths that difference cannot be ignored but must be stamped out and made to fit the model. If the model and the body disagree, it is the body that must give way. And this is the case whether it's intersexed infants, cross-dressing teens, or genderqueer adults.

It's Always the Same Movie if You Don't Change the Reals

Part of the problem of applying notions of truth to the body is that lurking in the background is always the idea of what is real and authentic. Now, since I keep getting called "sir" these days, maybe I should create a whole new category called M-to-F-to-M, where I finally get to be Real:

You know you're a real M-to-F-to-M when...
* You mother still calls you "Richard."
* You tell your boss you're transexual and he asks, "Which way did you go?"
* You look at your girlfriend's naked butt and wish you had a good strap-on.
* Your lesbian girlfriend looks at your naked crotch and wishes you had a good strap-on.

We're back to different orders of knowledge here. What can it mean to say that my sister's femininity is real but that of a drag queen, a cross-dresser, an effeminate little boy, or an M-to-F is not? Why do we say that the masculinity of a Sly Stallone is real but that of an F-to-M, a stone butch, or a woman bodybuilder is not?

This kind of knowledge is still politics going in drag. It's about power. By creating notions of realness and dividing bodies along a binary of real/false, bodies like mine are kept disempowered. And indeed, in places as diverse as my last job, the Michigan Womyn's Music Festival, my local women's events house in Miami, and the next women's room I have to use, I run smack up against the Real. Realness is not only about naturalness and the distinction between the groin you were born with and the one you bought yourself for Christmas. If gender is about language and meaning, then Realness is also about ownership, about who is allowed to use what meanings legitimately.

For instance, a drag queen is seen as appropriating women's symbols. No matter how convincing the illusion of femininity is, it's still an illusion, because by definition, the femininity is copied, not owned. The same is true for a transexual. No matter how "real" an M-to-F *looks*, she will never *be* Real.

✱ Queer bodies are always defined by gender norms that are constructed in their absence. In fact, such norms are constructed only *by* their absence, because if they were there at the inception, the norm couldn't exist. It would be queered from the start.

It's particularly intriguing to hear charges of Realness coming from lesbians and feminists. Barely 100 years ago suffragettes were not considered to be "real women" because they shunned passivity to invade men's social prerogatives. Only 40 years ago, lesbians were accused of not being "real women" because they didn't want to marry men and become mothers. Twenty years ago femmes were ridiculed for not being "real lesbians" because they looked like straight women—yet another kind of displacement that ceded femininity to heterosexuality.

And, of course, through it all, any man who slept with or desired the same sex gave up forever the hope of ever being a "real man." In fact, the United States may be the only country in the world where we are so insecure about gender that the words *man* and *woman* have no meaning unless they are preceded by *real*.

Realness circulates in so many different contexts because it is very politically effective. As a form of knowledge, it empowers some bodies, discourages others, and teaches all to stay within the lines.

Double Vision

"Can I ask you something—are you a man or a woman?"
—attendee at women's conference

"Not always, but sometimes I think I am."
—smart-ass author

What is it about binaries that so captivates our thinking: men/women, gay/straight, M-to-F/F-to-M, white/black, real/artificial, male/female, lesbian/feminist. Whoops…sorry. Scratch that. If there are more than two genders, it's a cinch that, with our bifocal glasses, we'll never see them. Actually, that's backward. Two-ness is not something "out there" but a product of the way we see. We look for that two-ness. Our categories assure that we see it. That's why no matter what gender I do, the only question is "Are you a man or a woman?" because that exhausts all the available possibilities.

When we pick up complex things—like desire or gender—with primitive mental tools like binaries, we lose nuance and multiplicity. Binaries don't give us much information. But then, they're not supposed to.

Quick: What is the meaning of masculinity? Mannish, not feminine, right? What about being straight? That means not being gay.

To say that I'm still really a man is only meaningful in terms of my not being a woman. I am feminine only to the exact degree that I am…not masculine. I am gay only as much as I'm not straight or to the exact number of songs I've memorized from *The Sound of Music.*

There's really not very much meaning or information circulating here, because with only two possibilities, meaning is confined to what something is not. As a form of thinking, binaries prevent other kinds of information from emerging. That is why no other genders ever appear. Binaries are the black holes of knowledge. Nothing is allowed to escape, so we get the same answers every time.

Two's a Crowd

So in binaries all knowledge is broken down into two equal halves, right? Actually, no. Despite the name, binary thinking is not like two, like two halves of an aspirin you break down the middle.

At this point in my life, I have spoken to hundreds of people about my body. Some of them even standing up. In 20 years, not one has asked me anything about "gaining a vagina." If they mentioned my surgery at all, every one said something, often in the form of a crude joke that was related to my losing the big Magic Wand. Now, I'm as impressed with my genitals as the next person. Maybe more so. This is the same sort of question posed to F-to-Ms. It seems no matter what sex it is, it's about male.

At this point, it should surprise no one that binaries are about power, a form of doing politics through language. Binaries create the smallest possible hierarchy of one thing over another. They are not really about two things, but only one.

Consider Man. We understand Man as a given, universal, and inclusive. That's why we say "all of Mankind" or "the study of Man." Woman is defined as what is left over: sex, procreation, and mystery. In this sense Woman is always "Other." Confined to what is not-man—sex, procreation, and mystery—Woman is always genderqueer. In terms of color, this would be equivalent to Asian being racially queered. Asians are seen through the lens of Orientalism. What is Western and white is universal, while the Orient as Other is confined to the mysterious, exotic, and primitive.

The second term of a binary exists only to support the first term. Thus Woman functions not as an equal half but as a support and prop, derivative from and dependent on Man. So both terms of the binary are really in the first. This gives the first term of any binary a lot of power. It defines the terms in which we talk. By doing so, it is itself insulated from discussion. We debate what Woman is, what women want, etc., etc. ad nauseam. But Man is immune from such debate. We endlessly debate the "meaning" of blackness, but whiteness—until very recently—is a given.

Only by overturning binaries and binary thinking will we really be able to open up more room for the second terms to come into their own, for things now obscured at the margins to emerge. But toppling binaries is not easy. They are very compelling forms of thinking. For instance, I can promote genderqueerness all I want. But questioning "real" sexes and genders, whether male and female, man and woman really exist, just leaves me looking like a fool.

And as long as I can't question the existence of normative sexes and genders, it will be *my* body and my gender that are on the firing line, that I will be forced to define, defend, and write books about, over and over again.

Genderqueerness may be a failed project from the outset. Our challenge is not promoting genderqueerness—as if it weren't already another way of promoting normative genders—but rather challenging the whole narrow, outdated notion of applying binary norms to bodies and genders.

Seeing Through Transparency

In the beginning was the Word, and the Word was with God, and the Word was God…and the Word was made flesh….
                                        —The Gospel According to John

In the beginning was Sex, and Binary Sex was with God, and Binary Sex was from God…and Binary Sex was made flesh, and it became The One, True Thing about everyone's body.
—The Gospel According to Us

As a panel member at a gay journalists' conference, I wanted to talk about issues, politics, gender-based hate crimes and job discrimination. But first audience members wanted to know what I "was." As reporters, they needed a label to identify me to their readers, not to mention their editors. The predictable questions flew. Did I consider myself transgendered? Was I presenting myself as male or female? Did I use male or female pronouns? Was I pre-op or post-op? Did I want to sleep with men or women (short menu in this restaurant)?

As I insisted on ignoring my personal life to focus on issues, their questioning grew more insistent. The more I deflected them, the more demanding they became. Finally several audience members became openly hostile, standing to verbally attack me with epithets and slurs, and finally physically assaulting me onstage with fists, chairs, and broken bottles.

No, wait a minute. I'm sorry. That was an *S/M* panel I was on. But at the gay journalism conference, my audience *did* repeatedly question what I was and express their frustration with my refusal to answer.

The question is whether language is transparent. Does it faithfully reveal the world, as though beneath a clear sheet of glass, or does it first create the world we say it reveals?

What kind of information did these journalists want?

Was I gay or straight?

Is it true I was transgendered?

Had I had surgery?

I wonder what in the world these things had to do with creating gender equality for all Americans. Is there anything I could say about my body or identity to those journalists that wouldn't obscure everything I really wanted to tell them? Are there any names for myself I could have given them with which I did not completely disagree, which wouldn't have made me complicit in my own silencing?

Our belief in language is based on our naive faith that the world is right here: finite, knowable, immediately and totally available to us. Thus what isn't named doesn't exist. What is named must therefore exist.

I'll See It When I Believe It When You've Named It

But is the world really "right here?" Do words really describe the world accurately, exhausting what's "there"? Or are they limited only to what is repeatable and shared, and thus communicable? What about all those messy spaces between words and around their borders? Many of them are populated by our life's more profound experiences. Can language capture why you prefer wearing a nice dress to a new suit, why you want to penetrate instead of being penetrated, why you enjoy having a chest but don't want breasts, how you feel when you're stoned (not that the author has any experience here), or why you like Big Macs but hate sashimi (Japanese for "tastes like shit")?

Indeed, what about all those messy spaces between words like *feminine* and *masculine* and around the borders of words like *male* and *female* that are populated by bodies that don't fit the language? Or any of us whose gender experience confounds words when we transcend the narrow, outdated language of norms?

Words work well for things we can repeat, that we hold in common. What is unique or private is lost to language. But gender is a system of meanings that shapes our experience of bodies. Genderqueerness is by definition unique, private, and profoundly different. That's what makes it "queer." When we force all people to answer to a single language that excludes their experience of themselves in the world, we not only increase their pain and marginalization, we make them accomplices in their own erasure.

It is bad enough to render them silent, even worse to make them speak a lie, worse yet if speaking the lie erases them.

A recurrent theme of this anthology is writers struggling with language used about them and against them, even as it struggles back, twists in their hands, erases their sounds. All of us have those small, private experiences that we can never truly put into words. Our belief in language tells us that they aren't as real, as important, as the things we can say and share.

But I think it's just the opposite. For nowhere are we more ourselves than in those small, private moments when we transcend the common reality, when we experience ourselves in ways that cannot be said or understood or repeated. It is to those moments that we are called, and it is to those moments that we must listen.

Changing the Subject

My Mother Made Me a Lesbian (She Can Make One for You Too)

Sexuality "did not appear until the beginning of the nineteenth century."
What had been some three hundred years earlier just so many disparate
urges, inclinations, and activities, were delineated as a problematic set of
traits and drives that supposedly define a central aspect of human nature.
——John McGowan, *Postmodernism and Its Critics*, 1991

What do we mean by *identity*? No one is perfectly gay, completely straight, totally womanly, or wholly transgendered. So what do we mean when we identify as such? Are identities real properties of people, or are they more like approximations, normative ideals against which we measure ourselves but never perfectly fit?

What about those of us who are Democrats or over 50: Why has sexual activity solidified into a social identity but party affiliation has not? Why do we consider the Human Rights Campaign an identity-based group, but not the American Association of Retired Persons? It is perhaps because we politicize bodies' age differently than we do their sexuality?

Is gayness an essential property of gay bodies, so that when we look in the mirror each morning we see a gay person staring back? Or is it rather a way we learn to recognize and see ourselves in the mirrors of others' eyes?

Perhaps all identification is a kind of displacement, a loss of self that is replaced by a reference to something else that one is not. But if that's so, identity is not a natural fact of bodies: it has a history. It emerged through specific kinds of language and knowledge that were a response to certain cultural needs.

Revolting Subjects

[I]t is already one of the prime effects of power that certain bodies, certain gestures, certain discourses, certain desires, come to be identified and constituted as individuals.
—Michel Foucault, "Two Lectures," from Power/Knowledge: Selected Interviews and Other Writings, 1980

The nineteenth-century homosexual became a personage.... The sodomite had been a temporary aberration; the homosexual was now a species.
—Michel Foucault, The History of Sexuality, Part 1, 1978

According to Foucault, it was in the 19th century that the homosexual was created. He doesn't mean by this that same-sex attraction was invented on the spot. On the contrary, for thousands of years people had known about disco, plaid shirts, show tunes, and whale watching, but sex was considered something one *did*, not something one *was*. But sex was an appetite, just like our appetite for food or money. If you liked one thing and not another, that was a matter of personal taste. People were still considered to have sexual problems, but not the way we think of them. If you used sex for humiliation or conquest, if you pursued it to excess or pined away in lust, then, yes, you had a problem with sex. But the problem was how sex was used, not its direction.

But in the 1800s scientists produced a new catalog of disease based on sex. It included: gerontophiles (old people turn you on), pedophiles (young people turn you on), onanophiles (you turn you on), zoophiles (Mr. Ed turns you on), masochists (a little pain won't hurt), sadists (especially if it's someone else's), necrophiles (don't ask), and of course the homosexual (don't tell). Such people were thought to be joined by shared emotional traits, physical dispositions, latent characteristics, childhood experiences, family histories, and so on.

A new kind of knowledge had been created, and along with it a new category of self-experience. It now became possible to experience one's self *as a homosexual* and to be identified by others the same way. And now we have a powerful civil rights movement based on this self-perception invented just 150 years ago.

As sex went, so did gender. Diseases like "transvestic fetishism" and "gender dysphoria" were added to the catalog. Individuals who transcend gender norms have been around since the first culture created norms and then tried to impose them. But we are now witnessing the emergence of a whole new class of people, once simply "queer," who now understand themselves *as transgendered individuals,* although the word did not exist 10 years ago.

FertilityQueers: Voices From Beyond the Sexual Binary

Two concerns: Is this really a big change in people's thinking? If so, how are such powerful effects achieved?

To the first concern, it's easy to respond that the idea of the "invention" of the homosexual is just "playing semantics." It may or may not be semantics, but it is not any sort of "play": The effects of such forms of knowledge are both profound and personal.

Quick: What is the name for the identity we use to refer to infertile women? How about women who have XXY chromosomes? Women who are masculinized because they produce too much testosterone? Mothers who like wearing suits and ties to work?

There are no such identities, because these are not bodies we want to track and control. But women who've had sex changes? We *all* know the name created to track *that* identity. But suppose, as with these other bodies, we didn't care about a woman's surgical history? Then such individuals would simply be "women," and the whole discourse around transexuality and the politicization of such bodies would not have happened, as it did not with these other kinds of women. Yet there is no doubt, had we given them an identity, categorized them socially and legally as not being "real women," and subjected them to widespread discrimination and violence, we would now be witnessing the emergence of a community of such individuals and a political movement to represent them, along with their demands for inclusion within feminist (and lesbian) organizations and anthologies like this one to promote their visibility.

How to Be Hip

Nor are the effects of such forms of knowledge confined to the political sphere. For instance, when I first decided to change my body, I was told I was transexual. I just wanted to change my body, but I was told the reason for this was that I was a "woman trapped in a man's body." I had a gender identity disorder. But I learned to think of myself as having a "birth defect," characterized by my new mental disorder.

When I entered the lesbian-feminist community of Cleveland Heights, Ohio, I was told I was still "really a man" or a "surgically altered she-male": in short, some kind of gender freak. I was kicked out of my apartment, shunned in bars, and barred from local events. Painful as this was, even worse was my buying into what was being said about me. I learned to think of myself as some sort of man-woman, neither male nor female: not even appropriate for my (lesbian) lover.

With the advent of transgenderism, I finally had a way of thinking of myself that gave me a sense of pride. I began to understand myself as transgendered. And, of course, at some point, that didn't work either, because like everything that preceded it, it didn't really fit.

It's not that I'm especially impressionable. To understand our bodies at all, we must make a stand somewhere. There is no neutral place, no position outside of language. We seek ways of understanding our bodies that solve what we perceive to be their problems.

In my case, the problem that was created about my body was its genderqueerness. And I sought ways of understanding it that would resolve that problem: some painful, some empowering. The problem could have been many other things. For instance, there's the gentlewoman who sat next to me on the bus, saying, "Please excuse my fat hips." When I asked her about this, she said, "I know, my feminist friends said I should think of them as nurturing and maternal." We had a long talk about her hips and my body and how miserable they'd made each of us.

Was she especially susceptible? I doubt it. But someone had explained to her that her hips were "width-queer," that they transcended some norm somewhere. She had internalized this as a problem of her body and sought ways of understanding it, just as I had, that would explain its "meaning."

Indeed, two things stand out most about our stories. First is how feminism's counterdiscourse on women's bodies has in its own way become as narrow and inflexible as the one from which it was supposed to free us. Second is how much the understanding of our bodies has colored how we feel about them. I doubt my wanting to change my body or that woman's hips had much implicit meaning. But the attachment of meaning is a powerful tool for making us experience ourselves in the world in very specific ways.

You Cut Me Up

Which brings me to my second concern: How are such effects achieved? As good progressives, when we think of Power, we imagine something above us, overwhelming, and harsh that we need laws to rein in. This works well with big, institutional power, like the police powers of arrest, the power of courts, and the government's power to spy on us or restrict our speech. But that kind of power doesn't go very far in explaining that women's hips or my body. After all, there was no central registry tracking us, no government agency compelling our experiences.

For that kind of power, we need another model: discourse. I seldom use the word, because when I do, Clare thrusts two fingers down her throat and makes rude gagging sounds. Academics may overuse it, but I think it's useful here. Discourse simply refers to power "from the bottom up." This is the kind of small power exercised in hundreds of little everyday transactions.

Think of the body's surface as a sheet of cookie dough. Because the dough has no inherent meaning, you can cut it all into circles, stars, or squares, or a mixture of different shapes all at once. When you're done, no doubt the cookies are "real." But there is no "truth" behind them, nothing to be learned from why one is a star and not a triangle, and no shape was any more *there* beforehand than any other. What truths there are lie with the cutter, not its product. Discourse is the cookie cutter.

But wait. All this is too abstract. Why don't you take a break for a minute, go down to the corner newsstand, and buy a *Times*?

News to Me

Fine. Does the man ahead of you hold the door for you as you leave your building? Do people step aside when you walk down the crowded street, or do they unconsciously expect you to step aside?

When you get to the newsstand, does the newspaper vendor address you as "Sir," "Ma'am," or "Miss"? Perhaps he finds you sexually confusing and stumbles awkwardly over pronouns. When he hands you your change, does he look down in respect, meet your eyes, or perhaps refuse to acknowledge you at all? Does he smile in friendliness or frown in disgust? If he's the guy you always see, before you leave, does he swap a dirty joke or ask about "the wife and kids?" Or maybe he flirts just a little, asking if you've lost weight and telling you that you need a young man in your life.

Even in this tiny exchange, a small fraction of your day, are piled up one interaction after another that stamp us with our sex, gender, or class. This is not power from the "top down," but from the "bottom up." It is not the big, familiar power of concrete buildings and visible institutions, power that is both massed and massive. Rather, it's the power of what is said and thought about us: the small, diffuse, invisible power created and instantly destroyed in thousands of little, insignificant exchanges.

It is through just such interactions that fat hips and queer bodies are made, interactions that tell us what we are, what we mean, and to what names we must answer.

Help! Youths Are Escaping the Stable!

But if this power of discourse is created and destroyed over and over again, then it must be inherently unstable too. What happens if it "fails"?

What about the homosexual? Could some people who are gay simply fail to acknowledge it? Not going into the closet, but simply refusing to answer to the name?

That is exactly what is happening among queer youth. As we've seen, identities are created in response to the politicization of bodies and desires. Eventually a countermovement emerges—as it did with homosexuals and now is doing with gender—to fight that politicization. But as this countermovement becomes successful, a paradox ensues. The more successful it is, the more unstable the discourse becomes. Gays show up on TV, in movies, as politicians running for office: Gayness is no longer so "queer."

Sexual orientation becomes less of a problem. (Recall that we asked at the opening if identities were a real feature of experience or an approximation of an ideal.) Young gays and lesbians don't walk down the street holding hands like we did, terrified, self-conscious, and staring rigidly straight ahead. They just walk around holding hands openly like their straight classmates. As the oppression that defined gay identity shifts, so does the meaning of the identification. Young queers face new possibilities, they can be other kinds of individuals, they can explore other selves.

Luckily for us, one of the selves many have used their new freedom to explore is gendered. Increasingly, numbers of youth are asking, "If I don't have to be gay anymore, what other selves are there for me to explore? Who might I be in another gender?" Gender, the old battleground, is quickly emerging as the new battleground and the new playground, for today's youth.

Put Down That Clipboard or I'll Shoot

The ways in which we formulate notions of selfhood out of the models of subjectivity available to us, shape our behavior in the world...
—Patricia Waugh, "Modernism, Postmodernism, Feminism: Gender and Autonomy Theory," from *Postmodernism: A Reader*, 1992

Do not demand of politics that it restore the "rights" of the individual, as philosophy has defined them. The individual is the product of power.
—Michel Foucault, *The History of Sexuality, Part 1*, 1978

We are used to taking the side of individual rights against institutional and governmental power. And we have centuries of political thought and experience to guide us in such struggles. But as Nancy Fraser notes, "Talk of rights and the inviolability of the person is of no use when the enemy is not the despot but the psychiatric social worker" with a clipboard. (Nancy Fraser, *Unruly Practices: Power, Discourse and Gender in Contemporary Social Theory*, 1989, p. 44)

With discourse, we're talking about a completely different kind of power—one that creates individuals. Our old political and theoretical tools don't apply. If the homosexual and the transgendered are themselves the product of certain kinds of power, we need new kinds of political action that will call into question individuality itself. Our problem is not fighting for the rights *of* specific individuals, but rather fighting for the right to *be* different kinds of individuals.

In other words, the question for genderqueers is, Do we want to fight *as genderqueers*? Or do we want to question the whole project of queerness? Do we want to make genderqueerness OK, just as gay rights is making gayness OK? Or do we want to attack the notion of normative genders itself?

The question is not as trivial as it sounds. For instance, a transgender movement devoted mostly to the problems faced by transexuals has the capacity to help a lot of embattled people. Yet it will leave out many people who are often gender-queered but not trans.

Do we want a transgender struggle that focuses on the rights of transexuals to change their driver's licenses, get surgery, and transition on the job? Or do we want a movement against the gender stereotypes that affect all Americans? This is not a rhetorical question. As gay rights continues to mature, the fight for gender equality looms as the next major civil rights struggle on the horizon. Our answers to such questions will have enormous power to shape what comes of it.

Deconstructing Trans

We're Just Like You, We're Just...Different

When a lesbian—perplexed at the furor over trans inclusion in her organization—asked me, "Where were transpeople 20 years ago?" I told her, "They were there, but they were gay."

I wasn't being snippy, but accurate. In the '70s they *were* there, and they *were* gay. But in just 20 years, they were neither.

Gender should have been the quintessential issue for both gay rights and feminism. And both owed a substantial debt to genderqueers: from outspoken suffragettes to radical dykes; from the genderqueers who rioted at the Stonewall Inn, to nelly boys picked out for assault.

But in the late 1970s and the '80s, both the gay and feminist movements turned away from gender as a primary issue, both for social and political reasons. The political reason was that following the success of black civil rights, minority rights turned definitively away from freedom of expression in favor of "immutable characteristics": things you can't change even if you want to.

If there's something socially undesirable about you that you *won't* suppress, then it's a matter of choice and not the law's concern. But if it's something undesirable that you *can't* suppress (race, disability, ethnicity), then the law should offer you protection. This has short-changed the right to self-expression. It has made social legitimacy an effect of helplessness before your own sexual and gender orientation

55

and whatever biological foundation you can put forth to explain them.

In the gay community the focus on immutability has led to promoting sexual orientation in a way that is completely removed from gender expression. Gay men never act effeminate, don't wear pastels, don't brandish limp wrists, and wouldn't be caught dead lip-synching to Barbra Streisand's Broadway album. Lesbians aren't butch, don't ride motorcycles, never sport crew cuts, and only wear combat boots if they've just come from Army boot camp.

In the trans community, just the opposite is the case. Gender is promoted at the expense of sexual practice. It's OK for me to say I'm changing my body because of my "gender identity." But it would be considered superficial, even perverse, to say I was doing so because having a more feminine body would turn me on. Among cross-dressers, it's acceptable to say that I wear women's clothing to "explore my feminine side," but not because it gives me an erection.

That's the political, but there's also the social reason these movements turned away from gender. Looking gender normative is vital to social acceptance. That's why few things are more uncomfortable than seeing someone whose gender you can't discern or more socially unacceptable than being a man who looks and acts likes like a woman or a woman who looks and acts like a man.

When gay activists began asserting , "We're just like straights, we just sleep with the same sex," that "just like" was shorthand for "gender." It said, "We look and act just like your parents, your friends, or your boss: Don't be uncomfortable with us."

And when feminists began explaining, "We're not trying to be men," the phrase "trying to be men" was also shorthand for "gender." It said, "We're just like your wives, mothers, daughters: Don't be uncomfortable with us either."

While the intervening years have proven this to be very successful rhetoric, they've also proven that it isolated genderqueerness as a civil rights issue. That was the price of social acceptance for two new and often-threatening movements.

It's fair to say that "transgender" was created by the gay and feminist movements. Its emergence became practically inevitable from the day those movements began moving away from gender.

A Hard Man Is Good to Find (But That Has *Nothing* to Do With My Gender)

Most remarkable in gender's evolution as an issue has been the widely accepted separation of gender and sexual orientation, even among transgender activists. But is desire really distinct from gender? Only if we confine *gender* to *gender identity*, as many gay organizations have done.

But watch any butch with big biceps, tight jeans, and a lit Camel walk into the local gay bar. Or a butch queen at the gym spending hour upon hour pumping and primping so he's buff enough to catch the eye of that cute new number with the tight butt, long eyelashes, and rippled abs. Or watch them in bed, one raising his butt, spreading his legs, and moaning to arouse the other. It is only through such gendered behaviors that sexual orientation is consummated, that it makes any conceptual sense. These behaviors are how we make ourselves attractive to others, are attracted to them, and make love.

Moreover, sexual orientation will always be tied to genderqueerness, because desire *itself* is gendered. A man having sex with a man or a woman having sex with a woman is itself the most profound transgression of gender norms conceivable. It is at the heart of homophobia.

It need not harm gay political aspirations to admit the obvious: That if it is gender-feminine to pull a dress over the male body, it is gender-feminine to pull a man down on it as well.

The Queerer Sex

Where is feminism in this today? Why has transgenderism remained the source of long-running tensions within feminist ranks? Gender-queerness would seem to be a natural avenue for feminism to contest Woman's equation with nurturance, femininity, and reproduction: in short, to trouble the project of Man. Yet feminists have been loath to take that avenue, in no small part because queering Woman threatens the very category on which feminism depends.

Man is the universal. Woman is defined by her opposition to Man, by what she does not have, the Penis, and the one thing she has that Man does not, reproduction and sexuality. Thus, to be androgynous is not gender-neutral but male. Man is the default sex; womanhood must continually prove itself by artifice, adornment, and display. In a culture centered on Man, Woman will always be the genderqueer. This has made Woman an inherently fragile project. Feminist and lesbian communities have remained deeply unreceptive to the new barbarians at the gate—F-to-Ms, M-to-Fs, passing women, cross-dressers, drag kings and queens, and tranz youth—who seem to threaten the very foundation of Woman, while male communities feel no such concern. A bearded, muscle-bound F-to-M evokes nothing like the same resentment, anxiety, and concern for authenticity in a men's group that either he or an attractive, curvaceous M-to-F does in a women's group.

It may take a new generation of young women to take queerness to its natural feminist conclusions—women for whom such queerness is not a threat but a new kind of feminist freedom.

Only Half the Man I Used to Be

"Transgender" origins lie in the search for a name for people who didn't want to change sexes (as transexuals do) or occasionally change to clothing of another sex (as cross-dressers do) but who wanted to change their genders: live full-time in another sex without medical intervention. Over time transgender came to be used for anyone who "transgressed gender," including—according to who you ask—cross-dressers, transexuals, and the original transgendered but also butch women, effeminate men, intersexuals, drag people, and genderqueer youths.

The term has not been without its conceptual awkwardness. Defining a class of people by "transgressing" norms would seem in some way to reinforce those norms. In addition, it defines people by what they are not—normal men and women. However, *transgender* has undoubtedly enabled many despised and marginalized people to come together around a common voice and a way to identify that is empowering and constructive.

Most cities now boast a local transgender group, and today, transgender conferences are being held somewhere in the United States almost every month. There is even a kind of tenuous artistic legitimacy, as transexuals find their way into movies like *Boys Don't Cry* and *Hedwig and the Angry Inch*. With this legitimacy has come political activism: Transexual activists now pass local ordinances, educate policy makers, and win lawsuits. And while transgender's increasing acceptance has not stopped the flow of blood from trans murders and hate crimes, there is reason to hope.

Let Me Hold That Umbrella for You

Transgender was intended as an umbrella term, then a name of inclusion. But umbrellas don't work well when one group holds them up. Today, trans activism is often focused on the problems (bathroom access, name change, workplace transition, and hate crimes) faced by those who have been most active in its success: postoperative male-to-female transsexuals (any similarity to the author is purely coincidental).

Yet there is little being done today to address the needs of drag people, butches, cross-dressers, transsexuals who do not seek surgery, or (besides the Intersex Society of North America) intersexuals. Cross-dressers especially have suffered from lack of representation, although they number in the millions and experience severe problems associated with child custody, job discrimination, hate crimes, and punitive divorce precedents.

Thus has transgender, a voice that originated from the margins, begun to produce its own marginalized voices. And in part because—as an identity organized around "transgression"—there is a growing debate over who is "most transgressive."

In Surgery We Trust

How does one decide such questions? For instance, as one transsexual put it, "I'm not this part-time. I can't hang my body in the closet and pass on Monday."

There is no doubt, from one perspective, that cross-dressers enjoy some advantages. They are large in numbers, most only dress occasionally, and they can do so in the privacy of their own homes. Does that mean they would live that way if they had a choice? Does it really make them "less transgressive"?

In fact, nobody wants men in dresses. There are no "out" cross-dressers, and almost no political organization wants them or wants to speak in their name. "A man in a dress" is the original "absurd result" that judges, juries, even legislators try to avoid at all costs when rendering verdicts or crafting laws. "Men in dresses" isn't the next hit movie: It's a punch line in the next joke.

Among genderqueer youth, it is no longer rare to hear complaints of being frozen out of transgender groups because they don't want to change their bodies. In an identity that favors transsexuals, changing one's body has become a litmus test for transgression. And even that litmus test is not always applied.

For example, one would assume that preoperative transexuals (or the increasing number of nonoperative transexuals) would be considered more transgressive, as would transgendered people of any stripe who don't "pass" as binary males and females. A 6-foot, 3-inch presurgical transexual woman with a deep voice and 5 o'clock shadow is doing the hardest, loneliest, and most dangerous gender activism there is. The same could be said for a 5-foot, 2-inch butch with a pear shape, small hands, and high voice who insists on having her masculinity recognized, acknowledged, and respected. Yet these are not the individuals who are highly prized as "most transgressive." In fact, as with most communities founded on oppression, the opposite occurs: those who can pass are most highly valued, as are those whose surgery makes them legally male or female. Since trans activists have loudly and justifiably complained about being "most transgressive" and about being consigned to the bottom rung of gay and feminist concerns, so it is doubly unfortunate to see them developing hierarchies of their own, in which transpeople must compete for legitimacy and in which their own margins sometimes go unrecognized. Indeed, like assertions over who has more "privilege," debates over who is most "transgressive" are a form of reverse discrimination that seeks to confer status based on who has it worst.

Which is to say, debates over identity are always divisive and never conclusive. They are divisive because at heart they are about conferring status, always a zero-sum game. For one person to win, another must lose. They are inconclusive because there are no objective criteria by which to decide. Winning such debates is always a function of who sets the rules and who gets to judge. And since postsurgical transexuals are most often in a position to judge, at the moment, the rules tend to favor their life experiences.

You're Indescribable

Transgender is now commonly used in two ways: as both an identity and a descriptive adjective. As an identity, it faces the same question as gender itself. Is it transgression about something we *are* or something we *do*? So far the answer has been definitely "something we are." This has created an interesting collision between theorists who understand gender as a doing and many transexual activists who claim it as a being.

The arguments being used to promote the theoretical importance of transexuals are undercutting those being used to advance their political legitimacy.

Organizations seeking to add transgender issues to their work add "gender identity" to their mission statements: a psychiatric term related to transexuals. But when we equate transgenderism with those individuals who can claim *their* gender is a sign of an internal, binary essence, we privilege transexuals over other genderqueers who cannot make similar claims. Moreover, we diminish those who conceptualize their transcending of narrow gender stereotypes as a matter of the right to self-expression.

If a boy is repeatedly beaten up after school for being a "sissy," can he plausibly claim that his "sissyness" results from some inner identity? What about a big-breasted femme who is sexually assaulted for being perceived as "sexually provocative"? Does the fact that they cannot claim their transgression to result from a "gendered identity" make it any less meaningful? Some gay and trans activists would reply yes.

While transgender identity is promoted as including butches, femmes, and drag people, it is hard to find many who so identify. Perhaps one lesson is that when an identity cannot be applied equally, those who are less equal refuse identification.

And while there are undoubtedly millions of Americans who frequently transcend gender roles—from ballet-loving quarterbacks to suit coat–wearing soccer moms—the identity remains inhospitable to them as well.

Too Queer for Words

Some trans activists have tried to correct these limitations by "embracing the contradiction." They emphasize the big-tent approach of transgender-as-adjective and assert, "We are *all* transgendered." This rings true, but does it also ring useful?

If people refuse a term as identity, is it more likely they will accept it as a description? And if not, of what use is describing people with an adjective they reject? The emphasis on transgender as a description also harks back to the idea of *all* gender as drag, as a kind of displacement of self into binary norms. Yet many transexuals reject such arguments. They understand—and want others to understand—that their gender results from a core identity, a true self that is not the result of some external norms.

Moreover, many transgendered people are attracted to the term because it is not openly inclusive, because it *does* name a specific group of people. They accept *transgender*'s wider use when it leads to greater social acceptance. But they would deeply resist the guy in the next cubicle who wept over last night's Super Bowl loss to the Packers, saying, "Yeah, I cried...I guess I am transgendered."

In fact, GenderPAC's reaffirmation in 2000 of its mission to be a human rights group for all Americans drew angry rejoinders from many trans activists who wanted a gender rights group that was exclusive to them. Among the loudest voices were those who had been calling for gay organizations to be transgender-inclusive and were now attacking a human rights approach for not being exclusive enough. In retrospect, it is difficult to see how excluding gay, feminist, or straight Americans is ethically superior to excluding transgendered people...or anyone else.

The only group today using transgression in its widest and most uncritical descriptive sense is queer youth, who consistently prefix anything genderqueer with "trans" or "tranz." Many such radical youths are taking civil rights to the next level: finally making the long-delayed connection among gay, feminist, and trans politics.

It is still an open question if *genderqueer,* a word promoted to resolve some of these issues, will yet create its own hierarchies and exclusions. Looking over the many debates about which authors and voices belong in this anthology, my bet is it will.

The New *Gay*

What began as the "gay community," then the "lesbian and gay community" (make sure not to erase women, put them first to make up for historic injustices), then the "lesbian, gay, and bisexual community" (append bisexuals whenever we remember to, don't forget they get oppressed too for sleeping with the same sex, wish they'd finally choose one sex or the other and stop passing themselves off as straight when it's convenient), has finally become—for all practical purposes (except when one was being quoted in *The New York Times* or on CNN, you know, something important)—the "lesbian, gay, bisexual, and transgender community."

The term *LGBT* is still uncomfortable for some people. Some gays and lesbians can still be heard asking quietly, in their more politically incorrect moments, "Why—I mean, I know, I shouldn't even think this, let alone say it—but why does changing your gender/sex belong in a movement about sexual orientation?" A good question if you think that sexual orientation and gender are separate. An even better question if you are fortunate enough to look, well…straight.

But there is no denying that after a persistent 10-year struggle, the *T* in *LGBT* is here to stay. Will the new gay embrace of transgender be successful? Will gay organizations actually devote any real resources to transgender, and if so, will they give us anything more than transexual rights?

On this, the jury is still out. Although a few organizations have led the way, most organizations have not brought to bear anything like real muscle, and what muscle there is continues to be channeled into "gender identity" and transexual concerns.

In the meantime, butches, queens, fairies, high femmes, tomboys, sissy boys, and cross-dressers have completely vanished from civil discourse. They are never mentioned in public statements by any major progressive organization. For political purposes, they have ceased to exist.

Gender itself remains invisible as a progressive issue. If it is mentioned at all, it is carefully confined to transgender. In effect, *gender* has become the new *gay*. It is the thing we no longer speak about in polite company. I think here of school bullying, which is all about gender. People are paying attention to it now because, unfortunately, some victims shot their classmates. These are terrible crimes. But is the gender-bashing of school-age youths new? Hasn't it been a regular feature of schools since there were classrooms and young boys in them? Or did we just overlook it because sissy boys are not a gay, feminist—or now gender identity—issue?

With gender stretched across the whole surface of individuals' relations with society, maybe it's time to quit attacking the problem piece-meal, waiting for the next issue to appear on the front page of *The New York Times*. Maybe it's time to acknowledge gender stereotypes as a problem we all share, a central concern, a way to come together: a human rights issue for us all.

Stories

Queens in Exile, the Forgotten Ones
Sylvia Rivera

Sylvia Rivera is the founder of Street Transgender Action Revolutionaries (STAR), a veteran of the Stonewall uprising, and a long-time political activist. She lives in Brooklyn, N.Y., with her partner, Julia, and works at the Metropolitan Community Church in Manhattan.

My mother was 22 when she decided to off herself. She was having a shaky second marriage; my stepfather was a drug dealer, and that was one of the reasons the marriage was on shaky grounds. He threatened to kill her and me and my sister. I was 3 years old.

She mixed rat poison into milk, drank it, and gave some to me. I believe the brand was JR Rat Poison, and it came in a light reddish-orange tin. When they took me off to get my stomach pumped was the last time I saw my mother alive, because after being in the hospital three days, she died.

She drank her poison, and I drank only part of what she gave me because I didn't like the taste of the milk. I added sugar to it. I didn't know what it was, but it just didn't taste right. I remember seeing her laid out in the coffin. Back in those days you had to wake a body for three days. It was like sheer torture, but in my mind she was sleeping. My grandmother told me after I was grown up more that I tried to wake her up, that I disturbed her in her coffin. One of the last things she told my grandmother on her deathbed was that she wanted to kill me because she knew I was going to have a hard life. And she pinpointed it, because it has not been an easy road. I've enjoyed the struggles, but I've also had my bouts with trying to off myself.

I was very effeminate as a young child. Life wasn't easy with my grandmother because she always told me that she never really wanted me, that she wanted my sister. My sister was taken away from her when my stepfather put her up for adoption. My grandmother never forgave me for that; she wanted my sister because she was a girl, and I was a boy.

I basically grew up without love. I guess in her own strict way my grandmother loved me. She did want me to acquire a good education. She insisted in putting me in all-white Catholic schools. And she didn't want me to learn the Spanish language. It upset her when I spoke to her in Spanish.

She wanted me to be a white child. She was a prejudiced woman. I mean, dark people, African-American people, would scare her. She came from Venezuela. She would have a little gesture or say something when black people would come on the subway or something; she would either rub her arm and say, "Look at them, they're coming," or she would call them "blonds" and look dead in their direction. She was a very racist woman.

She did not approve of my mother's marriages because both men were Puerto Ricans. My father was a very dark-skinned Puerto Rican. My stepfather was not as dark. My grandmother didn't like the idea of me having Puerto Rican blood. It would have been better if I had just been a Venezuelan child.

I was wearing makeup in the fourth grade. I did it because I liked makeup, and I didn't think there was anything wrong with it. I remember being questioned about it by my teacher, and I said, "Yeah, my grandmother knows." Of course it was a lie. She didn't know because there was a woman who was taking care of me out on Long Island, and I would put on my makeup on my way to school. I knew I could wear it home and take it off by 5 o'clock without having any problems because there was nobody in the house.

So to me it was normal. I really didn't get much of a slacking from the kids. I remember only one child, and he was the sixth-grade bully, who called me a faggot because I always played with the girls. At the time, I was either playing hopscotch or doing double Dutch. And I just went off on him. I beat the daylights out of him, and I don't remember much of it, but I do remember the confrontation in front of our principal. The principal asked me, "Why did you beat him up?" I said, "He called me a faggot. Do I look like a faggot to you?" I was painted, you know, and had on these tight, tight pants. I didn't know what a faggot was, but I felt insulted. I had already had sex, but I thought it was all part of just being who you were.

I only felt how unusual this was when I was back on the lower east side with my grandmother where I had to go on the weekends. It was a male-dominant culture. Of the boys I hung around with, I slept with one. The other boys knew where I was coming from. Every once in a while there were remarks. A lot of the women would make innuendos. A woman one time patted me on my ass and said, "Huh, your ass is getting big, that means you're getting pumped," and I took offense at that because I knew when I was home—you know, on the lower east side—that there was something wrong with what I was doing. My grandmother used to come home and it smelled like a French whorehouse, but that didn't stop me. I got many ass-whippings from her.

Before I even left home, I was turning tricks with my uncle for money. We didn't have much money, and I wanted things my grandmother couldn't buy. In the beginning I didn't know who I was attracted to. I'd look at men in old movies and get fascinated by them, but my sexuality was aroused when I was 7 years old. My cousin was baby-sitting me, and I always found him attractive. He offered and I accepted.

As I've grown up, I've realized that I do have a certain attraction to men. But I believe that growing up the way I did, I was basically pushed into this role. In Spanish cultures, if you're effeminate, you're automatically a fag; you're a gay boy. I mean, you start off as a young child and you don't have an option—especially back then. You were either a fag or a dyke. There was no in-between. You have your journey through society the way it is structured. That's how I fit into it at that time in my life. Those were the words of that era. I was an effeminate gay boy. I was becoming a beautiful drag queen, a beautiful drag-queen child. Later on, of course, I knew that Christine [Jorgensen] was already around, but those things were still waiting in the backs of people's minds.

Being on my own at 10 years old, on the street in Times Square, was frightening. I had to be resourceful. I had already experienced the hustling scene with my uncle. I had found my way to 42nd Street by the comments made when my family used to go to Coney Island. The adults would say about people who got on at 42nd Street who were effeminate and wearing makeup, "Oh, look at the *maricóns*," and I would have to turn my face away because it hurt me to hear that. They would say, "This is where the *maricóns* come and they make money." Of course, that registered in my head, and I found my way back there and dipped and dabbed and made money selling my body. So when I left home to 42nd Street for good I wasn't seasoned, but I knew what I had to do to survive.

I was adopted by a few young (but older than I was) drag queens. They helped me out. We hung out all night. Chickie lived with her mother in Brooklyn somewhere and she knew that her mother went to work at a certain time, so she'd bring three or four queens home and we'd crash and get out of there before her mother came home. It was like roaming from house to house, or I'd stay in the hotel room the trick would rent.

I was afraid, but I didn't really think of it because I needed to survive. I found it disgusting, though. I used to go home and scrub myself clean. This was in the early '60s. The drag scene was a night life. We basically didn't go out during the day. I guess we had to hide. Also, if you're out all night, you don't want to be out during the day.

But it was dangerous on 42nd Street. We all stuck together. The police were constantly chasing us. We had a code: If one of the girls or one of the boy hustlers spotted a cop, word was passed down that "Lily in blue" was coming. This meant we would disappear. So a warning of "Alice in the blue gown" or "Lily" meant to disperse.

I was too young to go to the few clubs that existed, but there were many house parties. They were called rent parties. There was always something going on. And it was fun, you know, because people needed money for their rent. Fifty cents, a dollar…you helped somebody out and you might end up crashing there some time. That was basically the scene for the youth back then, except for the drag balls. But you had to be a little older than I was to start going with that group of people.

You had drag balls up in Harlem and you had them downtown. We had the Phil Black's ball, we had the April in Paris ball…those were the two main ones. And there were balls constantly going on. I know the April in Paris ball used to be held at the Manhattan Center on 34th Street.

Balls gave us a social affair. If you didn't go, you just weren't part of the in crowd. And what talent you saw there! There were women who spent a year sewing and designing their costumes, just to get ready for one ball. And the hairstyles with 20 wigs…I'm exaggerating—we'll say seven or eight piled on top of one another. Being brought in in a gilded cage carried by half-naked young men. It was something extravagant and beautiful, something you don't see in balls today.

We had cross-dressers, but I didn't even know what cross-dressers were until much later. The street queens have always been prostitutes to survive, because some of us left home so early, or it just wasn't feasible to be working if you wanted to wear your makeup and do your thing. But there was that division at the balls where you had drag queens who were not from the same side of the tracks we were. Some of them were very affluent.

There were always drugs on the streets. In the early '60s there were a lot of ups. I got my Benzedrine supply from my truck driver customers. I was fascinated by speed. Besides alcohol. But those were my drugs of preference back in the mid '60s to early '70s. And then I changed around. I did a lot of heroin. I did heroin for about five years. Actually I've done everything that's been put out, especially in the '70s…LSD…basically everything, even to modern-day crack. But I haven't done ecstasy. And most everything I've kicked on my own.

I just sobered up off booze two years ago. I'm sober for the first time in my life without any alcohol in my body, and I've been drinking since before I left home. I started dipping at home, drinking booze about the age of 8. I always drank booze, besides taking all the other drugs. I'd mix my drugs and my booze together. It was something I thought was going to kill me. I thank my lucky stars. Somebody must be watching. Some higher power has been watching me 'cause I've tried to off myself at least six or seven times. It just wasn't meant to be.

I met Marsha Johnson like a year after I hit the streets. Marsha, I believe, was seven years my senior. It was Halloween night and she had just come out of the Port Authority because she still lived in Jersey with her family. She was dressed up in drag. A bunch of Spanish queens started going, "Oh, look at Marsha," and this one queen named Louisa snatched Marsha's wig. Well, Marsha wasn't going to have it. When she caught up to Louisa up on 42nd Street and Sixth Avenue she beat the living daylights out of her.

Then one time I was walking across Sixth Avenue and she was standing there on the corner. She called me to her side, we introduced ourselves, and a very strong sistership was born. She took me out to eat. She was standing there hustling even though she was working as a waiter at Childs' Restaurant. But she always had to make extra change, as she always said.

And later on we would see each other at clubs or at different gatherings. She knew my first lover and came to my apartment out in Jersey. We stood by each other, had each other's back for many years. And even back in the days of pre-Stonewall, we would sit on 44th Street, a lot of us girls like Marsha and Vanessa, Miss Edwina, Miss Josie, a whole bunch of us, would sit around in a room. We'd be getting high or something and we'd start talking politics. We'd start talking politics and about when things were going to change for us as human beings.

After Stonewall, Marsha and I just kept up the struggle. We saw the need after being out on the streets at our ages. We needed to help our own people. Even when we were living on 44th Street, Marsha always took in people, gave them a place to stay. At that time, before Stonewall, everyone always had a house full of people, people crashing because there was no room. If one queen had a place and you were her friend, she would gladly let you sleep on her floor or share her bed. There would be not just the two of us; there would be maybe four or five. And everybody was sneaking around not wanting to get caught by whoever we were renting from.

There are two stories of how Marsha died. One is that she supposedly committed suicide, and the other is that somebody murdered her. They fished her body out of the Hudson River at the end of Christopher Street nine years ago. It was very shocking for me when I got the telegram. Actually I was really pissed at her because our pact was that we would cross the Jordan together. She would get angry with me when I tried to off myself, so we made a pact. That's why I find it hard to believe she committed suicide.

Marsha had been on SSI (Social Security Disability) for quite some time because she had several nervous breakdowns. She had been locked up several times in Bellevue and Manhattan State. Her mind started really going. She had a doctor who did not diagnose her syphilis right away. So when they finally caught it, it was in the second stages. Marsha lived in her own realm, and she saw things through different eyes. She liked to stay in that world, so with that and the syphilis infection...and then her husband, Cantrell, was shot by an off-duty officer. He was shot to death and she really went over the edge.

She managed to come out of that one, and then she lost it again. She came over to my house dressed like the Virgin Mary, in white and blue, and she was carrying a wooden cross and a Bible. She came in and started preaching the Bible to me and we had a few words. Then she took the wooden cross and hit me upside the head with it. If it had been any other queen, I would probably be in jail, 'cause I would have killed her. She drew blood because the nail wasn't completely bent, and she put a gash in my head.

The next day I heard they arrested her and locked her up again. So she had several breakdowns. Bob Kohler, who was very close to her and to me, says that she committed suicide. He was closer to her the last few months. She always would go down to the end of Christopher Street, supposedly talking to her brother and wanting to go talk to her father in the water.

And there is testimony that some guys were messing with her and they threw her in the river. The police couldn't prove it. So I'm still stuck in the middle. When I heard that she was murdered, I couldn't understand why anybody would kill her. Marsha would give the blouse off her back if you asked for it. She would give you her last dollar. She would take off her shoes. I've seen her do all these things, so I couldn't see someone killing her. I know there are crazy people out there. I know there are transphobic people out there. But it's not like she wasn't a known transperson. She was loved anywhere she went. Marsha was a great woman.

Being arrested for "loitering with the intention of prostitution" became a routine, you know, 'cause I knew I was getting out the next day. The process is that they'll keep you, they'll process you, and you'll go in front of a judge. The judge will most likely dismiss the charge 'cause they go by your record. In all the years I was out there hustling— and that's between hustling and still doing politics—I was blessed because I was never arrested for prostitution. It was always "with the intention" or just standing out on a corner, loitering. So I never got arrested or did time for prostitution.

The judge paid people like me no mind because I had no convictions. Cases would be thrown out, so it would never be on my record. Most of the girls had records, so that's what the judge would go by. To get busted for pros you had to do a solicitation—or they entrapped you. A lot of the girls would ask me how come I wouldn't go with a customer, and I suppose it was because I got the wrong vibe. I believed he was the Man.

"Aw," they'd say, "you always saying that."

"All right, when he comes back around you take him. I'm not jumping in the Man's car." Of course I'd see them 15 or 30 days later and I'd say, "Oh, so we were on vacation again, huh?"

"Yeah, I shoulda listened to you, Sylvia."

I go by what I feel. What my spirits tell me, I'm following. Every time I went with what my spirits told me (except for two times, and both times I had to fight my way out of a situation), I was right. My instincts would-say no, I'd rather starve to death. And the girls wouldn't listen. And Marsha used to be the same way. I would tell her, "Don't go with that man."

"Aw, Miss Thing, stop…"

"I'll see you when you get home in 30 days."

But I was lucky. The only time I did time was for possession of heroin. And the cops who arrested me told me, "We couldn't get you one way, so we figure we had to get you another way." The cops in the area I worked at that time, which was downtown on Chrystie Street by the Bowery, were angry because they could never bust me for pros.

I did get into cars with undercover agents, not realizing until too late. I had one cop pull a gun out on me and say, "You're gonna do me or I'm gonna take you in."

I'm like, "Fine, take me in, I don't care." Then I pop the door open to jump out of the car.

He says, "If you get out of the car, I'll shoot…"

I say, "Aw, you'll be doing the world a favor, one less queer in the world, one less junkie…one less ho!" And I got out very grandly, walked to the corner, and then ran like a bat out of hell.

I was bold; I would take these chances. Why should I give this man a blow job, not knowing whether he's going to take me to jail or not? I don't like the idea of giving free service. I'm not out there to give anyone free service. At that time I was a heroin addict and I had a bunch of kids to support in STAR House. I had no time for games.

And there was another incident. I told the man where to park and he didn't, just kept on going and running through red lights. He said, "I'm taking you in for pros." And I said, "No, you're not." And he was going at a high speed. I popped the door open and threw myself out of the car, rolled, then hit the street running.

I was untouchable until the heroin thing. For that I got sentenced 90 days. That first night I fall asleep and my bullpen is packed with men. I wake up sick as a dog because I need a fix and I think, *Aw, shit, I'm fucked.* And there's one guy I know from the streets, so he gives me some protection, for a while. But when they take him upstairs to the Tombs, I'm left alone with all these other men. And suddenly they start hitting on me. "Come on, mama. I been in here for a year. I need a good piece of pussy," and blah, blah, blah... And I'm like, "Oh, no, we're not having this."

So I get knocked around a couple of times. I fight back, I holler for the C.O., and he comes to the cell. "What's the problem?" And I say, "These guys are trying to take me off," and he very nicely tells them, "Enjoy yourselves, boys, have fun." So I have to think fast. "O-o-okay...but we only suck dick. I'm sorry, I just don't get fucked up." Well, I guess they were dumb, because if some ho—you have a woman cornered and this woman is telling you that all she does is suck dick— then you know she must have an ulterior motive.

The one I ended up giving head to regretted it. I didn't stop biting that boy's dick until I drew blood, and they beat me so hard on my head for me to let go. That gave me a reputation. By the time I got to Rikers Island that evening, it was "That's the crazy bitch that bit that boy's dick. Leave her alone." It's always good to play crazy.

But it is rough for some of the girls, because they give it up. And once you give it up, you gotta give it up to every Tom, Dick, and Harry. So automatically you try to protect yourself in the hope that you don't get killed in the process, or you give it up and be used for all the time you're in jail. So I'd rather take the easy way out. I'd rather be dead than be subject to that. I'd always managed to protect myself.

Jail is not a happy place for transwomen and gay boys. It's a very unhappy place. Even though you're segregated, kept out of the general population, you have boys who would sign the papers that they were homos. I used to find that fascinating, that every time I'd been arrested, they'd have this big stamp that stamps all your records HOMO in big red letters. I used to crack up about that. I said, "Jesus, couldn't you just put it in a little box?" No, they got to put it all over in red letters.

You asked to be segregated. Drag queens didn't have to ask for it. We were automatically segregated. But anyone could say they were gay and they'd let them through. So the boys would try to run your quad, except that when you had a bunch of queens on one floor, it was very hard for the men to dominate. A lot of times there were fights on the quad with the boys 'cause they would try to rule and the girls would not have it. It's like, "This is our property and we don't wish to be here, but this is our vacation spot and you are here...I guess...because you want to get your dick sucked..." Many of those boys who claimed to be straight and signed the papers as homos were the first ones to fall down to their knees when you were in the cell with them or turn on their stomachs wanting to get fucked. There's a reason behind everything.

I thought about having a sex change, but I decided not to. I feel comfortable being who I am. That final journey many of the transwomen and transmen make is a big journey. It's a big step and I applaud them, but I don't think I could ever make that journey. Maybe it comes of my prejudice when so many in the late '60s and early '70s ran up to the chop shop up at Yonkers General. They would get a sex change and a month, maybe six months, later they'd kill themselves because they weren't ready. Maybe that made me change my mind. I really don't know, but I always like to be an individual. In the beginning I decided that not getting the operation was because I wanted to keep the "baby's arm."

My first lover taught me how to make love to another man, and in my youth I was always supposed to be the bottom. This is the way I thought a relationship was...an effeminate gay boy was solely to be the bottom. My lover was a butch-looking boy, very butch. Actually, no one even knew he was gay.

He showed me how to make love. He said, "When you're with another man, this is the way men make love." It was very hard in the beginning. He would ask me and I would refuse to make love to him 'cause I didn't think he was telling me the truth. But he knew exactly what I was doing. After we would make love he'd go out, and he'd tell me, "You wait for me to leave to masturbate, to jerk off when we can be doing that together. That's what love is about."

People now want to call me a lesbian because I'm with Julia, and I say, "No. I'm just me. I'm not a lesbian." I'm tired of being labeled. I don't even like the label *transgender*. I'm tired of living with labels. I just want to be who I am. I am Sylvia Rivera. Ray Rivera left home at the age of 10 to become Sylvia. And that's who I am.

I will be 50 years old this coming Monday. I don't need the operation to find my identity. I have found my niche, and I'm happy and content with it. I take my hormones. I'm living the way Sylvia wants to live. I'm not living in the straight world; I'm not living in the gay world; I'm just living in my own world with Julia and my friends.

The night Stonewall happened everybody was out partying. People were mourning, even me. We were mourning Judy Garland's death. Some authors have said that the riot came out of Judy Garland's death, but that's not true. Judy had nothing to do with the riot. Nor was any of it planned. It was something that just happened.

I guess there was tension in the air. It was a hot, muggy night, in the 80s or 90s, like when most riots happen. I don't know how many other patrons in the bar were activists, but many of the people were involved in some struggle. I had been doing work in the civil rights movement, against the war in Vietnam, and for the women's movement.

The bar paid off the cops at the beginning of the week, supposedly, on Monday night. A lot of bars were run by the Mafia. They paid off the police in the sixth precinct. Inspector Pine, who officiated the raid on Stonewall, had just been given his job as head of the morals squad. They were out to bust all the corruption in the police department and also close down these bars.

So the Stonewall was the first place he hit on in his new job. I'm in a book with him by David Isay. He says he thought it was going to be a routine bust. That's why they went in with only a few men. But to his surprise, we fought back. As he put it, "*Those* people would never give us any problem, because they had a lot to lose." So this night was different. This was the start of our talking back, speaking up for ourselves.

They came in; the lights went on. People ran for the bathrooms and got rid of their drugs. We stopped dancing. People started pairing off with someone of the opposite sex to try to make it look as "normal" as we could. And here the law walks in and it's, "Faggots here, dykes here, and freaks over here." The queens and the real butch dykes were the freaks.

Then we were proofed. You had to have on three articles of clothing that accorded to your gender. That was a law. So females had to have three pieces of women's clothing. It could be whatever, as long as the cop decided to accept it. At that time, the '60s, we called it *scare* drag. We were out a lot during the day with makeup, blouses, women's slacks—but no tits. We called it scare drag so we could say we weren't in drag.

To that point it was a typical bust. They proofed us. We went out the door. But no one dispersed. 'Cause usually we'd go somewhere and have coffee and come back in 15, 20 minutes. The padlock was cut off, and it was back to business—drinking watered-down booze, buying drugs, and dancing.

What people fail to realize is that the Stonewall was not a drag queen bar. It was a white male bar for middle-class males to pick up young boys of different races. Very few drag queens were allowed in there, because if they had allowed drag queens into the club, it would have brought the club down. That would have brought more problems to the club. It's the way the Mafia thought, and so did the patrons. So the queens who were allowed in basically had inside connections. I used to go there to pick up drugs to take somewhere else. I had connections.

The main drag queen bar at that time was the Washington Square Bar on Third Street and Broadway. That's where you found diesel dykes and drag queens and their lovers. Oh, yeah, we mixed with lesbians. We always got along together back then. All that division between the lesbian women and queens came after 1974 when Jean O'Leary and the radical lesbians came up. The radicals did not accept us or masculine-looking women who dressed like men. And those lesbian women might not even have been trans. But we did get along famously in the early '60s. I've been to many a dyke party. And transgendered men back then were living and working. I met many who were working and living as men with their female lovers. They were highly respected. The lesbian community today has a lot to learn from the old ways of the lesbian community.

I didn't really get involved in gay politics until 1970. After

Stonewall, I was getting my news from the *Gay Power* newspaper, and I was at the founding of the Gay Activists Alliance. That was the first real political meeting I went to. They were just getting their platform statement, their mission statement. I saw an ad in the paper, and I called the number and said, "Hello, do you take drag queens?"

They said yes and I got Miss Josie, and off to this meeting we go. First thing we get there it's "What's your name?" and I'm, like, "Sylvia." And the guy at the door said, "Don't you have a boy's name?" And I'm like, "Who? What?" So right away that was a setback. But I got involved, and the reason I stayed with them was for the gay rights bill. That's when we started petitioning for the gay rights bill, the New York City bill. And I felt comfortable being there.

That first meeting was where I met one of my best girlfriends even today: Bebe. She was sitting there, and I started talking to Josie in Spanish. I said, "Hmm...she looks like one of us," referring to her as a drag queen. She was a young child. We were just 19 years old. She turned and answered me in English, "I understood everything you said about me, and, yes, I'm one of you. I'm like you." And we became the best of friends.

The reason I stayed in GAA was the simple fact that I liked the idea that we, as an organization, were going to change the world. And there was a place for us. I fell right into the grand scheme of things. I remember I was out petitioning, I'd been doing it for a couple of weeks, and I remember that on April 15, 1970, I was petitioning on 42nd Street. I hadn't picked up why no gay men had come into the Times Square area. I figured that while they were up on 72nd Street, where most of the gay men were living at that time, or in the Village, I could take care of 42nd Street—my home turf.

There was a "Stop the War in Vietnam" demo and people started coming. The cops had dispersed the demo, and I'm standing out there collecting signatures, and two cops come by, and they say, "You have to move." And I'm like, "Why? All I'm doing is collecting signatures. I'm petitioning for gay rights."

"It's against the law."

I said, "What? I thought it said in the Constitution we have the right to acquire signatures..."

"You don't have an American flag."

"What does an American flag have to do with me collecting signatures?"

"You have to have an American flag."

I said, "It wouldn't make a difference. I've been to jail with poor Rosie over there, who is always being arrested with her American flag and her Bible for preaching the gospel." Rosie was a right-wing Bible-thumper. Well, I got arrested for petitioning for gay rights.

That's how my whole activist career started. Besides, I didn't consider that night at the Stonewall to be so important out of all the other movements going on. Getting that first arrest for something that I believed in was...wow, what a rush!

I bailed myself out of jail, and went to GAA the following day and told them what happened. We had a press conference, and Arthur Bell—may his soul rest in peace—grabbed me out of that meeting and dragged me to his apartment up in the 60s. And he says, "I'm going to put you up on a pedestal. You will be a star." I'm like, "Yeah, yeah, yeah..." So we did an interview on the bus, and then he followed me for about a week on 42nd Street, collecting signatures from people: mature women and men, couples, heterosexuals, and gay people. That's how things started for me.

And I was happy at GAA for a while. But it wasn't my calling. I found out later on that they only believed in acquiring civil rights for the gay community as a whole. Which is fine. They did a lot of good just concentrating on the gay issue. But they left the queens behind.

I enjoyed Gay Liberation Front better because we concentrated on many issues for many different struggles. We're all in the same boat as long as we're being oppressed one way or the other, whether we are gay, straight, trans, black, yellow, green, purple, or whatever. If we don't fight for each other, we'll be put down. And after all these years, the trans community is still at the back of the bus.

I despise that. I'm hurt and get depressed a lot about it. But I will not give up because I won't give the mainstream gay organizations the satisfaction of keeping us down. If we give up, they win. And we can't allow them to win. The reason we, right now, as a trans community, don't have all the rights they have is that we allowed them to speak for us for so many damn years, and we bought everything they said to us: "Oh, let us pass our bill, then we'll come for you."

Yeah, come for me. Thirty-two years later and they're still coming for me. And what have we got? Here, where it all started, transpeople have nothing. We can no longer let people like the Empire State

Pride Agenda, the HRC in Washington, speak for us. And it really hurts me that some gay people don't even know what we gave for their movement.

It's like I was saying all this year during pride month: "It's not my pride, it's their pride. It's your pride, not mine. You haven't given me mine yet." I have nothing to be proud of except that I've helped liberate gays around the world. I have so many children and I'm still sitting on the back of the bus, still struggling to get kids into proper housing, and to get them education, to get them off drugs.

That's why we decided to resurrect STAR at the beginning of the year. Something has to be done. You need a grassroots organization that's willing to ruffle feathers and step on toes. STAR was born in 1971 right after a sit-in we had at New York University with the Gay Liberation Front. We took over Weinstein Hall for three days. It happened when there had been several gay dances thrown there, and all of a sudden the plug was pulled because the rich families were offended that queers and dykes were having dances and their impressionable children were going to be harmed.

So we ended up taking that place over. That's another piece of history that is very seldom told, even in regular gay history, about that sit-in. Maybe that's because it was the street queens once again who were still hanging around from 1969 with some of the radicals like Bob Kohler. He is a radical who is 75 years old and still out there working very hard doing his thing. He's been an ally to the trans community since I knew him and before I knew him. He's insulted and offended when the gay community doesn't turn out for our demos.

STAR House was born out of the Weinstein Hall demonstration, because there were so many of us living together, with Marsha and myself renting two rooms and the hotel room, and even then we still didn't have enough room to house people. With the help of GLF and Gay Youth, we threw our first fund-raiser and raised enough money to go to the Mafia and rent our first building. You can say anything you want about the Mafia—yes, they took advantage of us, but when we needed them, they were there.

They did open up tacky places for us to party in. And they got us a building for $300 a month. They were there for us. Marsha and I and Bubbles and Andora and Bambi kept that building going by selling ourselves out on the streets while trying to keep the children off the streets. And a lot of them made good. A lot of them went home. Some of them I lost; they went to the streets. We lost them, but we tried to do the best we could for them. The contribution of the ones who didn't make it out into the streets, who wanted something different, was to liberate food from in front of the A&P and places like that, because back then they used to leave everything out in front of the store before it opened.

So the house was well-supplied, the building's rent was paid, and everybody in the neighborhood loved STAR House. They were impressed because they could leave their kids and we'd baby-sit with them. If they were hungry, we fed them. We fed half of the neighborhood because we had an abundance of food the kids liberated. It was a revolutionary thing.

We died in 1973, the fourth anniversary of Stonewall. That's when we were told we were a threat and an embarrassment to women because lesbians felt offended by our attire, us wearing makeup. It came down to a brutal battle on the stage that year at Washington Square Park, between me and people I considered my comrades and friends.

This was at pride. It was the year Bette Midler came to sing "Happy Birthday" for us. It was happy for the mainstream community, but it was not happy for us. They tried to stop drag queen entertainers from performing. I was angry because I had been scheduled for many months to speak at that rally. So I'm stubborn, and I wasn't going to have it. Because for four years we were the vanguard of the gay movement, and all of a sudden it was being taken away. We were being pushed out of something we helped create.

I remember this man telling me, a straight man who was my boss at the time, when I was working in Jersey—he said, "Ray, the oppressed becomes the oppressor. Be careful. Watch it." And I saw it. And I still see it. I literally had to fight my way up onto that stage. I was beat. I got to speak. I said my piece. And I basically left the movement for many years. I didn't come back into view until the 20th anniversary. And that was with David Isay's *Remembering Stonewall*.

He found me where I was in Tarrytown. I was living and working there. And then along came Martin Duberman and *Stonewall*. But I was really hurt in 1974. I tried to kill myself. I had 60 stitches on this arm after that incident. And I wasn't ever going to come back to the movement. But you know who held fast to her word was Lee Brewster. When she got up and spoke after I did, she took off her tiara, threw it into the crowd and said, "Fuck gay liberation!"

What people fail to remember is, here's another drag queen who has not been recognized as a hero in our community. She put a majority of the money up for the first march in 1970. Lee Brewster changed the drinking laws for gay men to be able to be served in public at a regular bar instead of an after-hours club. She did this. Lee Brewster, with her own money, changed the laws on the books in New York against criminal impersonation that was held over drag queens' heads.

When she died and I wrote an obituary for her, these freaking gay rag newspapers didn't even have the balls to put in her accomplishments—even after her death. Yes, I'm angry with this fucking community. I wish sometimes that 1969 had never happened, they make me so angry. But it happened, and I have a whole lot of children. One of my most beautiful moments, all these years, was in 2000 at world pride when the Italian transexual organization in Bologna invited Julia and me to participate. I got to speak to all those people that have oppressed our community. Because it's not just here in the United States with the mainstream community but all over.

It's astonishing to see how history repeats itself. But I reminded all those 500,000 children out there that day that if it wasn't for us, they would not be where they're at today. They wouldn't have anything, none of them, from one corner of the world to the other. Because it was our community, the street kids, the street queens of that era, who fought for what they have today. And they still turn around and give us their backs.

So STAR has been officially restarted since January 6, 2001. What happened is, we were at church services at the Metropolitan Community Church and they were calling for monitors for the upcoming trial of Amanda Milan's* assassins. So I spoke to Julia during this whole thing, and Reverend Pat was giving a sermon about it, and I thought, *We can't let this just die. What are courtroom monitors going to do?* I said we got to keep Amanda in the public's eye. That's the only way people are going to realize the plight we're going through.

---

*25-year-old transwoman murdered on Manhattan street June 20, 2000, by assailants who cut her throat.

And during the sermon Reverend Pat talked about the three kings. And he said, "Who are we to say that the three kings were not three queens? Only queens would get up in the middle of the night and throw elaborate stuff into bags and travel to the other ends of the earth not knowing where they're going, but they knew they had to be there. And they followed the star."

So I told her, "We have to do it."

That whole day was telling me what to do—the sermon and the fact that Amanda's murderers were coming up for trial and we had not kept pressure and visibility on it. We were three queens following the STAR. And that's it. The only word I changed was *Transvestite* to *Transgender*.

We raised a lot of hell back when STAR first started, even if it was just a few of us. We ate and slept demonstrations, planning demonstrations. We'd go from one demo to another, the same day. We were doing what we believed in. And what we're doing now, the few of us who are willing to unsettle people and ruffle up feathers, is what we believe in doing. We have to do it because we can no longer stay invisible. We have to be visible. We should not be ashamed of who we are. We have to show the world that we are numerous. There are many of us out there.

Unfortunately, many of us have to live by night, because of the lack of laws or protections. A lot of transwomen are standing out on street corners or working clubs. And many of them are highly educated, with college degrees. Many of us have to survive by selling our bodies. If you can't get a job, you have to do whatever it takes to live.

I live at Transy House now with Julia. We've lived there for four years. It's a communal house run by Rusty [Mae Moore] and Chelsea [Goodwin]. They started it eight years ago and run it after the model of STAR House. Chelsea was one of my original children at STAR House. It's a safe house for girls who are still working the streets. It gives them a roof over their heads without having to hustle for money. They pay $50 a week if they can afford it. If not, they help out around the house. One girl cleans up for her board. The only rules are no drugs and no business done on the premises by working girls. And one of the political things we do is lobby for the legalization of medical marijuana for cancer patients and AIDS patients, along with the struggle for transgender rights.

It's a shame that more people in the trans community don't open up houses like Rusty and Chelsea are doing with Transy House. We get calls all the time from city and state agencies looking to place people, and we have to tell them, "Look, we're constantly filled up and we're doing this by ourselves without support from anyone." There are lots of shelters for people with AIDS but no safe house for people without AIDS. There's no safe shelter for these kids, so they end up sleeping on the streets. It hurts to see this still going on after 30 years, when Marsha and I first started trying to do something about it.

I'm happy that I've seen this new civil rights legislation introduced in the New York city council. It's historic, and I'm glad that we all came out in numbers at the hearing because it made an impression, even though the major news media didn't cover us. Octavia St. Laurent said it last year at Amanda's funeral. "Men have rights, women have rights, children have rights, gays have rights, lesbians have rights, animals have rights...we ain't got shit."

Before I die, I will see our community given the respect we deserve. I'll be damned if I'm going to my grave without having the respect this community deserves. I want to go to wherever I go with that in my soul and peacefully say I've finally overcome.

Editors' Note: Sylvia died on February 19, 2002, from complications of liver cancer. She was 50 years old.

Vision

Aaron Link

Aaron Link is an artist and writer. He has reared cockroaches, wran-
gled butterflies, become a professional mask maker, and had surgery.
Currently, he is directing a theater troupe of homeless young adults in
Portland, Ore., and working on a book called What Becomes You, *from*
which the essays "Scars" and "Freaks" are taken. He is glad to be the son of
Hilda Raz.

I am losing the vision in my right eye. There is nothing wrong with my
right eye. My two eyes see two different pictures of the world. This is
true for everybody, but in my case the two pictures are unusually diver-
gent, so that my brain does not know how to fuse them into a single,
three-dimensional image of the world. Instead, I have double vision.
When things get too close, I cannot see them clearly, and my brain deals
with this problem by choosing the eye that offers a clearer picture of the
world. The images seen by the weaker eye do not fit this picture, so I do
not see them. The condition is called amblyopia. In Greek, the eye wan-
ders. In English, people call the wandering eye lazy. The condition
makes you miss what you are reaching for.

Amblyopia can blind you on one side. After many years of not seeing
the images the weak eye sends, the brain forgets about it altogether. Right

now I can only see out of my right eye when my left eye is closed.

The cure is to shut the eye your brain trusts and keep it shut until your brain learns again how to see. When I write, I wear a patch over my good eye. I fight to see past incandescent darkness. Somewhere in my brain something is saying it is better to see nothing than to see through a strange eye. I asked my eye doctor about the cure for amblyopia. He told me it has to be done in childhood; after about age 30, he said, it does no good to try to change. I am 31 years old. However, I did go through puberty only recently, so I wear a patch over my left eye. Amblyopia is the most common way to lose sight in America.

It is 1980. I'm in high school. The teacher has given us an assignment in my drawing class: Draw a self-portrait of how you will look 20 years from now.

Staring at the paper, I have the germ of an idea. After a pause, the teacher says, "Oh, and you can't draw a tombstone or a graveyard or anything like that. It's a clever idea, so I let it go the first time, but now it's already been done." So much for the germ of my idea. I don't want to disappoint the teacher. For the next two days I stare at an empty sheet of paper, because I cannot see what to draw.

Earlier. There are three stories about the mystery. In the one I find first, a scientist explains how a person can become invisible. Not everyone can do it. They have to become special, like him. He's an albino. The way he explains the process, most people have a shape that's colored in, and their colors will protect their forms from invisibility. I know this has got to be a symbol for something, because I color in my hair and eyes and skin and I know that the process will work on me. The story says the scientist is insane. In the end the regular people get together and kill him. I've noticed a lot of stories end like that. I'm paying attention.

I find the second story because it has the same name as the first, so it makes me curious. Maybe this book will have a different formula. In it, there's a man who lives in a secret place and nobody notices him. Down inside his secret, he has 1,369 lights. He says, "Without light I am not only invisible, but formless as well; and to be unaware of one's form is to live a death." (Ralph Ellison, *Invisible Man*) Something turns on in my vision, but then the story doesn't talk about the secret lair full of lights anymore; it goes out into the world, and out there I do not understand and do not want to go.

The third story is science fiction, which means it's not supposed to be real. It tells me that people make other people invisible; it's not something you do yourself. When they make the man in this story invisible, the first thing he does is go into the girls' showers. I'm in junior high school by now. I get this. All the girls know he's not supposed to be there, but they can't do anything about it because he's supposed to be invisible, and if they notice him, then they'll be turned invisible too. Being invisible would be great, the story says, except that you get lonely. This story tells me that if the doctor sees you, he won't help you, and he'll leave you to live or die on your own. This is the other thing that's wrong with being invisible.

When I'm 17, I tell my mother I want surgery. She tells me I'm insane. I go to a mental health counselor. He can't see me, but a voice in the room troubles him. I've read the part of the story about people being killed by invisibles and the part about invisibles being killed by people. The story says that sometimes you can defeat the real people, but they'll always kill you in the end—if you let them know you're there. I decide to live or die on my own. I'm invisible for a long time. It's a lifestyle choice, like the man in the room full of lights.

In 1995 I start taking testosterone. There are no pictures of people like me. I look and look through books of gender theory, autobiographies of heroic transexuals who won't let anybody take their picture, and medical literature. Medical literature has no pictures. I suppose that inviolable natural law makes it impossible to photograph the invisible. At any rate, doctors seem unable to see me. The only picture I can find is in a "body modification" magazine. There's a picture of a person who has had all the evidence removed—no breasts, no genitals, no hair, no color in the skin or eyes, a shaved head: invisible. I shut the magazine and find my partner. For a long time I look into this strong, square face, hold it close to both my eyes, watch each hair's summer colors run to blond beard around the lips the way in winter I turn toward the sun.

After a while I can pull on my leather jacket and go out into the rain. On my way home, our gay neighbor says hello. He introduces us to his new friends. "They'll be your neighbors," he says to them, nodding to us. They are a lesbian couple, and he wants them to feel at home. "These two women are your neighbors." My partner has all the evidence: a body whose image changes, eye to eye. I take my vision home. I hold my partner close to both my eyes. I hold my photograph of Boris Karloff in *Frankenstein*. He's beautiful.

Someone shows me a photograph. There is a picture of a naked man, in a lesbian sex magazine. I would never have seen the photograph. Not that I don't look for naked men.

I don't see lesbians and their sex magazines. They don't see me either, but I don't expect to see a naked man in them the way they expect to see a naked woman in me. In the photograph, the naked man stands quietly, erotic and beautiful and utterly without shame.

He is rippled with muscle and striped like the small Sumatran tiger. It is a self-portrait; in the absence of images, he has become the photographer. When I see him in person, half a year later, 500 people are giving him a standing ovation. The photograph disappears. Bookstores and libraries do not keep such things. Images lost rapidly from the retina can be preserved permanently in the mind.

I've had surgery. Another neighbor asks if I'm OK; he saw me come home in an ambulance and he's worried about me. I tell him I'm getting well. We chat a little. My mother tells me I shouldn't talk to him; he wears a fundamentalist Christian T-shirt. The next time I see him I no longer wear the bandages. He stares at me for a long time. I watch his eyes strain to focus, which can give you a vicious headache. Then his vision resolves. I watch myself disappear in his eyes.

There's an absence in your vision. Everybody has one, a blind spot where too many nerves converge to leave room for the delicate process of sight. To protect the integrity of vision, blind spots have to pass unnoticed; if you could see them, they would be bounded darkness, hanging in the mind. Cameras do not have blind spots, but they are moved by mortal vision, moved away from pictures the eye does not resolve. Since my surgery, I have watched them move thoughtfully away from me at events whose theme is pride. The pride of my neighbors is being preserved. It is a lifestyle choice, like being invisible.

It is possible to see your blind spot. I have tried many times, but it is an effort. You have to sit down and pass some object across your field of vision slowly but continuously. The object can be anything: a pen, a part of your body. Note the point at which it disappears and the point, farther on, at which it appears again in your vision. The length of time the object is invisible does not mark an event that happens to the object but the size of the blind spot in your own eye.

Freaks
Aaron Link

The first thing I remember about waking up after sexual reassignment surgery is an attendant asking me urgently, "Where do you hurt?" I gave him the answer that was excruciatingly obvious: I told him my balls hurt like hell. He looked quickly away, then asked if there was anywhere else I might be hurting. In that moment, it occurred to me that he didn't believe me. And it wasn't my pain he didn't believe in; it was my balls. He knew they were there, of course, in theory, but they weren't going down too smoothly in what we like to call real life.

So I'm lying on a hospital gurney in excruciating pain, thinking we have a little dysphoria problem here, a little trouble dealing with reality. This is exactly the same problem we've always had, a little seminal semantics. Only this time, the other person is the one with the little fucking problem dealing with reality. The little miracle of surgery is the way the surgeon can take your mental disorder and graft it on to someone else. The attendant was attempting to reject the transplant. Under the surreal light of the recovery room, I kept thinking, *Clap your hands if you believe in fairies, everybody.*

Later that night we got to duke it out with the immune system of the hospital staff. Some cells ignore the intruder while others refuse assistance to the foreign body in their system. In the morning the discharge nurse neglected to provide necessary postoperative care instructions and devices, tried several times to forget our prescriptions for painkillers and antibiotics, and giggled hysterically through the entire process. The transplant, so to speak, survived nevertheless.

When we got home, I discovered that my surgeon had equipped me with a jockstrap printed with the Stars and Stripes. Jack Armstrong, the all-American boy.

I had a dream just before my surgery in which I looked into a mirror in a hotel room on my way back to Los Angeles. I was tall and blond.

When I started sprouting thick black hair in unlikely places, I realized that I'd seriously thought that having a sex change meant I was going to get a whole new body. I had mine all picked out; I found it in the ads at the back of *The Advocate*. Receding hairlines and shoulder hair—and a pattern of beard growth that consistently causes strangers to stop me on the street with the assumption that I have a special knowledge of farming with a horse-drawn plow—had not been on my list. You do not get a whole new body. The body that you get is yours.

My cousin is the kind of acrobat who carries 10 people on his shoulders while riding a bicycle; imagine this act captured on scratchy black-and-white film from the vaudeville era. I seem to have become my cousin's action figure.

Realistically, what do I look like in the mirror? What I look like in the mirror is no Greek statue, but a Roman copy: a little thin in the limbs, a little too thick in the middle for perfect symmetry, a bit awkward, but handsome, workmanlike. Most of the Greek statues you see in books and museums are really Roman copies. We are serviceable renderings of a lost ideal.

Of course, there are also the big scars across my chest, the tight balls, the little dick that lies comfortably in the fold between my testicles. That too.

The type of genital surgery I had is called metoidoplasty. Unlike phalloplasty (the construction of a penis from whatever other body parts the surgeon believes you can spare), metoidoplasty wasn't developed for men who'd had their dicks shot off in the war. Like my black hair, it operates on the assumption that you have an inheritance to begin with, like it or not. It is a modification of your existing sex organs; the one you get is yours. I decided on metoidoplasty after seeing a photograph of the finished procedure. A photograph of the finished procedure is what you call a porn shot of a transexual. Like most men, the gentleman in question was a size queen, and he made damn sure he was at full extension before his groin, thighs, and one highly suggestive hand were preserved for posterity. If you've seen car ads in which a man presses his nose to the dealership window, slack-jawed with lust, and murmurs, "I want one of those," let me assure you that, on the scale of desire, new cars are overrated.

In other words, I thought the picture was erotic.

A friend and I once saw a film clip of a vaudeville act. On the scratched old black-and-white stock, a buff man dressed as Rudolph Valentino drank kerosene and breathed fire. I was spellbound. The next night at a party, I listened to my friend describe the regurgitation with disgust, as throwing up stuff. That is what he did. Beauty is in the eye of the beholder.

Periodically I see artwork depicting hermaphrodites: abstract pillars filling a room, with one bullet-bra point down low and two high up. Movies with names like *Tits and a Dick*. A TS man named David Harrison wrote that he'd planned to appear in a porn film once, but the producers canceled it. No possible source of erotic appeal. The sex organs of lovers remind me of clusters of ripe fruit, soft and pendulous as French plums. In the mirror I am reminded that hands of burro bananas have their own delicate charms.

Realistically, you might find something like it in the photographs of Joel-Peter Witkin. It would fit nicely between midgets and cancer victims, posed against the velvet drapes, illuminated by a sepia-toned lantern, something with fringe, some dried fruit, memento mori. In interviews, the photographer stresses his sympathy for his subjects. I do not see him standing among the other freaks in his pictures.

At the party, three of us sat around a book of photographs by Edward Muybridge. He was a photographer of the vaudeville era who invented a procedure for taking photographs in rapid succession. Against a black background ruled with regular white lines for measurement, Muybridge photographed galloping horses, leaping cats, flying vultures, and hundreds of people who were mostly in the nude. Woman walking, carrying bucket. Hod carrier climbing ladder. Woman with hand to mouth, walking down incline. Man throwing 70-pound boulder. Paralytic child walking on all fours. Across the page, the picture sequences resemble strips of film from an old movie.

We sat around the block, admiring the curve of the hod carrier's back, smiling at the languid air of a woman watching her companion smoke a cigarette in a chair, laughing at the runner in his jockstrap and modest little tasseled cap. My friends remembered a sequence of a legless boy climbing down from a chair. They pointed at the particular frames that had inspired them with horror. The moment at which he lifts his right hand. The moment at which he reaches forward, the strong muscles in his shoulders outlined against the light. I am looking at the frames, the shudders of my friends, the abstract shapes dissolving into light. The moment I remember is the moment when the paralytic child, trotting on her hands and feet across the sea of shutters, has turned to face the cameras. She is grinning with delight.

Because most of his models posed nude or nearly nude, Muybridge was accused of being a pornographer by his contemporaries. Because the men typically wore jockstraps, while the women wore nothing at all, he was said to be exploiting women. His response to his critics was his body itself. On the frontispiece of his photo collections, a tall, stooped old Scotsman with a shock of white hair and an incredible beard rises from an old crate, his face in shadow. He strides purposefully toward the camera, arms swinging ("The normal stride of a biped consists of two uniformly executed steps. Shakespeare recognizes this fact in *The Merchant of Venice*, act III, scene 4: 'I'll…turn two mincing steps into a manly stride' "), his freakish, impossibly pendulous testicles dangling in the air against the grid of measurement.

Scars
Aaron Link

There are two major scars on my chest. Each is about seven inches long; the right one is slightly above the surrounding skin. Though the scars themselves are delicately sensitive, the skin just around them is slightly numb. I am told all this will fade with time. Each nipple has been moved and grafted into the right place. Around them shades a faint pink scar.

There is a great deal of concern about scarring in chest surgery. One of the classic books that include information on transexual men was written by a medical doctor some years ago. In it there is the phrase: "In spite of the rather poor cosmetic appearance of the surgery, many post-operative patients insist on going bare-chested in public." This, in the doctor's words, is an example of "poor reality sense," a symptom of my illness. The first time I went bare-chested in public a young woman gave me "a citation for being too good-looking." This was part of a fund-raising ploy for a charity; she used this line on men when soliciting donations. I gave her $5. Poor reality sense, I suppose; it was all the cash I had.

I have never been concerned about my scars, though many people are. They look exactly as they should; I have known them for a long time. When my brother was 5, the doctors took him to surgery to repair a birth defect. He had a hole in his heart. They opened him from breast to spine, reached in between the curve of his ribs, and stitched it up. When I look at the shining pink curve in the mirror, what looks back with enormous force is the familiar geography of childhood, the place I used to rest my head on the person I loved most in the world. My two scars together are the same length and curve as his. I did not expect any of this.

My brother says he does not think much of his scar. The surgery that saved his life had only one lingering effect. He is afraid of needles. I sit down to write with bright green fluid on my leg to numb the skin. Every two weeks I give myself an injection in the large muscle of the thigh. I will do this for the rest of my life. The needle my medicine requires is startlingly large, 20 gauge, like the needles used to inflate footballs, or the ones with colored glass heads that you see in junk shops, the ones labeled "hat pin." Though it is difficult to start through the skin, when it comes out it doesn't leave a scar.

When I last saw my brother, his scar had flattened and faded with the years into an almost imperceptible white line. A lot of things we used to share have faded. His chest is no longer the contour I remember; his height came tall and late, and has been reshaped by a gravel road at high speed. Ten years ago, he was thrown from a car and almost died for the second time. I've almost died once. I went to the hospital, and emerged with my brother's memory imprinted on my skin.

My mother has a scar on her chest too—where they took the cancer out. It is long but small, almost invisible compared to my brother's or mine. She has no feeling in the skin on that side of her chest and no nipple there. I share scars with her exactly as with my brother; my two equals her one. My scars are in the center, my brother's on the left side, hers on the right. Growing up, I never looked like any of my family. We have a joke now. The scars are how we know we are related.

Scars

Hilda Raz

Hilda Raz is editor in chief of the venerable literary quarterly Prairie
Schooner, *professor of English at the University of Nebraska, and a poet and
writer. Her recent books include* Trans and Divine Honors *(Wesleyan
University Press poetry series),* Living On the Margins: Women Writers on
Breast Cancer *(Persea), and* The Best of Prairie Schooner: Essays *and* The
Best of Prairie Schooner: Fiction and Poetry *(University of Nebraska Press).*

You'd never know one of my breasts is a silicone sac. And the two top
scars, from the biopsy and the mastectomy, are pale and thin. The hysterectomy left a low smile on my flat belly, hipbone to hipbone. When
I show Aaron, his eyes take everything in. Is he wondering why I both-
ered with reconstruction? But no. He wants a reconstructed chest, flat
like my right side but shaped like his brother's. For years he has been
weight-lifting, developing the pectorals we all have, his unscarred. And
his surgery is called chest surgery, chest reconstruction, not double
mastectomy. I try to teach him about scars.

I remind Aaron that his brother John's heart-surgery scar is raised, a
keloid scar, but mine isn't. No reason his will be.

At this time in his life—he's 30—I had expected to show him something else. How to fold contour sheets or keep the linen closet neat.

Instead I'll show John how to fold contour sheets. My younger child, Aaron, and I tromp out each freezing morning of his visit home—a long visit to teach me about transexual surgery—to feed the ducks at Holmes Lake. He is teaching me his new name, Aaron. Later, we bake bread as we always do together. We both know how to test the dough, braid the long snakes we roll out together with floured palms. I tell him again the story of his birth as we weave the braids into loaves. We have been doing this kneading, this storytelling for years. I remind him that he is named now for my papa, as he would have been born male. The choice of his new name is his own. I tell him about my vision when he was inside me. I saw myself reading to my two small sons. At his birth, I raised up to meet Aaron, met Sarah instead. "What's wrong?" I asked the doctor. "Nothing's wrong," he said. "You have a daughter." And I wept with joy and relief.

Today, as we tromp and knead and talk, I ask the same questions, express the same fear he meets patiently every day. Why can't I understand what he is teaching me? I can't teach him what he'll need to know—what I know about surgery—because I can't seem to learn what he wants me to know. Each night I tuck him into Sarah's bed, perch on the side of the mattress and let my palm find his rosy cheek.

I hold it as I kiss Aaron hello, Sarah goodbye. Each morning, I put on my snow boots and walk out to meet my child in our kitchen, drink our coffee, set out to find the ducks again. Our boots mark the new snow side by side, never again in the same tracks.

A Conversation With JT LeRoy

JT LeRoy, author of Sarah *(Bloomsbury, 2000) and* The Heart is Deceitful Above All Things *(Bloomsbury, 2001) has achieved cult status at the age of 21. This conversation was recorded in November 2001.*

GenderQueer: You've been quoted in an interview saying, "When I wrote *Sarah* I was male-identified. Now I'm not. I don't know what I am." How do you see yourself?

JT: It depends on the day, really, and what clothes I'm wearing. I don't like to pigeonhole it. It's private. Sometimes I'm in the mood to be referred to as she. It feels natural to me to go back and forth. I've been doing this since I was a little kid...with my mother...going back and forth. I thought everyone did that too. Checked with their parents. I just really thought that's how it was. If I referred to myself as "she" or peed sitting down at my grandparents', I'd get in trouble...people freaked out. But it's fun to be able to wear what you want to and not have to worry about what society says you can't do.

GQ: It was so great hearing you on that NPR interview, saying how you liked to go out sometimes as a boy and sometimes as a girl. I'm in awe of that.

JT: Well, it's still scary for me. And it can be dangerous. It's not like I'm really out and proud about it. I'm not ashamed either…it just is. It's not something I have to justify. It's dangerous. *Boys Don't Cry* was coming out as *Sarah* was in galleys, and I didn't see it because people told me it would freak me out. When I finally saw it on video, it did. It's true. What's worse is the shame around it. I'm not only getting beat up, but I'm feeling shamed that I'm also taking the beating.

GQ: Have you been attacked a lot for going out as a girl?

JT: Yeah, a lot of times, but not always for that. I've been beaten up a couple times for that.

GQ: Doesn't it seem crazy that people care so much?

JT: Yeah, there was a party…. Bono really liked my book and invited me to a U2 concert. I went back to the hotel and their private party and Robin Wright, Sean Penn's wife, kind of cornered me. I went up to give her my book, and she grabbed me by the shoulders and demanded, "Are you a boy or a girl?" She was really upset, right in my face over and over: "*You a boy or a girl?* Why are you wearing a wig?" Luckily, I was sorta buzzed at the time, so I didn't freak out, but it was like, "Why the fuck do you care?"

People just want to know, one way or the other; they need a solid answer. They can't just let it be. They get really mad at you. They want to know one way or the other.

GQ: You've gone from working truck stops to shoots for Abercrombie & Fitch, from one kind of shooting to another. Is that hard, taking that rush of one kind of recognition to the other so quickly?

JT: I know, it's kind of bizarre for me because I have a hard time being around people, so this is kind of new…it's spooky. It is fun to be dressed up. It was weird when I did the *Vanity Fair* shoot. I spent basically two days being in three kinds of female outfits. It was fun being a girl for two days, as Cinderella, then a geisha. And at the end of the second day they shot me as a boy with my face beat up, and the assistant photographers who had been kind of flirty with me…they just freaked out. I mean they knew, everyone had been referring to me as "he," but for them to actually see it…it just freaked them out. They really changed toward me.

GQ: What do you think *Sarah* does for people who don't fit in the binary boxes?

JT: It makes people care about people they wouldn't normally think about except in a negative way. I created an imaginary world in *Sarah* where there's no judgment; it just is. Of course, no truck drivers would want to trick with transgendered prostitutes. I created a world that was my fantasy. There are transgendered people who work truck stops, but they work separately and it can be really dangerous.

GQ: Are there truckers who wear Victoria's Secret bras?

JT: Of course, they do it all the time, but they do it with their straight girls. A lot of them wear panties…. They don't identify themselves as trans.

GQ: When you were tricking, did your tricks know you were trans?

JT: No, no… I always felt like if I couldn't pass, I wouldn't do it. You know, I'm always impressed by people who have deep voices and male characteristics. I think I only have a few male characteristics…my hands and my neck. There are people out there in the world, I think they're brave…

GQ: Well, I speak from personal experience, and it's like…what are my options? I'm a public librarian. I'm asked to declare my gender at least a dozen times every day…

JT: But I think it is brave, because there are lots of people who feel that they're really women but don't really pass, so they don't try. They're too scared that people will raise an eyebrow to them and think, *I know what you really are*…and have people think there's something wrong with you.

GQ: There are times, especially with young kids, around 13, 14, when they hit puberty they know what's going on and they try to put me in my place…. They go out of their way to humiliate me in front of their peers.

JT: What do they say to you?

GQ: You know…I've been called everything but a Reuben sandwich, but I've been doing this for so long, it's just…you can say anything…just don't…no physical contact, OK?

JT: That's so fucking harsh…. You know, I think that's brave. When I go out, I don't want anyone to know.

GQ: You've got the voice. I tuned in to the NPR program after it started and I just assumed I was listening to a young Southern girl.

JT: Yeah, I think starting young definitely helps. I think a lot of my getting into being like a girl was a reaction to a lot of men who took advantage of me as a boy. You know, the pedophiles. There was a way that I think I used them as much as they used me. It was a symbiotic relationship. My being feminine happened gradually, kind of slowly.

GQ: How old were you when you first started tricking with your mom?

JT: It happened kind of gradually, with my mom's boyfriends. It started not being a big deal, and I saw the power and the money in it. It always felt normal to me. If you're born in a fucked-up situation, it just seems normal to you. I don't know if I can pinpoint an age. I started having sex with men and it started not being a big deal. You know, how do you define tricking? I started trading it for stuff…. But a child's body is sacred, and I really don't think adults should be having sex with children, because the power imbalance is just too great. Even if the child is into it and everything. The power imbalance is too great.

GQ: I admire the way your characters adapt to that power imbalance, to being powerless. Maybe I read this into your story, but I admire the way Sarah adapts to being used. If there ever was a trans hero, it's Sarah.

JT: Yeah, I'm disappointed that the transgender community hasn't taken up *Sarah*. There's a magazine I found, a national transgender magazine, and I called them up twice and told them about my book…that it was coming out, and they were like, "Yeah, whatever…" I mean, how many fucking books come out that are about transgendered folks that are for the mass market that aren't just preaching to the converted? I mean, little old ladies read my book. I hear from parents all over the world…straight people, a lot of women, and here I call this magazine and they blow me off.

GQ: The problem is that there are two kinds of different questions presented by *Sarah*. One is the quality of the writing, which is top-of-the-line literary, but the other is the subject matter. Trans organizations want legitimacy, and hookers are an archetype they want to get away from. So there's this, "God, we love the writing, but raccoon penises and truck stop trannies is not something we're going to promote and have associated with us." I mean, politically you want to focus on the most disposed people, but at the same time…and it's a class issue too.

JT: But I looked at prostitutes in *Sarah* like they were artists. They're as respectable a profession as chefs, like the ones at the Dove. While the straight ones over at the Three Crutches are trailer trash. The trans characters are very noble; they are respected and revered in a way that in real life they're not. I mean, a lot of people in the South and remote areas are kicked out of their homes and they lose their jobs and they end up tricking. They end up getting the shit beaten out of them. It's like they are the lowest rung.

In *Sarah* I totally reversed that. They are the most valued. I don't write about it with any shame. There is absolutely no judgment. That's one thing I'm really proud of. I never once said, "We all know that sex is really bad, and we all know that prostitution is really bad…"

I didn't write *Sarah* to be political. I wrote it from my experience. I've heard from a lot of transgendered people, and I know…. I didn't set out to write a transgendered novel. I didn't know what *Sarah* was going to be about. I started writing about raccoon penis bones, and this thing just grabbed me by the throat. You know, they teach the book at, like, Harvard and Duke—along with Sophocles—and I get professors calling me up with analytical explanations about all the universal truths it hits on, and I wish I could do the Pee-wee Herman thing and say I knew that, but I didn't. I just wrote from deep inside my soul and this is what came out.

I tell people, if you really want to know about me, everything you need to know about me, everything in my heart came out in *Sarah* from my unconscious mind. That's the essence of who I am. A lot of it was people I knew and a mishmash of experience. It means a lot to me to be recognized. I feel shut out of a lot of families. And to be recognized and welcomed in means a lot to me. I guess that's why I wanted more support from the transgender community. Not to be held up or something, just to be recognized. But it took a critical mass of street people reading it to bring it to the attention of the trans community, and I think that's really funny. In a way it's wonderful, you know, because usually it's the other way around.

Dutch
Debbie Fraker

Debbie Fraker lives in East Point, Ga., in a polyamorous and gender-variant family of four women. Her work has appeared in Southern Voice *newspaper,* Etcetera *magazine,* The Chattahoochee Review, *and other publications.*

Greg and I got divorced without giving much explanation to my family after being together for several years. My grandmother was one of the few family members who assumed I was doing the right thing for myself. She said that I should do what I felt I had to do.

My mother, of course, accepted my decision easily. She had left Daddy just the year before, partially emboldened by a women's studies course she had stumbled across in a local continuing education program. She took it after the ceramics class and before the introduction to basic photography. At first I was cynical about the idea of a women's studies class at a community college, making jokes with Greg about it. I didn't expect her to get much out of it. But she gained confidence from her interactions with other women, and the praise she received for her writing made her realize she was smarter than she thought. She finally began to understand that she could make it on her own if she wanted to. And she simply packed up and left.

My split with Greg was a little bit more dramatic, since I finally had to tell him I'd been having sex with my "best friend," Gina. I tried to give up Gina, and he tried to forgive me, but neither of us succeeded. Since our breakup took place in another state, my extended family didn't hear much about the details. Thank goodness. Even though I was happy with my new life, I wasn't proud of the cheating and lying I did to get where I was.

My family certainly would not have been happy about it. They had all fallen in love with my handsome, charming husband, and they missed having him around. Aunt Celia said if I couldn't live with Greg, I probably couldn't live with a man. I've never asked her if she really knew what she was saying. Five years later, when I took my new wife, Elaine, to a family reunion, Mamaw accepted her as family. She never questioned our relationship or ignored it the way others had.

Lane and I felt a little uncomfortable at the reunion because it was her first visit with my family. Mamaw seemed to know how nervous we were, and she called Lane over to sit with her. "Come here and keep me company, honey," was all she said.

After a few minutes of quiet, Mamaw leaned over and quietly asked Lane a question—as if they were conspirators. "Has Annie told you about her Aunt Evelyn?"

"No, I don't think she has," Lane answered politely. I had told her about my grandmother's arsenal of stories, and I'm sure she was ready to listen sweetly to something that held no interest for her.

"Evelyn was a little mannish," Mamaw started. "In fact, she preferred to be called Dutch. That was what most of the guys down at the hardware store called her ever since they were kids in school together. I just never could get used to that name." Mamaw clucked disapprovingly and shook her head. "But she did everything she could to make herself look like a man. She wore overalls and kept her hair cut short. Of course she had those big bosoms, so she didn't really look like a man." Mamaw sighed and looked off into the distance as if she were still trying to explain this to Evelyn herself. "She was my brother's wife's sister. When Cora, my brother Ted's wife, moved out of her family's place, Evelyn, the older sister, just stayed and took care of things. It was that old gray house out toward Straw Plains on the way to the lake. When their daddy died, Evelyn took up the farm chores because they needed doing. We never thought nothing of it. She had always helped her daddy work the fields since she was a little girl. She was good as any man with the kind of work she was doing.

"One day Evelyn brought home a friend, Lizzie, to help her with old Miz Caldwell. Lizzie moved into the house and took care of Evelyn's mother as if she was her own. She took care of the house too, better than Miz Caldwell ever had. When Miz Caldwell died, it was Lizzie took care of the funeral and had all the relatives over to the house after for the wake. Nobody thought a thing of it when she stayed on to help Evelyn out. Oh, there was talk sometimes. Like when Old Mr. Peabody told some of them guys, 'That Dutch, she acts like she thinks she's a man.' I heard he even said something rude that wasn't repeated to the ladies. But when Mrs. Peabody heard about it, she said, 'Wilbur, you're just jealous 'cause Evelyn always gets a better price for her tobacco than you. You just hush up,' and he did.

"Lizzie stayed on with Evelyn until Evelyn died. Everybody in town was shocked when Lizzie insisted that Evelyn be buried in overalls. But that was all she ever wore. We reckoned maybe she didn't have anything else for Lizzie to dress her in. Nobody ever saw her in a dress or a skirt. But nobody questioned Lizzie's right to stay on in the home place after Evelyn was gone. Lizzie didn't have any family around here. In fact, I don't think any of us knew where she came from before Evelyn brought her home. Nobody in Evelyn's family needed the old place, so they just left it to Lizzie.

"When Lizzie died a couple of years later, my brother Ted took care of her funeral and everything, just like she was family. You know, when he went in that house after she died, he said it looked just like a show-place. Everything was neat as a pin, not cluttered a bit, even though she'd had some trouble getting around that last year. He found some little knickknacks of his mother's sitting around, along with some other stuff he didn't recognize. It was all carefully tended with loving care. There were little white crocheted doilies on the arms of the chairs that were all as clean and bright and neatly pressed as if they'd just been made. Lizzie must have made them, 'cause Miz Caldwell couldn't even sew a straight line."

Mamaw finished the story and looked quietly across the room where the family was gathered. Lane sat in stunned silence, unsure how to reply. After a minute, Mamaw spoke again. "Do you think Evelyn and Lizzie might have had a relationship like yours and

Annie's? Well, it doesn't matter now, I guess." Then she nudged Lane and pointed. "Look at that, that child is going to hurt himself. Would you please get that truck off the table so he doesn't keep trying to reach it?" Lane gratefully did as she was asked.

When Lane later relayed the story to me, I was as surprised by it as she had been. It was a completely new story to me. I tried several times to find the old gray house, but Mamaw hadn't given me much to go on. Why hadn't I just asked her where it was when she was still alive to ask?

Vignettes
Charlotte

Charlotte, a resident and native of Atlanta, is locally famous for her 20-year transition. She's a Vietnam vet, holds a third degree black belt, and was a regionally and nationally rated competitor. She builds and repairs furniture and guitars.

I was 3, maybe 4. My mother was a beautician, and every Tuesday was her day off. On that day she and I would put on our Sunday best and take a bus to Atlanta. This was the early '50s, when going to Atlanta was a dress-up event. As we sat on the bus I would always take her clip-on earrings off and wear them. Once we got to town I would give them back, but that ride on the bus was terrific. My favorites were the ones with the emerald-colored stones set in round clusters.

I was 5. While my mother was at work I stayed at home with the maid. My favorite activity was to lock myself in my parents' bedroom and play with my mother's clothes, shoes, and lipstick.

At age 10, in the fourth grade, I always spent recess with the girls. I liked their company better, and I knew I wouldn't get into a fight. There are two other boys who stand out to me from this time. One was a red-haired, freckle-faced boy, just slightly overweight, who spent recess with me and the other girls. The other was a new kid. He was the most feminine boy I had ever seen. He played alone. He switched schools eventually, so I never got to know him.

Later that same year the entire class was playing softball and my teacher, Mrs. Porfilio, was pitching. She called me a sissy in front of the class. This was about the same time the physical abuse from my older brother had gotten so bad I wasn't allowed to be home alone with him. I went to the beauty salon immediately after school and stayed until mother got off work.

I was 13, in the eighth grade, out of school for a holiday, and nobody home but me. I wore my mother's clothes and stained my lips with her lipstick. My dad got home from work first, and there I was. I had changed out of the dress in time but had forgotten about the lipstick. I missed three days of school. The event was never mentioned.

At age 18, I registered for the draft. On the verge of being drafted the next year, I joined the Air Force. I wound up volunteering for duty as a sentry dog handler and going to Vietnam. While I was in Saigon, I came out to a prostitute who took me to a seamstress and helped me get a dress made. We went to a cobbler and had some shoes made to go with the dress. She took me to her apartment and gave me a chance to wear my new clothes. She was a very sweet and kind human being.

I got a letter from home with a clipping out of the newspaper about a doctor from my hometown who was arrested for being dressed as a woman.

I spent every night in 'Nam walking my dog on the perimeter of Tan Son Nhut Air Base, thinking about living my life as a woman while empty flare canisters and 122M rockets slammed into the ground around me. Even the ferocity of the Tet offensive in 1968 couldn't distract me from my inner life. It gave me an indifference to the violence that made the other dog handlers afraid of me. At times they needed to be.

At 22, I had been home from Vietnam for about eight months. I was not surviving military life at Eglin Air Force Base in Florida. I finally asked for professional help and drove over to the base hospital to talk to a psychiatrist, hoping he would cure me of my mental torment. I came out to the shrink and was immediately relieved of duty and processed for discharge. He told me to accept myself for who I was. He said that as long as I dressed in private, it wouldn't make any difference. My diagnosis was "anxiety reaction with psychosexual confusion." I was honorably discharged for medical reasons.

I got home a month later, went to the Veterans Administration Hospital, and saw a bunch of shrinks there. I went once a week and talked about everything under the sun except my gender issues. After a year and a half my therapist retired, so I was bounced to someone else—a woman.

Shazam! I suddenly felt I could open up and talk about the real stuff going on in my head. She lasted two sessions. I guess it was the castration fantasy that pushed her over the edge.

Then I had sessions with a man again, and he thought some sort of B.F. Skinner behavior modification therapy was the answer. As time went by I began to feel that this man was not my advocate.

I graduated to the level of getting dressed and going out shopping. I went to a little dress shop about two miles from home and was pulled over by an Atlanta police officer for failing to come to a complete stop at a stop sign. When I produced a driver's license with the big M in the sex line, I found myself arrested. My car was impounded and I was strip-searched in front of male and female officers. They took me to every floor of the jail to parade me in front of every turnkey and inmate before they put me in a cell. Thankfully, I was alone in the cell.

The charge was "impersonating a female." As soon as I got a lawyer, I found out there was no such law. I didn't pursue a lawsuit against the police because I didn't want to wind up on the front page like the doctor from my hometown.

At 25, I became convinced that I had two options: I could either learn to like myself for who and what I was or I could die. It took me another three years to wind up at the Harry Benjamin Clinic in New York City, where I got my first prescription for Premarin.

At 30, I had electrolysis. I was back in Atlanta and completely out of the closet. I had friends. I worked at the Magic Pan restaurant.

At 34, I was still on hormones but got married to a woman who started out OK with my gender identity. Eventually I found my way back to the closet and no longer had friends who knew me for who I was. On the day my wife told me she wanted a divorce because she didn't want to be married to a woman, I had an automobile wreck that put me in the hospital from mid October until early January.

For a couple of years my gender issues vanished. I quit taking hormones, but I felt like I had lost my soul. I spent a year just getting through the anger. During the time off hormones, my wife (who had stayed with me due to the uncanny timing of my wreck) became pregnant.

At 39, I became the father of a gorgeous, wonderful little girl and became a stay-at-home dad.

At 40, I was hit with a case of depression that sent me back into deep soul searching and medical intervention. I got back on Premarin and started antidepressants.

At 45, I was still on hormones, still with my wife and daughter, but home life was a mess. I was a mess. I struggled to find some transgendered friends and eventually met Dallas Denny.

At 48, I was no longer able to pass as a man, regardless of my clothes or hairstyle. My cowardice no longer stood in the way. I transitioned without transitioning.

Now I am 51 and I'm going to pick up my daughter from theater camp. It's a lovely summer afternoon. I get there early and park in the shade, leaving the engine running and the air conditioner on. I lean my head back, close my eyes and am about to doze off when I am startled by someone tapping on the car window. I roll my window down, and this woman says, "Hi, sorry to bother you, but aren't you Hanna's mom?"

For simplicity's sake, I nod yes. She continues, "I'm Katie's mom. Katie has enjoyed spending time with Hanna and I was wondering if it would be OK with you for Hanna to come over on Saturday and spend the day with Katie. I'm sorry, my name is Karen, and you're…?"

I've been letting people assume I'm Hanna's mother for convenience's sake, but it has never come this far. All the campers have a list of other campers, their phone numbers and parents' names. I know Karen has a sheet of paper at home with our phone number—and Hanna's mother's name.

"My name is Angel. It's nice to meet you. I think Saturday would be great. Hanna has talked about Katie every day on the way home." So now I am Angel…my wife, a woman who will find no humor in this.

Forget asking Hanna to call me anything other than "Daddy." We haven't gotten that far yet. I writhe in agony for two days over what to do. I call my friends and ask them. I go to my transgender support group and tell them. After the laughter subsides, everyone agrees that

Charlotte

I should call this woman and explain that I misled her only to keep from making her uncomfortable. I do this. And Saturday with Katie never happens.

I recently had to put my mother in a nursing home because she has Alzheimer's. As I was going through her things, I found a pair of clip-on earrings, the emerald-colored stones set in round clusters.

Loving Outside Simple Lines
Sonya Bolus

Sonya Bolus is a high-femme poet, artist, mother, and lover. She lives near San Francisco with her son and cat, and is committed to creating and sustaining language and community that allow us all to live in integrity.

Leaning over you in bed, I run my hand across your shirted torso, caressing breast and muscle, smoothing abdomen and flank. My touch on your female body does not emasculate you. You are not a woman to me. You are butch. My fingers tell you I understand.

My stone butch; I am prepared for you to pull away every time I reach for you. I don't understand the strange sense that guides my approach to you, but it is innate, instinctive, natural.

You gaze at me with trust and wonder that you can let me touch you so freely. I tell you I could make love to you for hours. I, young and novice femme, could make love to you, skilled and knowing butch, for hours. And you, tough from years of living as you do, lie quiet beneath my touch.

Sometimes I have to trick you. We pretend you are fucking me, so you don't have to think about what I am doing to you. I make my body available to you as a distraction.

Sometimes I use words: "Let me suck your dick." Whether I go down on a dildo or a cunt, I am sucking your dick. I see it. I feel it. I know it. We both believe in this absolutely, and there is a shift from role play into another kind of reality.

Always, I give you my body, completely. I luxuriate in how well you know my needs, how well you match me and capture every strength and grace I hold within. I give over to you, and you take me to total release, drive me to sexual madness, then bring me back to safety in your embrace.

Without knowing that anyone like you existed, I searched for you. And now that I've found you, I feel such relief to know that you are real. Now I want to know the wealth of your mind, body, and soul, the hell of being you in this world, and the joy that also comes from living outside simple lines.

You ask me to marry you. "Yes" is my answer. And I say yes to life. I say yes with my eyes wide open. You will be my husband, for you are butch, and I can call you no other way. You will be my husband because you are worthy of that title, far more than any man I have known. You'll not own me, but I'll be your wife. I am already your femme and your girl, and I feel my own strength and power as never before. I marry you, and it is more than words or license or tax break, more than a church wedding or a white dress/tuxedo affair, more than a political statement, commitment ceremony, holy union. Marriage with you is life. You extend your hand to me. I step into your world and unite you to mine.

Comes the day you tell me you want your breasts removed. Top surgery. Chest reconstruction. I am oddly not surprised. I think I always knew we would do this together someday. And somewhere in me, though you have not said it aloud, I know this is the first step of a profound transition.

I love you. So I go with you to the computer, and we look up different transgender Web sites (places I have already been because I knew that someday you would want this information). We read about procedures and options. We have an animated and revelatory conversation. But inside me, a deep, overwhelming panic begins to build.

I want to scream, "I love you...as you are!" My desire for you is not confused. I'm a femme who loves butches, who knows butches. I understand your body. Why can't that be enough?

Ever since I met you, I have struggled to reconcile your breasts with your masculine face, your cunt with your masculine presentation, your body with your masculine soul. I have wanted to "figure you out," using an intellect fettered by narrow expectations, so implicit in my culture that even I have rarely, if ever, questioned them.

You, simply by existing, question all gender assumptions. Gradually I have learned not to try to understand you with my intellect but instead to trust my heart, so clear in its acceptance and love for you.

Yet now, I fear, I want you to agree with me: "Perhaps if you had been recognized, accepted and validated as you are, maybe now you would not want to alter your body." Please, my eyes beg. I want there to be an easier way. I want that you should not need to do this. I want even the possibility that there might have been a chance for you not to need to do this.

You patiently shake your head. "The world is only part of this," you tell me. "The rest of it is inside me."

And my heart knows better. I know you better. You were transgendered before socialization tried to force you to choose "one or the other."

"Are you a boy or a girl?" has been ringing in your ears from earliest memory.

"What do you think?" you flip to them now, tired of explaining. Confusion turns in their eyes. What they say is: freak. What they do is: turn away. Stare. Laugh. Spit. Kill. Beat the spirit from your heart.

You fight them. Survival. Best defense is Get Them First. Show your menace; you are not to be toyed with. "Dangerous" is the message in your eyes, clothes, walk. The razor edge walks with you. You anticipate attack or threat at every turn, exchange, and glance. You talk through. Survival. And "tough" encases your heart.

End of the day and your voice is cold. Your eyes, too old for your years. Tears backed up, held in at what cost? I draw you into the circle of my arms and feel your tension ease. You breathe, and I know you are quietly bringing yourself to me. You can hardly believe you can let it all down, that you can let the tears fall. You can. I know your strength; you have nothing to prove to me. Every part of you that they hate and fear gives me delight. In loving you, I am assured of my own normality.

It is this I fear losing.

The next morning I am driving to work. As I hand my $2 to the toll collector at the bridge, I try to calm myself. "Whatever happens, she will still be my Mary," I whisper again and again, like a mantra. But then

I realize you will not be Mary anymore; you will have a new name. And as if that were not enough, you will not even be "she."

We are in uncharted territory.

One night, several weeks later, I awaken to see you sleeping next to me. Your breasts—dusky in the half-light—are spilling onto the bed. Your breasts, which I never touch without knowing a part of you shrinks from my hand. Beautiful, womanly breasts.

Suddenly I can't lie beside you another moment. Tears from nowhere stream hot down my cheeks. In the bathroom I leave the light off, sit on the edge of the bathtub, double over in the moonlight. I rock against my confusion.

Anger. How dare you throw my universe into disarray! Just when I think I finally know myself! When I think I know you!

Fear. This is too much to ask of me! I can't bear this weight. It is impossible. I feel insane!

Betrayal. Who are you? Are you a butch only because there was no other choice! Am I really a lesbian? What does this mean? How can I be a femme if you are a man?

I want to scream at you. Hate you. Instead I stifle my crying in a towel until at last the tears come silent, flow gently. In the morning you find me curled on the couch in the living room. You hold me. Your eyes are so sad. You tell me how sorry you are.

For what? For being true to yourself? I don't want you to apologize for this. I don't know what I want!

I let you hold me, and it does feel better. But I berate myself for being so angry. For hurting you. I wish I could just get to the other side without going through the pain.

Every day I feel different: I drift in and out of anger and pride, excitement and fear. I grapple with monumental theories and insignificant—but suddenly important—consequences of your transition.

My greatest fear is of how this might affect my own sense of self. "Just don't ask me to be straight," I tell you. "It took me too much pain and time and struggle to come out queer, lesbian, and femme-proud. I can't go back." But you never step on or dictate my identity, and for this I am grateful beyond words.

Instead you inspire me to look with courage at my self-definitions. I see how they are true to me. I also see how they sometimes limit me. Though they have often given me security and a means to self-awareness,

I notice parts of myself I have suppressed: the attraction I once felt for men, the desire I feel now for other femmes, the need to examine my own "othergenderedness."

Some days I feel very alone in the world, like the biggest "freak among the freaks," and I turn old internalized hatred upon myself. Other days I feel like part of an ancient, unspoken tradition, as one who is particularly "wired" to partner a transperson. I feel almost sacred.

Months pass quickly. Every time you bleed, you feel a little more insane, and I feel less able to be your safe harbor. We go to meetings, get to know other transmen and their lovers and wives. We search the Internet for surgeons. We figure out which credit cards can hold the weight of this surgery. Time eases pain, it is true. I love your breasts, but now I release this part of you so beautiful and mysterious to me.

I am changing. Part of me begins to address this surgery with a note of erotic anticipation. I notice that much of my desire is linked to the disparity between your gender expression and your body. When you bind your breasts, pack a dick, when you wear a suit and tie, T-shirt and boxers, when you shift before my eyes from woman into man, I am aroused, excited beyond belief.

I relish the way you construct your gender despite the dictates this world links to your body, which further manifests your particular gender.

Christmas week we travel from San Francisco to Maryland for your surgery. We make love in the cheap motel room near the surgeon's office. I want to touch you, but you tell me you just can't. I could cry.

Later I ask if I can kiss your breasts goodbye. You grant me this, though I know what an effort it is. But I have to ask for this; I'll never have another chance. I kiss your nipples as tenderly as if they were made of snow. I let my tears fall onto your soft skin. I know I will always remember how your nipples quietly harden, even under such a gentle touch.

The next day we go to the clinic. You leave me in the hallway as you make your way to the operating room, looking back to mouth, "I love you." Your eyes are wide in fright, but you are smiling.

Then you are gone. I spend four hours waiting.

There is a strip mall next door. In the coffee shop, I write in my journal. In the drugstore, I buy you a card and makeshift bandages. I try to be objective about whether sanitary pads or diapers will be more comfortable and absorbent against your wounds. The lady at the checkout counter asks me how I'm spending my holidays. I tell her, "Quietly."

After three hours, I come back to the waiting room. It is a cosmetic surgery office, so a little like a hotel lobby, underheated and expensively decorated, with candy in little dishes, emerald-green plush chairs, and upscale fashion magazines artfully displayed against the wall.

A young woman comes in, frantic to get a pimple "zapped" before she sees her family over the holidays. An older woman comes in with her daughter for a follow-up visit to a face-lift. She is wearing a scarf and dark glasses. The nurse examines her bruises right out in the waiting room.

And you are in the operating room having your body and your gender legally altered. I feel like laughing, but I know it make me sound like a lunatic.

After a lifetime of waiting, I am finally called to the recovery room. You are woozy and weak but smile at me when I take your hand. I remember why I am willing to nurse you through this and anything.

Over the course of the next several months we embark upon a journey filled with dramatic peaks and valleys. You start testosterone treatments and your very thinking is changed, along with your body. Most profound is the change in your sexuality. You are more driven, yet more open and vulnerable. You want me like men have wanted me. Sometimes I am so frightened; it is only your love that makes sex possible.

And yet, if anything, you are more sensual to me now. On you, "more masculine" seems like "more butch." I never thought it possible that you could be more butch.

You strut more. Sometimes I find you looking at yourself in the mirror, curious and even delighted. I never saw you take such an interest in your body before. You let me touch you more.

There is a giddy feeling to our lives. Clothes shopping, making love, just being together in this journey is funny, surreal, and filled with a strange, joyful expectation.

And there are stray moments when I stop in my tracks, suddenly realizing my own transition, how I have also changed. How I am changing even now.

On one such day I make a word for myself: *transensual*. And in naming myself, I feel substantial—connected. I am reminded of when

I discovered the word *lesbian* and later *femme*. These words name me and help create me at once. My self has reached for these identifiers, found them and filled them out. Now I make them unique to me. Transensual femme lesbian.

I often bless this path you have taken, for your own sake and for mine; it has propelled me into my own journey, and I have found a part of me which needed to emerge. I see people, the world, differently. I am different.

I am trans-formed.

When you came out over 30 years ago, a young butch in the Chicago bars before the lesbian-feminist movement swept you up in its passion, did you ever long for this second chance?

When you burned your last bra and wore your last dress, did you ever think your path would lead you to this future?

When you swore to yourself as a child that you would somehow find a way to put your elbow in your ear if it would change you into a boy, did you ever think your wish would come true?

You are a boy now. And you are a transgendered butch with a 50-year history. Your politics and passion, your anger and hurt, your emotional capacity and human consciousness—these can never be erased. When I move against you, when I hold you to my breast, when I take you in my mouth, I take in your whole self. You feel my soul and I respond to you, as a femme, as a lesbian, as a transensual woman…as myself.

Tonight I wake up to see you lying next to me, your chest softly rising and falling with each breath. I hardly notice the scars, you are so beautiful. Sleep well, my butch, my boy, my man. I will be here when you wake.

World's Youngest

Mollie Biewald

When she wrote this, Mollie Biewald was a 15-year-old dyke artist with a passion for genderfuck, filmmaking, and 'zines. Now she's studying chemistry and genetics in New York.

I am 5 years old. My grandmother brings my brother and me playing cards. She takes them out of her purse, says, "Blue is for boys, pink is for girls," and hands me the pink deck. I am confused because, while it's true that I've worn more pink than my brother, I don't remember ever hearing that before. Still she's my grandmother and I, being an impressionable kindergartner, believe her.

I am 14, having just left school permanently, in a bookstore drinking smuggled coffee with a friend. When I moved I had to leave her behind, so I write to her almost daily, tell her everything that happens to me. After a few weeks of letters I realized I was consciously censoring myself on one issue, so I wrote her a coming-out letter, told her I was going to transgender meetings and tried to explain why I was nervous, because I knew she got the letter, but she hadn't mentioned it. We sit on the floor in the poetry section and I read random passages aloud to her. Finally she says, "I'm very…um…confused by your…uh…gender nonidentification." There's an uncomfortable silence for a minute, then I say, "Yeah, I know. Me too."

I am on the subway too late at night. A man much bigger than I am gets up and comes and stands in front of me, so I'm trapped in a corner. He stares at me, looks me directly in the eyes and says, "Are you a man or a lady?"

I say, "I'm a woman," in a scared little voice as tough-sounding as I can make it, but he doesn't hear me and asks again, "Are you a man or a lady? Or are you, ha, ha, ha, something in between?"

I look him in the eye, say, "I'm a woman."

He says, "Oh, really?" and doesn't move.

The train keeps moving; I avert my eyes as much as possible, even though he's right in front of me and the closest I can come to looking at neutral space is his foot. I glance up at him every once in a while; he's still there, staring at me. The train is almost empty. I think I'm gonna throw up. Finally it stops nowhere near my destination, but I stand up, push him out of the way with my arm, and run off as fast as I can. He screams something out the door at me, but I can't make out what he says because I'm already too far away.

I am 7, my parents have just split up, and I'm beginning to disappear into the emotionless happy-homemaker being that will almost consume me until I'm 12, 13, maybe 14. On the outside I'm suddenly a good, stable, "normal" little girly-girl, or as close to it as possible for me. I live to please. I learn to sew, clean, and cook. I grow my hair out. I dress up three times a year, Thanksgiving, Easter, and Christmas. My grandmother makes my little sister and me matching pink- and white-checked party dresses. I'm not completely gone, though. I'm a pirate for Halloween.

My best friend is a boy named Ben; we write crazy stories and fist-fight and trade clothes. When we're together, neither one of us has to be our "real" gender. We bake cakes, take a sewing class together. People tease us, say, "Mollie, is this your little boyfriend? Aw, isn't that sweet?" Before long I'm too much of a girl for him, and I don't see him again for years.

It's seventh grade. I've just moved to a rural town from Boston and turned 12. My hair is purple, not long enough for me to pass as a female. I stand out too much from the trendy-girl cliques and am almost instantly the school dyke. Three or four times a day I'm asked whether I'm a boy or a girl, and when I answer they laugh at me.

My home economics teacher refers to me with male pronouns for weeks; I don't know what to say, so I wear a skirt to school even though it's humiliating, pull my hair back with lavender barrettes no boy would be caught dead in. She doesn't notice. After a month I stay after school for a minute, walk up to her, say, "Mrs. Tripp, you, um, know I'm a girl, right?"

She turns bright red and says, "Oh, I'm so sorry. I thought you were a very...uh...*nice* boy."

I leave, and on my way out the principal screams, "Son! Son!" at me until I turn around, then grabs my shoulder, shakes me back and forth and tells me I'm not supposed to cross the street in front of the school. My mother picks me up and I burst into tears but don't tell her why.

I am 13, at a queer conference listening to a speaker tell his coming-out story. At first glance I assumed he was a lesbian in boy drag. I discover I'm mostly wrong; he's a straight man who was once a dyke, still physically a woman but considering his options. I go home intrigued but rather confused. That night I write: *If I'm transgendered, wouldn't I know it by now?*

Days later I get my hands on Kate Bornstein's *Gender Outlaw.* After reading it, thrilled and terrified, I write: *OK, OK, this is me. Now what the hell am I supposed to do?*

Kate's in town to do a play not long after, and I drag my mother along because I can't drive. I sit there in amazement for two hours, trying to absorb everything she says. My mother looks uncomfortable at first, staring at the man sitting in front of us who is dressed completely in leather and holding a whip. She whispers to me, "I can't believe I took you to this!" On the way out I say to her, "I'll always be your daughter. But I'm your son too." She laughs, says, "Oh, God, here we go again."

I am with a group of almost-strangers and one friend, on the way to my first dance. I'm in drag for the first time 'cause it's a gay prom. My friend and I link arms in front of someone's camera, me in an ill-fitting suit and she in a sequined gown. On the subway we're stared at—two flaming faggots, two straight-appearing girls, and one dyke who can't quite pass as a boy. We get there and I spend most of the time outside talking with a little goth girl I've just met who instantly tells me her life story. She leads me inside and we attempt to waltz to Madonna in a throng of dancing gay boys. A drag queen in gold lamé walks up to me and straightens my tie. Suddenly I'm invincible.

It is September, days before I turn 14. School starts, and in social studies I'm supposed to write an essay introducing myself to my teacher. I sit there for a half hour wondering what to say, then finally think, *Oh, what the hell,* and write a couple of pages about identifying as transgendered and my history of forced dress-wearing. I type it up and turn it in, not sure what's going to happen. My teacher doesn't mention it until a month later when I tell her I'm leaving school to go live with my father. She says, "Gonna wear some dresses while you're there?" I laugh and leave the classroom for the last time.

I am in English class next to my best friend at school. I take a bright blue tie out of my backpack, say, "Teach me how to do this." She gives me directions, and when I mess up she takes it into her own hands and does it for me. My English teacher, a homophobic straight man who referred to me as "G.I. Jane" until I screamed at him, stares at me, along with the jock boys who've spent the last two years harassing me for not being enough of a girl. I rip off the tie, put it back in my bag, and forget what she's just taught me. The next day when we walk into class, we're both in almost complete boy drag. She whispers to me, "What is this, the dress code conspiracy?"

I am 14, at BAGLY for the first time in a few months, where I had always gone as a girl. No one seems to recognize me. It comes time to split into separate men's and women's meetings. I stand in the middle, then begin to follow the girls. I stop and realize, standing there, that if I go with them, society has defeated me for the moment, made me feel shameful enough about not identifying with "my" gender that I can't speak up. I walk over to a person who I know identifies as transgendered, say, "Um, is there a transgender meeting?" He says no, but if I want we can have one. I sit down next to him, and for the next 45 minutes we have a tiny little meeting, the two of us and a 45-year-old transsexual woman. I say things I've never said before, amazed with myself. I leave beaming, knowing I'm never going to follow the girls again.

I am 6. My mother hacks off all my hair until it's short as my brother's, because it's become one huge knot and I refuse to comb it. She ties a ribbon around my head, but when I look in the mirror I don't look like a girl.

I am 14, in a barber shop with about 30 men and no women. I sit down and tell the guy standing over me exactly what I want him to do to my hair. He gives me a mean look, says, "You *really* think so?" and starts to cut. He presses himself up against my shoulder in a way no barber should and I want to scream, run out of there, but I'm frozen. I don't.

I sit there for 20 minutes staring at my blank expression in the mirror and his disgusted stare, try to take my mind as far away as possible, anywhere but here with a man much too close to me who hates me for not looking enough like a girl or a boy. He finishes finally. I look up to see he's done a truly half-assed job, cut all the places I told him not to. I get out of there, get home.

I carry the mail upstairs, sort it into a couple of piles, and find a package from New York with my name on it. I run off into my room and rip it open, pull out a lovely black T-shirt with dripping blood-red letters. I put it on and look in the mirror and I'm delighted, even if I do have a sucky new haircut. I dance around the house as the world's youngest Transexual Menace, decide the barber dude is gonna rot in hell anyway, so maybe I don't need to kill him. It takes me a few days to start wearing it in public, first around the house in front of my father, then at my mother's house. She groans, says, "Isn't that just asking for trouble?" I curtsy and say, "But of course."

Packing a Rod
Allen James

Dickless little fag
Allen James is a Skinhead
and he likes to smoke

Hi, my name is Al
But please do not call me that
I prefer AJ

One of the first significant, substantial purchases I made after starting testosterone was a Compact Colt .45 1991 A1 automatic pistol. It's just about the best penis substitute I've ever waved at a sex partner. I love my gun. *Can I get an a-a-ay-men?* You better fucking believe *I lo-o-ove* my gun. I love to take it apart and grease it up good and put it back together and admire it…oh, you sexy little death-machine… I suppose I oughta feel guilty or something, loving and fetishizing a firearm to the point of anthropomorphizing it. But I don't. And I won't either—don't matter to me whether or not I'm supposed to keep this a dirty little secret. I got a *dick* and I can *kill* you with it. Yeah, baby, *trip* my trigger, why dontcha. Heh.

I keep it next to my butt plugs in a black leather sheath. Got a big

125

ol' snap-on to keep it in, and the noise when I unsnap that fucker is unmistakable. Just ask the guy whose ass I fucked last night. *Ka-snap* and, hey, is that come or piss staining the front of your pants? Gives me an angry, rock-hard, two-inch hard-on either way, pretty boy. Only reason I didn't stuff it up your ass is 'cuz I couldn't find a rubber, and Lawd knows I don't wanna get Daddy's killer cock with the seven-round magazine wet…rust, dontcha know? Givin' me a blow job is serious business, believe you me. And when I come, it's dead-out *mind-blowing.* Hey, I made a *funny* back there, didn't I?

Dunno, maybe I have conflated butt fucking with murder, given the Plague Loose Upon the Backrooms and all. Since I'll never know the joy of callously injecting wasting death into a beautiful man through my dick, maybe I've settled for second best. Well, hell, I'm doing my best, y'all. And since I'll never have a dick that'll poke out the top of your goddamn head every time I slam it into you, second best is just about all I'm capable of.

I am pissed off about my weenie. And, yes, I go to the gun range and make *big destructive noise* about it. I got a collection of strap-on fuck sticks that is by no means unimpressive, and I hate every goddamn one of them. D'you get it? I gotta *tie a fake dick around my crotch* in order to fuck like the man I'm trying to be, and it pisses me off. *You* try being a fag with no dick, see how *you* like it. And the available surgery *sucks.* I do not want to go through life waving Frankenstein's Cock at prospective sex partners any more than I wanna spend my life stuffing my underwear full of condoms and hair gel. Am I compensating by carrying a firearm? You better fucking believe I am.

Shortly after purchasing my gun, I discovered that I am a size queen. Now I want a shotgun.

I hope better surgical alternatives come along sometime soon, 'cuz I can't fit a howitzer in my bedroom.

Not as if You Felt That Way, But...
Allen James

Not as if you felt that way, but...as if you needed to feel that way...but never had...and you weren't even sure what...that way...was supposed to feel like. It's a lot like that.

I find myself getting irritated whenever I spend any time with large groups of other gender-variant people. I get sick as hell of hearing about their need for "acceptance," their sad desire to have their existence and the decisions they've made validated in some way by someone else. Piss on that mess. The day that magical someone else whose approval I'm expected to beg for is the person who has to save money for my surgery and sticks this damn needle in *his* leg on *my* behalf is the day I'll kowtow to him.

I knew, the day I finally got off my ass and actively pursued medical methods in hopes of changing my gender, that I'd end up inhabiting my own personal freak show. How can someone be surprised by the reactions of other people to the decision to change one's gender? C'mon, folks, we are the stuff of which successful *Jerry Springer* episodes are made. Figure it out already, and stop crying about how "Mommy and Daddy say I'm going through a phase! *Wa-a-ah!*" For fuck's sake, if you're adult enough to make this decision, you ought to have some idea of the social and familial consequences, right? How can the whole "Everybody *looks* at me so funny now" thing possibly be a surprise? I guess if you're used to inhabiting a personal universe in which you are the only entity who matters in any way, the reactions of Those Other People may be a bit surprising. Like I said, if you're grown up enough to do this, you're grown-up enough to live with the inability of other people to look past their own preconceptions about gender. Maybe.

Gender, as far as anyone who has never been really, fundamentally conflicted about it is concerned, is a given value. It just *is*, as far as the majority of humans even think about it. To the lucky people whose meatsuits fit their beings, the idea of *questioning* one's given gender is bizarre and absurd. We're walking punch lines, us tranny types. Funny, sad, nuts, weird. Our national culture, at least in America, is really not designed to accommodate major differences and is definitely not set up to encompass such base-level questioning of the nature of gender as is inherent in the decision to change one's own. Shit, y'all, in America, culture is mostly designed to stimulate sales and to facilitate the flow of capital from the haves to the have-nots and then back to the haves. We just have the shitty luck to be a statistically insignificant consumer niche, not worth the trouble.

I digress. As I was saying, the idea that gender is mutable is so foreign to most people that they are literally incapable of even imagining it. Describing one's own need to effect even the smallest change is made intensely difficult by the lack of fully descriptive terminology, and by the lack of social models that exemplify gender-variation without relying on stereotypes and jokes.

Dunno, seems to me I've been needing to be male or more male or a man or like a man, or something other than female or not a woman for so long that I'm not really sure how I feel about being the sort of man I am. What a sentence. Anyway, I have never, for a single day, felt sufficiently comfortable as a woman to consider it the state I was supposed to inhabit. Even when I *tried*, I just could not do it. It's not easy to describe, this feeling of "I'm not supposed to be in this body." I lack the accuracy of description necessary to impart fully the overwhelming, mind-numbing wrongness of it.

Everybody has been in an incredibly uncomfortable social situation of some sort, right? Well, imagine feeling like that *all the time*, even when you're alone. Thinking back to my life pretestosterone, the primary emotion I can recall feeling is profound embarrassment. Shame, if you prefer. Not at my feelings of maleness, as one might expect. No, I was ashamed of and embarrassed by my biological gender—to the point that I was mostly nonfunctional emotionally.

Wow. I had no idea I was such a drama queen.

I'm a homo, by the way. Prior to starting hormones, I was a big, ugly bull dyke. Can you say "armor"? Other than having open, running sores on one's face and all exposed skin, the "megabutch, man-hating, leather jacket–wearing, 300 pounds of seething anger" persona is probably the most effective mode of preserving personal distance I'm aware of. I suppose I should insert a disclaimer of some sort here. I'm not going to though. So there. This is *my* rant. You wanna rant about me, feel free. I'm in a long-term relationship with another homo FTM, and one or two of my acquaintances have seen fit to suggest that I am not really an FTM because of it. "Have you ever considered that this is all just elaborate fetish play? Maybe you should reconsider..." Bite me. Just because *you* lack the intellectual facility to look past genitalia to the person it happens to be connected to is no reason for you to presume to challenge my existence.

A Life
Shirle

Shirle wishes to remain anonymous. She works in the same corporate office in New York City where she has worked for 30 years.

"In that mute lightless city where I wander, I see you in the distance. Your shape is misty but I know your walk, I know you're on your way to where we used to live, meaning to meet me there. I hurry after and blind-windowed buildings rise and dumbly topple. Streets twine like coupling snakes and somehow I've forgotten our address. All I can count on are kindly daisies nodding by your grave."
                                                                    —Lucy Cores

I was brought up in an upper-middle-class family. My mother and father were both gay. My mother was a surgeon; my father was a stockbroker. I was born, well, the term for it is hermaphrodite. I was born with a complete compliment of male organs. The only female organ I have is a clitoris. My mother said she would never raise a male child, so she had me partially castrated. My father was very effeminate, and the only time my mother ever had sex with him was when she wanted a child. She made it very clear to me that she had been the aggressive party. He lived in the right side of the house and she lived in the left.

He had his men friends in on the weekends and she had her women friends in on the weekends.

My mother sexually abused me all the years I was living at home. My first remembrance of this was at the age of 5, and the reason I think that's so clear in my mind is that it was my birthday and my father gave me a pony. I had a beautiful day, with a birthday cake, but no friends. I was never allowed friends. That night, as I said, was the first night I remember my mother abusing me. She came into my room and she started soul kissing me and before I knew it she was all over me...sodomy and the whole bit. When she was through with me she said, "Now, you little bastard, go back to your childhood."

Every single night...every single night. I was never in my body. I always felt during this time...I used to project myself somewhere, anywhere, but I wouldn't allow myself to be conscious of what she was doing. Down deep I don't think I even knew it was wrong...or I thought it was wrong...I don't know what I thought. I didn't understand what she was doing. In the beginning I loved her very much, and then I grew to hate her.

I was educated by a tutor. Never went to public school. I did receive a good education. I guess Mother didn't want to be ashamed of me. I had an older sister, six years older than myself, who died at 21. And I have a younger sister, 10 years younger than myself who followed in Mommy's footsteps. She's a surgeon. I haven't spoken to her in years.

Well, anyway, I had a teddy bear. I can't remember the teddy bear's name, but I had the little teddy bear all the while I was living at home, and I used to hide him under the bed when she would come in because I felt he was too young to see such things.

My mother gave me away at the age of 10. I'm getting a bit ahead of myself, but at that time I went out in the yard and I buried my little teddy bear in my favorite spot under my tree house that I had built myself. And I just buried him there before I was taken away.

My father never had meals with us. She and I would sit at the dining room table and have our dinner. And my father would have his dinner on the other side of the house. We had a cook. She was from Germany. She was Jewish and I loved her dearly. She was so kind to me, and I'm sure the woman knew something was going on, but I guess she was afraid to say anything because my mother was looked up to as a god in that New England town. Her patients idolized her. Everything looked just right from the outside. Beautiful New England home, acres and acres of ground.

I never lived with my younger sister because she was born after I had left the house, but my older sister I loved dearly and was very close to, but she left home and went to live with my grandmother. And she knew there was something going on...I know she did, but she didn't understand how to handle it. And I used to beg her to come back, to come back to me. My grandmother was very well-to-do, and she used to come by and visit me occasionally. I don't know if she realized what was going on...I really don't know...and don't know why she took my sister and didn't take me.

I just detested my home, absolutely detested it. It was like a museum, a house full of antiques. I wasn't allowed to sit here, I wasn't allowed to sit there. I just never felt I belonged. It was not a house to live in.

Some days my mother would take long lunch hours when she had office hours and I'd be with my tutor in the morning, and then at noon she'd send me up to bed, and she'd take a long lunch period and come up and spend the time with me. Needless to say what went on. And then I'd go back downstairs, and my tutor would be back from lunch and I'd continue my schoolwork.

During this time my mother would have her women friends on the weekend, and most of them were doctors; they were all professional women. She used to share me with them. There was one woman and she was wonderful to me. She was so kind to me. And I loved her. When she would come, she would ask my mother if she could have me. I'd sleep with her, and she never hurt me...never. She used to hold me in her arms and...just be loving to me.

My tutor was always concerned because I was getting urinary infections all the time. She didn't realize, I'm sure, what was happening, but she was very worried about me because of my health. Now I understand how it was happening because it happened later in my life, which I'll explain.

At the age of 10, Mother gave me away to a friend of hers who was a surgeon. She was chief of staff of one of the big hospitals in Manhattan. She lived on Central Park West, and she was a very wealthy woman. Her mother was French and her father was German, and she spoke with a charming accent. I learned to love her. I loved her dearly, and the complete period of time I was with her she was sexual with me. Ah, at times she was so kind and gentle and loving to me and at other times she was cruel, absolutely cruel. I believe she was an alcoholic.

One evening she took me out in the living room and put a bottle of imported scotch on the coffee table and she demanded that I drink. She would have one and then I would have one. Of course, after two I blacked out...I was only a kid. But she felt this was making me strong. I had to be strong for her.

At that time I was going down to the Village into the bars. Older women...I was very attractive to older women...and they'd pick me up and take me home and I'd wake up the next morning and they'd either drive me home or send me home in a cab. One night I went with an older woman and she drugged me and I was violently ill. She took me out on the street and, as you know, Joan, in those days they were called butches, today they're dykes...but this gal saw me and she had a car nearby and she asked me where I lived. I told her and she took me home and I fell into Edie's arms when she opened the door, and that was one time I was so glad I was living with a doctor because I was violently sick. She had to pump out my stomach and all the rest of it.

One evening Edie came home and she was in one of her violent moods and she had sex with me and I started hemorrhaging. She called a doctor friend of hers, a woman, to the house because she was too intoxicated to know what she was doing for me. This woman saved my life, literally, because I was bleeding so badly. Of course she knew what was going on... She knew exactly what was going on, but no one did anything about it. Just nothing was done about it. And as I said, I'm ashamed to say that I loved her dearly but...I was terrified of her also.

She had an apartment on Riverside Drive. She didn't live there. I later realized it was a lesbian whorehouse. She used to have professional women coming from all over the city, and she called it a woman's gym...a gymnasium.

Edie never took drugs; she just gave them to me. She would usually give me a shot of Demerol or something and send me up there in a cab, and I had all kinds of little outfits. There were little boy outfits like Peter Pan...knickers and all...costumes...they were costumes...and she'd send me up there a couple of nights a week. I was the entertainment, so to speak. Then when I came to hours later, they'd send me back in a cab. And the doorman used to come out and take me upstairs.

So he also had to know there was something going on, but people were frightened in those days…I guess…they were afraid to go forward and say anything.

When I was 14, I started growing a beard. Edie said, "We cannot have this; I have to do a complete castration on you." So she removed the testicles. And then she pumped me full of female hormones. So I started growing breasts. But believe me, my thinking was far from womanly. They can change one as far as physical is concerned, but they cannot change the mind or the brain or one's thinking. I loved women and I always did and I always will. I love the scent of a woman. I love the touch of her skin. I love everything about her, and no matter what they did to me, they couldn't change that. So anyway that's what she did to me, and she herself operated on me.

And there were times, very happy times, with her. In the mornings she'd take me over to Central Park. She used to go horseback riding every morning before she went to work. And she'd take me with her, not every morning but occasionally. I had a pony that I used to ride. And, as I said, I had some very wonderful times with Edie when she was kind and not a beast as she was at other times.

I stayed with Edie until the age of 16 when I met Les. My Leslie, I was so lucky. And I met her in the hospital, at Mount Sinai. I was there overnight and so was she. And it was so strange. We were both from Milton, Mass. But Leslie was 24 years older than I was, and we never knew each other. We were in a semiprivate room. And I was very shy. I had a bed next to the window.

Leslie came over to me and sat on the side of the bed and talked to me for an hour or so. She said that she had never seen such sadness in a person's eyes as she saw in mine. And when she saw Edie come in she said that she knew…she knew right then and there that Edie was the person who was hurting me…even though I had just introduced her to Leslie as my doctor, as my surgeon.

Leslie knew. And that night she talked quite a bit to me and told me she was a writer and that she had been in the Army Air Corps. She'd been a pilot in the Second World War. She told me a great deal about herself. She was a flight commander, and she had all women pilots under her. And she said most of them were gay. She got out of the service as soon as the war was over because she was an extremely aggressive person. She told me that she went in to do a job, she did the job, and then she had to leave because she couldn't possibly take orders the rest of her life. That wasn't Leslie.

She'd had so many careers. Leslie was one of the most interesting people I ever met. She used to go to supper clubs. She knew all the people who entertained at the supper clubs. And she worked for *Vogue*. This was all before she knew me. She worked for them as a fashion consultant and she used to write articles. She had a Ph.D. and she used to write medical articles. And she wrote for radio. You wouldn't remember this, of course. She wrote scripts for *One Man's Family*. She also wrote biographies for radio of different famous people.

I think the very first time I met Leslie I never felt she was a stranger. There was a love I had for her. I know this sounds crazy. But I had a feeling of love for her. And when she put her arm around my waist, I was elated. I was just thrilled. So Edie took me home later that day and I think it was about three months before I contacted Leslie.

It was on a Saturday in May that I next saw her…and I went down and she took me out to a beautiful dinner and then to the theater. I forget the play we saw, but it was a little theater in the Village. And we went home and she asked me how old I was. I told her I was 21, but of course I wasn't, I was just 16. And she said to me, "You look very young. So please tell me if you're not 21. I can get in a lot of trouble." So I promised her I was 21.

We sat and listened to music, and she said, "I only have one bedroom—do you mind sleeping with me?" and I said, "No." Of course I was very excited. We showered and went to bed, and I thought she was sleeping, so I sort of snuggled up to her in back. She was on her side, and all of a sudden she turned around and she started kissing me. Well, it wound up, we made love, and it was wonderful. The next morning…I called her Miss Gordon all the time…I don't know if I said this previously on the tape or not, but the next morning I was still calling her Miss Gordon, so she said, "Honey, you can call me Leslie now." And she started laughing. So the next day she said she would have to take me home, and I really didn't want to go.

She did take me up to the apartment, up to Edie's apartment, and I was there for at least another week or two. And then Leslie called me and asked if I'd like to spend the weekend with her. And I don't think Leslie knew the setup or the situation—I don't really know—but she asked if I'd like to spend the weekend with her and I said yes.

All that week I was looking forward to it. She was meeting me at the bus in Washington Square, and I remember I brought a dozen red roses and she was so touched by that. She was so surprised when she saw them...but she loved them, she just loved them. And thereafter I gave her a rose every single week.

It's hard for me to say the way I felt as far as my sexuality is concerned. I always considered my gender identity to be male, even though I felt complete and comfortable as a lesbian with Leslie. Now I feel like a male, like I did when I was very young. I wear tailored clothing, androgynous to male, but sometimes I wear skirts and makeup. I wanted to have a male organ, and I was thinking of doing it, but I'm not because it would be too emotionally upsetting. I couldn't go forward with it.

But when I was young, I can't say how much I wanted to be with a woman, and be with her the way I was born to be with her, I guess. That's trite, but that's how I felt. I used to agonize over that, and I used to refer to the part of my body that they took from me as Peter. And one night I was in bed and I was thinking of Peter, and of course he was cremated. I used to think of how horrible it used to be... He took on a life for me. I used to think of how horrible it must have been when he was sitting in the corner waiting, not knowing what was going to happen to him. And the flames engulfing him. And...he was gone forever. And how I missed him. I've missed him all my life—even when I was with Leslie. I used to cry sometimes. She didn't understand. I wanted to father a child so badly. I wanted to be what I was meant to be.

Of course, she knew what I was, and I said how I had always wanted to be what I was born to be and she said, "Honey, if you were still male, you wouldn't be with me," because, she said, she was strictly "a woman's woman." So then I felt differently about it because I felt that she would not have had me, and she would not have. I loved her so much. I wanted to be what she wanted me to be.

The gay world was kind to me; they accepted me at that time. But now there's no acceptance for me. Gay women have told me they want no part of me when I tell them or they find out. I had one woman tell me, "I don't want to hear about male organs. Forget it."

But, anyway, when I lived with Edie I tried to take my life. I slashed my wrists. Later Edie did plastic surgery on my wrists so it wouldn't be seen. She found me, I was hemorrhaging. And she saved my life. I'm glad she did because I would never have known Leslie. At the time I didn't want to live; I hated her for saving me. I just felt I couldn't stand it anymore. I thought I was the only one in the world.

Leslie finished my education. She sent me to the Art Students' League because she knew I was interested in art, so I went to the Art Students' League for two years. And then she sent me to New York University to study business administration, which served me very well later on. And she wanted me to go for my master's but I wouldn't because I didn't have enough confidence in myself.

I learned so much about life, about the world, about so many things from Leslie. She had such a zest for living, even to the day of her death. She was very strongly opinionated; people either hated Leslie or they loved her.

She wouldn't waver. She'd listen to all sides of the story and then she'd make a decision, and she wouldn't waver from it. I respected Leslie for that. I respected her very much and looked up to her for that. She taught me so much. Practically everything I learned in life and about life was from Leslie.

When I became 20 years old, I told Leslie I had to work. She just wanted me to stay home and take care of her and she'd take care of me financially, and she did.

Later on, when I was going into business and earning a salary, I never spent a nickel of my pay. She put it right into the bank in a separate account for me. We used a joint account. All of the money in it, of course, was Leslie's. And she bought everything for me. I never needed money. She bought my clothes, paid my doctor, paid my dentist. I never had to carry money because I never needed it.

We did everything together. We even did our food shopping together. And once or twice a month, however, she'd go on business trips, and maybe she'd be gone a week or so. But when she was home, we were always together—except when she was working, of course. And then she demanded "complete privacy," as she used to put it. She'd be in her study for hours at a time, writing away. Most of her writing then was medical articles and medical documentaries.

When I was 19 years old she gave me the greatest thrill of my life. She took me to Paris. And oh, it was wonderful. We spent three weeks in

Paris. And we traveled all over France. Leslie loved Paris because she'd been there numerous times. It was the first time I'd ever been to Europe, and oh, God, what a city. There's just nothing in the world like it.

Leslie used to say Paris was her first love and New York her second. And we just had a fabulous time. I'll never forget that. It was the thrill of my lifetime.

We settled first in the Village for about six years. She had a charming apartment. It had a beautiful big wood-burning fireplace, and we could stretch out in bed and look up at the sky and the stars and the moon and…oh, it was something special.

We had a wonderful life in the Village. The Village was wonderful in the '50s. You know that, Joan. It was great, except for the hate around, which definitely existed. But we used to go to these little private places so we didn't have to worry about that.

Leslie would never take me to a bar, though. She took me once, and never again. And I used to beg her to. I will say, and I must say, we had an understanding between us. I'm not going to side-pass this at all… Leslie was a womanizer. She liked women. And she and I had a very clear understanding about this. I accepted it fully. It hurt sometimes, of course it did, but I accepted it because Leslie always came back to me. She told me she would never leave me and she loved me deeply, and she proved that more than once. There was no doubt in my mind about that.

I took full care of her. I did all the cooking. And I used to iron and wash her clothing, do her shirts…just took full care of her, and I loved doing it. I know that today this is frowned upon. But I loved doing it, and she took full care of me financially. That's for damn sure.

We just did what came naturally. We were not play-acting or…or playing parts or anything else. We just did what came naturally. And at that time that's what I needed. And at that time, apparently, that's what she needed.

Later on I told her, of course, that I would have to work. I couldn't possibly go on not working. I felt like a nothing after a while. I had to do something I was capable of doing. And for two years I worked as an artist, doing ceramic painting. And then she wanted me to get in the business world.

She felt I could make a much better living in the business world. And I did. So I went to work for a large company, and I started out in the sales department. And I trained to be a sales rep. And after sales I went into collections for this company, and after collections I became a public relations manager, in public relations, and absolutely loved it. So I was very happy in my work and very happy with my lover.

Leslie had one close friend at the time. She was chief psychiatrist at one of the hospitals in Manhattan, and after having lived in the Village, she contacted Leslie and told her she was going to open an office in East End Avenue and she wanted us to go and live with her and her lover. So we did. And it didn't work out too well. Leslie and she were very close, and May—that was Leslie's friend's lover—became violently jealous.

We were there a year; then we left because things were just not working out. Leslie and she were spending so much time together... They'd sit up till 2 or 3 o'clock in the morning...they'd just be downstairs in the doctor's office talking about all sorts of things. Anyway, May just couldn't put up with it, so Leslie decided to leave because things were becoming very difficult for...R.B....that was the doctor.

So when we left there, we went to live in Forest Hills, and we found a lovely apartment... It was a beautiful place at that time. Then after having lived a good number of years in Forest Hills, Leslie wanted to buy a home, so we bought a home in New England, a small college town in New England.

Leslie became head of a prep school. She was also writing, of course, and it was a beautiful area, and the house we bought was beautiful. They thought Leslie was my mother. We never said that, they just assumed she was my mother and we said...we didn't say yea or nay...but this was the assumption. One day I had to go to a doctor in town, a woman, for a minor problem...and she was in my confidence at the time...and I stupidly said we were gay. And she told the entire town about it, practically put it in the paper.

The next Christmas morning...we had had the furnace man there to repair the furnace...and Christmas morning, about 4 o'clock in the morning, Midgie, our beagle, came running up the stairs. She awakened us, or we probably would have slept right through it until the furnace blew...and Leslie ran downstairs. The fire was shooting out from the furnace...and the off switch was on the other side of the furnace, and Leslie shouted for me to leave the house and I wouldn't leave. I would not leave. I didn't care…I was going to stay with her. And she ran across in front of the furnace and her hands were burned…and she turned off the switch.

We learned the following day that the furnace would have blown had Midgie not awakened us and Leslie not turned off the furnace. And we found out several months later this was done to our furnace purposely.

A short time later, I had a horrible accident. A guy hit my car while he was stoned out of his head, and I was almost killed. So we got rid of that car and Les bought me another one. I was going home one night and…a couple of days before, I'd had the car in for servicing…and going home that night I lost complete control of the car and hit a tree. The state troopers came along and they checked the car out…not then…they just towed it off, and they took me to the hospital. When they checked the car out they said I was driving without a steering rod. So the steering rod had been removed from my car, and I was damn near killed.

We realized then what was happening, and I told Leslie that I had told this doctor…and she had a long talk with me and said that we'd have to leave, that she certainly wasn't going to put our lives at risk. So we left and we left a bundle of money there that we had put into the house. But, as Leslie said, it was better than losing our lives.

So we moved back to Forest Hills. And we were very lucky that we left in one piece. These were educated people, and it was just amazing, the hate, the subtle hate, I should say. It was never brought out in the open, but I remember I said to Leslie…I was so hateful toward straight people at that time, I detested them… I remember I said to Leslie, "But they tried to kill us for just loving each other." I couldn't believe it, that hate could run so deeply as this, although I should have known because it existed in the Village. But in the Village it was right out in the open. This was subtle and even more dangerous.

I mentioned that my younger sister and I have nothing whatsoever in common. She followed in Mother's footsteps. She's also a surgeon. Well, my mother died, and she died very suddenly. She had never been ill. They found her dead across her desk. It was an aneurysm of the brain, so it was instant.

Anyway, my sister contacted me and told me what had happened, requesting I get there immediately.

I could not go.

I called my sister and told her that I wouldn't be there. She said she would never forgive me as long as she lived. And she never has. When later she found out about my situation, she said something I can never forgive her for. She said that if that had been true…which she has her doubts about…I had never lived in the house when she was there…then I invited it. A 5-year-old inviting rape.

Leslie had never been ill…minor illnesses but never anything serious. She was an extremely strong person physically, mentally, and every other way. One morning I was in the bedroom getting dressed and I heard this scream…and Leslie didn't scream…and I ran into the bedroom and she wasn't able to move. She was on the side of the bed and she wasn't able to move. I said, "What's the matter?" And she said, "I don't know, I have excruciating pain in my back. I…I can't move."

I called our doctor, who was Paula. She told me to get an ambulance and take Leslie down to Memorial and have her X rayed. It turned out to be an extreme case of osteoporosis. She had simply turned in bed and fractured six vertebrae. She had complained of an aching back for years but never sought medical help for it. Nowadays, of course, they have treatment for it, but not then. There was so much bone loss that, looking at the X rays, you could barely see any trace of bone whatsoever in Leslie's back.

This began a long, slow decline. She was in pain almost constantly in the beginning, and had three doctors that were taking care of her in Manhattan. She was cared for in New York City for the first five years.

I had to take her down by ambulance because she wasn't able to sit in the car. She couldn't sit up. And it was strange…she could walk with a specially made brace. She had trouble walking, of course; she was able to walk, but she was not able to stand for any length of time waiting for a train or sit up straight in one place in a car. She wasn't able to do that. So I had to take her by ambulance three times a week. And the second month she became very bad and I had to have a private nurse. And she was on duty eight hours a day.

I think it was about the fourth year…we had a huge bank account. We had enough to take care of us for a lifetime, but it went very fast. When I saw it going down so rapidly it was terrifying. In her prime,

Leslie was six feet tall. At her death she was barely five feet. She died on March 29, 1992.

I've been in therapy for 16 years now. I went into therapy because I knew I couldn't handle Les's death alone. Four years before she died I saw the end coming. My therapist has been a godsend. She took care of the preparations for last rites for Leslie. She was with me during the service. And after Les's death, we had spent all our money. She bought my medication, which I couldn't afford. I was alcoholic at the time, and she helped me with that. She saved my life, literally saved my life.

There was a sign on Leslie's office door all the years that I was with her. It's an Indian prayer. And she loved this. It ends, "I seek strength not to be greater than my brother but to fight my greatest enemy, myself. Make me always ready to come to you with clean hands and straight eyes so that when life fades…my spirit may come to you without shame."

Leslie lived by this, and she also had something else hanging on her wall. "To thine own self be true." And this she also lived by, up until the very end. She always had the strength and the courage to be who she was. And I must say that about myself. I'm very proud of that.

Liminal
Peggy Munson

*Peggy Munson is a queer poet, essayist, and fiction writer who has pub-
lished widely in publications and periodicals including* On Our Backs *and
the* San Francisco Bay Guardian. *She is the editor of* Stricken: Voices
from the Hidden Epidemic of Chronic Fatigue Syndrome.

She knows I am a wild thing, pins me fast and hard. She grips me by
the throat the way you hold a street punk, firm hand in a V beneath my
chin. She tilts my cheeks from side to side like she's thinking about
slapping them or like she's surveying my baby-soft skin. She kisses me
hard on the mouth, then cocks my head back, holding me firm in her
grip. My heart races from excitement and fear. I begin that pitiful, auto-
nomic gulping. I practically drown in my own pathetic spit like some
diva junkie choking on vomit—20 years past her prime. Still, she holds
me there. Firm.

*The neck is the most fragile part of the vertebrate, the tenuous bridge
between mind and body. Every animal protects itself from being broken
there.*

One sharp gesture and she could easily do some harm. She knows
about my fear of entrapment. I'm so conscious of every fire escape in
my body. Her watchful eyes watch me breathe, working me like the

bellows of an ancient diving apparatus. "You think you are self-contained?" She wants to ask me to prove I'm not. When I swallow I feel a ripple in my throat. She tells me I am *dangerous*, with some kind of Mafioso blood running deep in the clogged arteries of my overindulgence. She tells me I am *trouble*. She expects me to hurt her someday, but she doesn't care. This is where things get tricky: Even when she has me pinned here, she is pure masochist. She doesn't know this yet. She's still banking on her superior strength.

I want her to almost choke me, and I want to squirm away.

"So give me a name, porn writer," she orders me. She wants me to come up with a name for her former cock, which still looks like a cock to me—but what do I know? I haven't seen the real thing for a while. She tried *girlcock* for a while, but that didn't work. *Clit* didn't seem quite right either.

"Call Webster's," I answer, and then she presses the V further into my neck. What do I know about the origins of words? I'm just a *user*.

Poised over me, she feels like she's a superhero intermingling with the mortal world. She likes my fragile mortality, how it contrasts with the early line drawings of her own metamorphosis. Her superhero has a name, *The Nomenclator*, because she names everything. She even had to rename herself when her boy name didn't work anymore. Yet she knows how I just like to watch words implode on themselves, perennially seeking the black holes after words. I am not a planet that needs saving. She's angry with herself for being *too late* to save me.

Her former dick is more Antichrist than Christ, more cockfighter than cock, so in my head I call it *galleros,* or cockfighter. She is the former boy superhero turned dyke who fights the big bad iron phallus of the patriarchy. But I also have to admit, when she's hardening in my hand I sometimes want things no dyke is ever supposed to want. I crave the Hollywood heterosexual fuck. I yearn to be the splayed blond whose lips were modeled after a cock ring. Sometimes I imagine circle-jerking with her in a gay buddy porn flick, groaning and coming fast and hard. And I want her firm clit, a clit any girl could find in a haystack. I want to massage her soft former testicles that feel like the sweet, tender insides of a cunt. I want the pink tip of her old cock, her clit-like cock, and the slit on the end like the ridge on some women's nipples.

"We could name it after one of the Kennedys," I suggest.

We have been talking about how Jackie O is such a suggestive name, how anything with "O" makes you just want to fuck it.

"You're assuming it's going to die a horrible death," she says. "Do you want that?"

"I only elongate," I say. "I never castrate."

She holds my neck firmly.

She knows I need a reason for being here. She knows my life is a lemming walk. I need to believe that every breath means something. She deconstructs my gender, tells me I have the kind of tomboy androgyny she really likes, but it is all *dyke*. She tells me I am what testosterone used to be for her, the rage that stampedes at the sight of red. I am all girl and tracheotomy, so much suppressed red screaming inside of me. And she is the antithesis of tracheotomy, talking like a manic boy even when she is choking on everything unsaid.

Of course, sometimes I make her quiet, real quiet, just ozone and anticipation and *wanting*. I like it when she's my tornado girl like that, deep in the profound vortex of her own formative cunt. I like it when I see her feeling that. I think I know when she feels it, because she gets all soft like she's transforming, turning inside out. It's such a power trip, but it also brings out every one of my nurturing instincts. And sometimes she does it to me.

Sex with her can sometimes be a *peleas de gallos*, a cockfight, pure raging animal testosterone from either one of us. Sometimes I think about going down on her with lipstick, smearing my garish makeup like some hyperbolic ravaged femme and sucking on her amazon clit until I make her come. She confuses everything I am, shakes the change out of my pockets and makes me want to barter with foreign currency. But then sometimes she is a total estrogen femme, and I just want to put her in an apron, give her a box of tissues, and watch her perform.

When we play truth or dare and I choose truth, she asks, "Am I a boy or a girl?"

I want to tell her she is all girl when I fix her up in a vintage lace dress and put leather cuffs on her wrists and make her answer the door. I want to tell her she is all woman when a servile Italian waiter calls us *ladies* and grinds pepper over our arugula salad. I want to tell her she is all boy when she goes around naming everything and solving mysteries like Encyclopedia Brown. And when she presses me down by the throat, like a girl trying to be tough, and then turns me over and spanks me, I almost want to call her "Daddy." It's all messed up.

"You're just full of shit," I answer, because we're acting like babies that day.

I know you are, but what am I?

I know you are, but what am I?

I know you are, but what am I?

I don't say this: You are something between desire and fear, how you hold me. Between force and surrender. You are beautiful, even hating the chiseled shadows on your face. You have chosen me because I will run; I have chosen you because you will stay. I love the shadows behind the shadows, how much they imply. Your color is the crayon between blue-green and green-blue and cornflower blue. Your eyes cancel instinct. Your gesture is the embrace. I like how you hold yourself accountable. I want to be held by you, held accountable.

Instead I say, "I'm just full of shit."

And she answers, "I know you are, but what are you?"

"I'm a fool." But this isn't good enough for her. She gives me her "You can't talk to royalty that way, court jester" stare and says, "But what are you?"

"I don't have to say."

She pushes my breath to a place deep behind my heart and says, "Oh, yes you do."

Do Your Ears?
Peggy Munson

We are bad boys, incorrigible, always burning red around the ears as if our minds are locomotives of naughty thoughts. When we see prim restraint, we think of ghost towns. If we pass barn siding, we crave matches. Eyeing the bulges in Levis, we concoct saddle horns. Even in my cramped apartment, where we must imagine open spaces, we want to pretend the world is our rodeo. We want to mount and ride everything.

"This is bad," he whispers. "We shouldn't do this."

"We're not doing anything," I say with a scowl in my voice, looking at him like he's the most presumptuous prick on the planet. "We're just friends."

We squeeze onto the narrow futon the size of a sleeping bag, and he says we must be quiet or we will get caught. The dads are upstairs with long-necked beers and pigskin hard-ons, preparing to go hunting. I want to tell him a ghost story, the one about the girl in the woods and the scary man. But this is an old story, one he's probably heard hundreds of times. So instead I hold him down and pretend to be a vampire. I prime the downy hairs and the knotty vine of muscle on the side of his neck with my soft breath, then sink in my teeth until he makes a girlish, high-pitched whimper and I tell him he sounds like a *fag* and besides, he should shut the fuck up. He can be hopelessly childish. I clamp my hard hand over his wet lips, hold him roughly, and growl into his ear. "Remember," I say, "the dads are going hunting soon."

When I was 6, I used to walk around with my shirt off in the summertime. "Don't you know you are a girl?" the neighbor boy asked me. "Don't you know girls can't do that?" But apparently no doctor ever gave me a thorough examination, because my friend finds something very interesting when he pulls back my hair.

"Look at this," he says tracing the hard cartilage and soft, dangling flap of my ear. "You have little boy cocks all over your body."

No, I want to insist. *You can't say that. I'm a girl.* But all of a sudden, he becomes a virulent Boy Scout singing a joyous anthem:

Do your ears hang low?
Do they wobble to and fro?
Can you tie 'em in a knot?
Can you tie 'em in a bow?

My friend is good at changing the meaning of everything. As if to prove that my ears really are cocks, he starts sucking and licking their erogenous rims. I become a Doberman on police alert, stiff for his hungry mouth. He's a practiced, prepared, good little Boy Scout, and he knows his way around an aural compass, licking his way from the pinna to the lobe. If the dads come down, he will tell them he was just examining me for ticks, like I'm some old mangy dog. He's a really bad liar, not as good as I, but they'll believe him because he always looks so fresh-faced and earnest. He even looks earnest when I push him away by the chin and hold up his face to survey his swollen lips.

But we aren't queers because we don't kiss and we don't touch each other's dicks; we only think about it. I hold him down by his pretty-boy, ruddy cheeks and tell him he's really naughty for giggling when he looks at me. I want to slap his cheeks playfully, but that would make noise, and I know he would just squirm and whimper anyway. I wrestle him so he is trapped beneath my weight and I feel the hard bone of my crotch pressing the crap-flap on the rear of his red union suit. I wonder for a second how his bare ass would feel against my body, and then I bite his red boy ears, lick the crevice behind the downy hairs, and amplify my whisper right over the ridge where everything echoes. "Be a good boy," I croon.

And he is quiet as a languid snowfall, like he's letting himself be covered in the perfection of a million unique snowflakes.

"That's it," I say. "You're getting it."

The story goes like this, as far as I can remember.

An agoraphobic woman lives in a rustic cabin, but the woods are a spooky place, full of trees that have probing arms and animals being animalistic. It has taken so long to civilize women. The woods bring back their feral impulses and make them think they are fighters, hunters, lovers, creators. They stop wearing bras, like '70s feminists crooning Carly Simon. After a few months they can divide medicinal mushrooms down to the genus, but they forget about the important rules of chromosomes.

So, along comes this archetype with a hook to set things right. A hook like a meat hook. The woman in the woods, braless and singing "You're so Vain," is sitting in her cabin one day whittling a piece of tender birch, making something that looks like a dildo. Everything in the woods starts to look like something else—I mean, to transform and mutate. Suddenly Mr. Hook bursts in on her happy scene. She screams and drops the knife. She looks stage left for a cue, and then says with fright in her voice, "Are you going to kill me?"

Everybody has heard this story before. Everyone knows how it ends.

Oh, but the half-carved piece of wood. The investigators on the scene of the crime mull over whether or not it is an important piece of evidence. They wonder if it is some sort of totem, if the woman was a witch. They wonder if she was building a crude knife, or a thimble. A psychologist, brought to the scene of the crime, explains that women sometimes carve things out of nothing. Women, he explains, get scared in the woods. Perhaps she was carving a little man. "But whatever," he says. "It is good for a doorstop, or kindling."

And, really, it is just a piece of nothing.

We curl up on my futon the size of a sleeping bag and pretend we are in a small hunting cabin, lying a floor beneath the fathers, reminding each other that we are the best of friends and best friends shouldn't fool around. It is something about karma. Something about making too much out of nothing, because friendship and sex and boys and girls are such radically different things.

All day he was my houseboy, and I was a stringent dyke sergeant. He crawled around in his teddy boxer shorts and mopped my floors with a sponge. He dusted cobwebs out of corners. He cooked me eggs with greens and red peppers and onions and basil. In his polished black boots and black 501s and tartan shirt and ALL-PURPOSE CHORE BOY badge, he ran errands for me. I kept a list on a clipboard and checked things off, giving him small rewards when he did a good job. After he washed and dried and oiled my heavy cast-iron pans, I let him unwrap a long licorice whip that was black and sinewy like the real thing. Previously, when I imagined giving him the licorice, I considered putting the end of it up his ass and making him parade around for me like a horse while I slapped him with a riding crop and made him gallop, then eating my way up to the sweet anise sting of his asshole. But I couldn't do that; we were just supposed to be friends, and he was only helping me with these chores as a favor.

So, after we unwrapped the licorice, we practiced shoving it down his throat like an intubation tube, first three inches, then four inches, then five inches, seeing how far we could make it go. And as his lips and throat became more practiced at opening for the licorice—and sucking on it—we both agreed he was going to make some leather daddy very, very happy.

Of course, at that moment, I wished I had a dick the size of Florida. I intubated his widening throat and I just wanted to say to him, like an evil doctor, "Suck my cock, slut."

Nightfall came early, and our bodies reached high tide, filling our insides with restless and hungry surf. I had to admit I liked seeing him on all fours, crawling around so servile and eager to please. I had to admit I was having a hard time with the "nonsexual boundaries" we had established in our friendship. I remembered myself as a young tomboy, ordering little boys to come up behind the propped-up dirty mattress on my cold, closed porch, then making them pull their pants down. As his knees darkened from my dirty floor, he looked more and more like the kid who always got shoved facedown in the dirt on the playground, humiliated and emasculated, then came up asking for more. His ears were crimson with exertion, and he smelled like dewy morning sweat. He smiled at me with eager lips as he tore up my house. I clucked my tongue against the top of my mouth, rolled my eyes, and wondered if he would have the patience to put everything back together again, or if he was one of those attention deficit disorder boys wandering from neighborhood to neighborhood looking for new places to ransack.

After a while he begged for a rest, and we sprawled out on my long yellow couch to talk about our nerdish high school years. We talked some locker-room talk about the people we had wanted to fuck and how and wherefore and why. I stroked his coarse, wavy hair that made him look like a Nordic seaman. I stroked it in a falsely platonic, slightly titillating way. After a while, I got up and retrieved an energizing houseboy vitamin and made him swallow it with a single gulp of water. After all, he still had to prepare dinner, and I knew boys could take care of others but not always themselves.

He was a good boy, the best, one of the most sought after boys in New England, so I had to keep him well.

At some point after he fed me dinner we were feeling bloated and logy, and we curled up together on the little futon like we were napping after a game of kickball, and then I started metamorphosing into his bad boy chum.

I tried to control myself—don't get me wrong. I tried because we had rolled through several processing talks that satisfied my lesbian *Roberta's Rules of Order* about how we shouldn't sexualize our friendship because that would ruin everything. I loved him, truly, like the brother I never had, and I didn't want to jeopardize our unique and beautiful connection. It was so nice just lying there with him, spooning my back against his strong front and pressing my butt up against his hard hipbones. I thought of innocent times when big, strong animals were free to roam the uniform land. *It doesn't have to be anything but comforting,* I would tell myself, but then I'd look at him sometimes and think, *My friend is really fucking hot.*

Do your ears hang low?
Do they wobble to and fro...

And after a while, those thoughts became a cacophony of singsong, pubescent voices, and when I pressed up against him and looked at the curve of the back of his ear, I turned hungry and mad as Van Gogh.

From the front he can't always pass, but from the back he is rarely read as a *she,* even though he hasn't done hormones or surgery. His neck is strong, and the hairs on the nape of his neck are cut close. Before I can stop myself or plead innocence, I am running my tongue up the narrow shaft of the little dick of his ear, and he loves it. His ears are so alive and so responsive. He whimpers loudly, so I have to hold his mouth firmly closed and squeeze up against his back and suck on his ear. He tries hard to be a good boy, to not make noise, but his body retorts every time I stick my tongue into his ear and lick the little hairs rising up there, those tiny soldiers lined up waiting for the harsh bark of commands.

"Hold still," I say. "*Shhh.*" We both know the fathers are upstairs polishing the barrels of their rifles and getting drunk, because they're going hunting at dawn. "You'd better just hope they're not hunting for little queer boys."

We are innocent like the prep-school boys in *A Separate Peace* who tumble together with rage and love and envy and beauty because they feel the omnipresent threat of wartime. We don't know what's going to happen, even when it starts happening. And when we are immersed in the tender moment of what's happening, we pretend to know nothing. I hold him tightly against my body so he can feel my androgyny and strength and narrow boyish hips. A lot of people quickly identify me as a femme, and I feel so relieved to be out of that dress. When he gets close to my face, he notices the wispy black hairs above my upper lip and tells me I have a little mustache. But he doesn't say it in that "Quick, buy a depilatory before you turn into a bearded lady" way but with a quiet awe. And when my lower lip brushes against the coarse stubble where he has shaved off his sideburns, I tell him right into his ear how much I love rubbing against that feeling on a boy. I love the way the landscape changes from soft and lush, to coarse and forbidding, just as I love the soft skin of dicks when they are hard.

I stroke the stubble with my lower lip, moving down and kissing him softly on the neck where I left bite marks before. I hold his chin firmly in one hand and tilt his head back. I suck and bite his neck up and down the lumpy burial mound of his trachea, where all of his secrets and screams and groans are buried. I love that part of the neck, where life and death collide and everything scared and primal rocks and coalesces. I hold him so I am slightly cutting off his breath—and I know he has to trust me—then suck and bite up and down his neck. I trace his bottom lip with my thumb so he can taste me slightly. I pull his mouth open, hook my thumb under his teeth, and hold his jaw open.

Then, for just a moment, I plunge my thumb deep into his mouth.

"Look at that," he gasps when I pull out. "Your thumb is a little cock too."

But I have already figured that out and am tracing the circumference of his lips to see how wide they can go, imagining what it would feel like to press something deep into his mouth. We wrestle and struggle for a while, but he lets me win. So I pin him down on the claustrophobic futon that reminds us both of freshman year in college when everything happened on single beds and when the sex was groping, surprising, ecstatic. I press my body hard against him, then tease his cute ruddy face with my lips, mouth, teeth. I exhume more whimpers and screams from his throat while I pin his hands back behind his head. Then I burrow into his armpit, rubbing my face against its warmth and nipping at the tender skin on the side. I feel his firm biceps. I hold his strong wrists. He turns me over and presses me against the wall, holds me there with his body, then he traces the outline of my hand like he is seeing it for the first time. He rakes his fingers between mine, and for a minute we just hold hands and breathe hard and look at each other. We are two boys who think that if they don't say the word *fag* out loud, they won't have to know what they are doing.

But suddenly I know exactly what I am doing. I am a bad boy and I just want to shove a cock into his mouth. I want to see how much he can take. I knock his face from side to side with my palm and lock him in a wrestler's hold under my bent arm and bite him really hard so he starts squirming away, sliding toward the edge of the mattress. Then I push his head roughly over the brink and I poise over him, and I slide my thumb deep into his mouth until it becomes a dick in its own right. First he is sucking like a baby on a pacifier; then he is sucking like he's giving a blow job to every president of the land of the free and especially every president of the home of the brave. Because now we have crossed out of innocence into blind courage, and I am fucking his open mouth with my cock.

I push into his mouth, firm and hard, pressing his head against the hardwood floor and tilting it back to get just the right angle. The back of his throat widens for me, and I am in the underbelly of the earth where narrow corridors open up into cavern rooms, and time stops because everything is dark and unspeakable and pure. And his lips suck the soft skin of my thumb and the hard bone at the end, and he feels so dirty and innocent and turned on. He nibbles a little, and then I push in harder and thrust in and out until I feel his gag reflex kicking in, then I pull out and give him a moment of rest while I stroke my wet thumbnail against his lower lip.

"I'm bad for biting," he says.

"Yes, you are," I answer, then I hold him down so firmly he whimpers with excitement. "But I love the way you suck me off. You're such a sexy boy." And he barely has time to register gratitude before I'm thrusting into him again with my thumb, and we are both moaning because it feels so good. I can feel all the curves of his throat and I stroke my thumb shaft down the top of his mouth and deeper, deeper into him. I press up hard against him, and the pleasure of taking him like this, of letting him please me just ripples through my body. Every time he whimpers, I whimper—then I silence him by pressing in harder. He's the bad boy.

"You're not as good at being quiet," I whisper to him. "I have to fuck your mouth to shut you up."

We have a lot in common with the dads and their guns, how we can turn anything into a cock. This is the men's secret, how rifles and long-necked beers can be dicks. But if they can be dicks, anyone can have one. Dawn is coming soon and we have to be quiet. The fathers don't look kindly on cocksuckers, and besides, dawn can cultivate regret, and I want to take my boy while he is sleepy and gaping with surprise. Right now he is fresh-faced and taking it like a man. We are in the dreamy, late-night space where friends can sleep with each other and thumbs can be cocks. And when I push into him, I do have a hardened dick and every nerve of it responds to every motion of his lips and tongue,and when he sucks the base of it, I feel steam rising off of my body. I feel so hot and sexed-up and erect.

I fuck him until his throat is raw and a chemist could stain several throat cultures from beneath the slide of my thumbnail.

Until my hand smells like his mouth and his mouth smells like my hand.

Until platonic love meets innocent lust.

Until he is weary.

And when we finally relent, our bodies curving off onto the floor, he says in a quiet, serious voice, "I *love* sucking you off like that."

And I say, "I loved it too." And then I smirk. "You're really hot."

I wonder how my friend has forgotten the story, how he can go around calling himself something different from what he has been called all along.

The story is a common urban legend. It travels from mouth to ear, from city to city. The ears receive the mouths; the mouths never receive the ears: This is how the tradition continues. It becomes so believable.

He wants to be alone to jerk off, so I retire to my bedroom. I can't sleep, so I write about the mouths receiving the ears. I write about how he loved it when I bit his ears, how they were red like the ears of a little scoundrel. I write about how I want to go deep inside them to the cochlea so he will hear the exact words I say and nothing will be lost in between. Then I lay the notebook beside my bed.

If the fathers go hunting, I think as I drift into twilight sleep, *if the fathers go hunting, my confession will be right by my body. If the fathers go hunting, someone will read it and know these complexities.*

When I wake up he is gone and my house is immaculately clean. He has put everything into place, everything lined up in neat rows, and laid food on the table like a good little helper, a leftover piece of Indian bread with ginger and honey. On the table is a note that reads, "I hope my performance as houseboy met your needs." I bite a corner of the *naan* and lick the honey off my hand, noticing I still taste a little like his mouth. I think about getting a new leather harness for some of my bigger, silicone dicks, but then when I reach for the phone to ring him up so I can praise him, I think, *I bet no guy every dialed with his cock.*

Do It on the Dotted Line
Raven Kaldera

Raven Kaldera is a trans/intersexual FTM, organic farmer and homesteader, a member of the board of directors of the American Boyz, and author of Hermaphrodeities: The Transgender Spirituality Workbook. *"Tis an ill wind that blows no minds."*

"Sometimes," the woman speaker said to her rapt audience, "we just have to draw a line between male and female." Her sincerity was apparent. Everyone in the room could feel it. It made them trust her. It made me sick.

I knew I was going to have to stand up and challenge her, and I knew I could do it in one of any number of ways. I could tell her I have a medical condition (congenital adrenal hyperplasia), that I'm the sort of person they used to call a hermaphrodite back in the olden days (like the 1950s), but that now we call ourselves intersexuals. I could tell her that I was raised as a girl and now live socially as a man, that I've seen both sides of that line and know its transience, its fragility, its vagueness. I could order her to define *male* and *female* and *man* and *woman* and then tear down her definitions. I could argue with her on the field of reason, but I didn't.

First of all, I knew her objections weren't stemming from any reasonable space. She was scared, plain and simple. Scared of finding penises in her restroom and testosterone in her girlfriends and proba-bly of a lot of other things too. No matter what I said, I probably wouldn't change her mind, because I wouldn't be addressing her fears—fears that were, in a sense, reasonable. After all, we are advo-cating an entire renovation of the gender system. We may disagree on what it should look like, but we're pretty much in favor of bringing on the drills and chisels. We shouldn't pretend otherwise; it insults the intelligence of the frightened masses. Yes, what you fear is true. And you know what? You'll live.

Second, I'm not just a medical condition. I'm a mythical beast. I know because when I was 10 years old, I found the word for what I am in a book of Greek myths and it said so. Two years later, when I hit puberty and grew breasts and facial hair, saw my hips spread and heard my voice crack, bled and got erect, I knew it was true. They said it was a myth, but here I am—a unicorn, a dragon, a monster, a piece of magic let loose on the world. Your reality gives ground before my undeniably solid presence. And I'm a *heyoka*, a sacred trickster, on top of it all.

So I grabbed the femme friend sitting next to me and hissed in an intense undertone, "Eyebrow pencil! I need eyebrow pencil! Now!" Coming from someone dressed as butchly as I was, it took her aback, and she fumbled through her purse as if I'd insisted that poison gas had been let loose in the building and I needed her lipstick to coun-teract its effects. She hurriedly handed me a brown stick, which I promptly used to draw a dotted line from my hairline to my chest. I'd have drawn farther, but I didn't want to open my shirt and show off my hairy breasts just yet. Then I pulled my knife out of my pocket and walked up to the female speaker who was still holding forth on the value of women's and men's spaces.

She saw me, and her eyes widened. With the weird face paint and the knife, I suspect she took me for some kind of crazy coming to stab her. I indicated the dotted line drawn on my face. "Here's your line," I said. "Here's your line between male and female." Then I opened the knife and held it out to her, hilt first. "Put your money where your mouth is."

She looked stricken, horrified, then turned and ran from the room. I don't know what was actually going through her mind, but I know peo-ple took her aside later and told her about me, about who and what I am. I hope she got it. I hope she finally understood that whenever a line is drawn, it passes through someone's flesh.

There's a card in the tarot deck called "temperance." The often androgynous angel on it, shown standing with one foot on the water and one on land, is pouring fire and water back and forth between two cups. I feel like that much of the time, one foot in each world, frantically juggling opposite elements. Not just male and female either; there are also the separate countries of hormones and culture, intersex and transgender, spirituality and intellectualism, queer and transexual, and so forth. The lines aren't stable; they move around, but they're easy to find. Just come and look for me. Where I stand, there's the line. Where I move, the line goes with me. I live on it. It is imprinted into my flesh. You can take my clothes off and see for yourself.

The angel on the temperance card always looks so serene, though. I wonder if I'll ever feel like that.

My mother freaked out when I started to become masculine at puberty. I was the oldest, and she'd wanted a daughter so badly... I didn't have the heart to tell her that I already knew the secret: No matter what was done to me, I was never going to be anything other than what I was. But my parents had this tendency to beat their kids whenever we did something they didn't like, including things beyond our control, so I plucked and shaved my beard, took my hormones, and tried to dress to deemphasize my broad shoulders and long, muscular arms. I tried to dress and walk femininely, even when I was swearing like a sailor or arguing like a lawyer. I tried hard to find something positive about living as a woman. After all, women kept telling me they were really the superior sex, right? And then there was the solidarity of being oppressed. That ought to be worth something in the high moral ground department.

But it just didn't work for me. I felt like an impostor, no matter what I did. I was afraid that no matter how hard I tried, they'd still somehow be able to look at me and strip away my mask. Sometimes they did. I was often accused of "male behavior," even when I couldn't figure out what was wrong with my behavior. My health deteriorated in reaction to the medications I took to keep my body from becoming masculine.

One night as I endured the massive hemorrhaging that threatened to put me in the hospital—a side effect of my artificial hormonal soup—I finally decided that maintaining my assigned gender was not worth ruining my health. I began to contemplate changing to male hormones. Once I'd faced the idea, there was no turning back.

I owe three people for my coming-out. The first person is someone whose real name I never knew; I walked into a workshop on sacred androgyny, and a large, heavyset, hairy woman with a body like mine (and a 5 o'clock shadow like mine—only mine was blond and didn't show) got up and told everyone about how s/he was an intersexual who'd found a spiritual calling in hir condition. I sat stunned, my tongue frozen in my mouth.

I'd always believed it was something to hide, a shameful, annoying thing. My husband and lover, who flanked me, didn't even know what I was. I'd hidden it that well. And here there was someone like me, someone saying that this was a gift from the gods? I walked out shaking all over. It took me a year to get the courage to tell anyone (and only after divesting myself of both my husband and my lover), but I owe it to that one brave mythical beast, my sister/brother. S/he called hirself Siren; I never saw hir again, but someday I'm going to find hir and buy hir dinner to thank hir for my freedom.

The second person is my lover of seven years, now my wife, who was the first person in my life not only to support my gender transgressions 100% but to encourage me. She sweet-talked me into growing out my beard, encouraged my masculinity, let me wear the dick during sex, and held me through bouts of body dysphoria. She is a male-to-female transexual, and she started dating me while I was still in the denial stage. But she had me pegged long before I knew my own mind. Somehow she knew I was the man for her, even when I was wearing skirts. I've already thanked her, of course, and I continue to do so every day. Her I owe for knowing that no matter what I did with my flesh, someone would always desire me.

The third person isn't a person exactly; it's a bunch of guys from a support group for female-to-male transexuals. I went into the group sideways, defensive, certain there would be deeply grooved differences between them and myself. After all, I was an intersexual, which was its own kind of pain. I was never going to think of myself fully as a man. (Many years and many testosterone injections later, now that I'm "sirred" on the street, I still don't. I'm a masculine androgyne, but that's as far along the scale as I'll go in either direction.) Instead I found we had many things in common. Those guys were my lifelines through the worst parts of my decision-making period.

I learned from them that I didn't have to be squarely on the opposite end of the gender paradigm in order to change my body, that I didn't have to live with the discomfort. Change was possible and reasonable and didn't need to be justified (to the people who count, anyway) except to say, "This is right for me now."

Thanks, Max, Henry, Julian, Mike, and Greenie.

It was one thing to think that my body would make things better, but nothing prepared me for how good it would actually be. Twelve hours after my first shot of testosterone, the chemical depression I'd had since puberty lifted, literally, on the spot. It was as if a gray cloud had been lifted from the world, and I laughed hysterically the entire first night. "Who needs Prozac!" I crowed. "I've got boy juice!"

Now, two years later, as I'm "sirred" on the street, scheduled for a double mastectomy, and living a very different life, I find myself on still another fence, that between the fledgling transgender liberation movement and the barely-out-of-its-shell intersex rights movement. As someone who is inarguably both, I find myself running back and forth, patting hands, slapping faces, cleaning up messes of misunderstanding, and explaining, explaining, explaining. This must be the 10th time I've found myself standing between two groups of arguing people who want to draw lines that bifurcate me.

Fortunately, I've become rather good at the whole thing over the past few years. Part of becoming good at it is just learning to accept it. Once when I protested to a friend about how I was tired of being constantly in the middle of controversies, she commented, "But you were born a controversy, dear. And there was probably a reason for that."

She was right. I am a sirocco of controversy, a mythical beast with a real self, a blurrer of boundaries and a builder of bridges, and sometimes the poor sod who gets to drag people kicking and screaming across those bridges. The toll in the middle is paid in the coin of self-awareness, and the troll under the bridge is forgetting who I am. We do it on the dotted line every time, we walkers between worlds. I see change sprouting from my hoofprints every time I look back, and I know with unshakable certainty that I am exactly where I need to be.

Fading to Pink
Robin Maltz

Robin Maltz is a queer femme scholar, mother, adjunct professor, and a doctoral candidate in the department of performance studies at New York University. Miss Maltz dedicates her essays to her stone butch, Marty Burns.

"Femme invisibility" is what my femme friends and I call it when we are misread as heterosexual. It happens every day for straight-looking femmes: the gaze of straight males expecting a deferential smile in return; the "Are you married?" and "Do you have a boyfriend?" questions from straight women; the camaraderie heterosexuals assume in our presence while other queers, even butches, look right through us; and the casual homophobia we're privy to by virtue of our invisibility. We are, after all, queers of a sort that has been around for decades as the femme half of the butch/femme couple, but since the 1970s gay liberation movement, GLBT pride means being visibly queer, and being visibly queer means compromising my femmeness.

A lesbian on a feminist Internet E-mail list once asked me, "Why don't you tone down the femininity and look more like a lesbian if you're a feminist?" I wrote back that queer visibility does mean a lot in shaking up the status quo, but it is not the only way. I use my femme femininity in ways that are insidious, a little trickier than just looking queer. I use my gender as a strategy against the assumption that femininity in a female means I am heterosexual.

I am persistently outing myself—to my students, to the local moms I encounter when I drop my kids off at practices, to my doctors, to my neighbors, to the man in the JESUS LOVES ME T-shirt at the supermarket who asks for a church donation. I am also marked as queer through my affiliations with queer organizations, my friendships, my writing, and the presence of my partner, a stone butch. I pointed out on the lesbian feminist Internet list that a mainstay of lesbian feminism is the notion that femininity is a trap of heterosexuality, a gender presentation imposed on women by men. I suggested that maybe it was time for lesbian feminists to rethink that position in relation to femmes.

On a more personal note, toning down or androgynizing femininity for a femme would compromise the erotic, romantic, and, dare I say, domestic sway a femme has in butch/femme dynamics. My femininity is rooted in who I am as a woman, as a queer, as a femme. I feel that I cannot escape it even if I wanted to. When I first came out I tried to "look like a lesbian." I laugh now thinking about how I swaggered under my short (but not short enough) hair, how I wore boxer shorts hoping it would infuse me with enough masculinity to make me no longer yearn to stretch out in a bikini on a warm beach or fantasize that a butch would press hard against me and lift my dress with her strong, certain hands. I believed in visibility, and I figured there was only one way to look like a lesbian, and it wasn't looking like a straight girl!

Butch/femme relationships and community have been historically vital in making our butch and femme identities meaningful, vital, essential, and soulful. At the end of the day, butches and femmes find home in one another. We validate each other's gender, sex practices, and desire—which are generally misunderstood or portrayed negatively by lesbians who reject butch/femme as heterosexual imitation. However, for the past several years, femmes have encountered a level of invisibility within butch/femme communities. Some of the butches in our Internet and real-life communities, especially the young butches, are transitioning from stone butch (which means a very masculine but not male-identified butch, most often a sexual top) to transgendered men or FTMs. That is, they are no longer satisfied (or maybe never had been) with being the "men" among collectives of butch/femme females but now aspire to be as close to male as possible.

There are a variety of distinctions between stone butches and FTMs, but one that directly involves femmes is the different ways in which these two masculine beings relate to their bodies. While stone butches dislike and disguise their female bodies, FTMs pathologize theirs, as if the body alone is a mishap that needs to be fixed through surgery and hormones in order to feel whole.

One of a femme's areas of sexual expertise is her ability to transform a stone butch's body through acts of imagination, so that a stone butch never risks being "womanized." A femme knows how to masculinize a stone butch's body; a phallic length of silicon is not a dildo or a sex toy but a butch cock, and a chest is a chest, not breasts. If a transman no longer needs masculine validation from a femme but rather by passing as a male, by body alteration, by blending into heterosexuality, is a femme still a femme? Or is she a significant other (a term for the partner of an FTM) who witnesses the gender/sex transformation instead of participating in an ongoing process of imaginatively re-creating gender?

The transitions of butches to FTMs have left some femmes in the lurch. Do they follow their lovers into passing anonymity? On a butch/femme Internet list, Marty, a stone butch, asks, "FTMs and transmen are female-freaks wanting to be read as normal men, and femmes are normal-looking women wanting to be read as freaks.... How could there not be a conflict?"

At this moment of instability in our butch/femme communities, what is at stake for femmes is a full circle back to the closet. This is why I find it essential that femmes create a queer presence, one that does not depend solely on visibility through gender presentation or the presence of our butches. While we can remain bottoms in our relationships, we need to exert authority about our own queer identity. Femmes need to give voice to our "journeys," our childhoods marked by peculiar sexual desire, unusual playmates, and the conflict of reading as a "normal" girl.

Since I have bottomed to the possibility of presenting femininity to the public, played straight, and having it read otherwise, I'm writing myself into visibility through autobiography. Autobiography gives visibility, voice, and authority to its subject, and it has been a valuable genre for transexuals, butches, and lesbians.

I have in front of me a photograph of myself. This one has been etched in my memory, and I wanted to share it with my butch lover for all its pink femininity. In my memory of this photograph, I am a tiny child on my birthday, my fourth birthday, the Fourth of July 1961, North

Hollywood, Calif. I am standing up straight—my mother told me to—hands behind my back, my soft brown hair swept up into a top knot and my blue eyes looking directly at the camera. My lips are parted and my head slightly lowered, a shy gesture that I have come to recognize as my own. I am wearing a bubble gum–pink sunsuit with a triangular hint of pink panty between my small thighs, my arms and legs bare, my toes curled and my foot arched out—another familiar shy gesture. To my side is a table set for my party with a pink tablecloth, pink paper plates, pink cups, and a pink-and-white birthday cake.

I wanted my butch to see this photograph. I wanted to show her that I was a femme well before I could imagine that the name *femme* would call me into being as a queer female. I wanted her to see I was meant to be in pink with a hint of panty showing. A naughty girl, grown up.

The photograph in front of me is not the one I have described from memory. My mother was sorry but the photograph had faded so there was barely any image left. "What a shame," she wrote. I called my lover at work to tell her my mother had sent my childhood photographs. She said to wait until we could get in bed and look at them. I was excited and wearing my pink flannel nightie because it was winter. I sat on the bed and waited. She took out the photographs slowly so I would keep smiling at her. "I want to see the pink one first. The one I told you about. My baby femme picture."

I squinted but could barely find myself in the photograph. There was a ghostly image in the center, and the pink was gone. So was the party table. I held in my 40-year-old palm what had been a photograph of me at 4 years old. It was white and blotched with gray, stained with smudges and dirt. I put the photo back in the envelope. My lip quivered. My butch took off my pink nightie and made love to me, her femme who was once a girl who loved pink.

My butch lover picked me up at school one Friday in the car. She said, "I have something to show you." In a clear frame was my picture, enhanced by a photographic laboratory. I have it in my hand now.

At first blush, the antiquity of it startled me. Much of the photograph is gritty white, unsalvageable, marred by amorphous watery shapes with a ghostly quality that seems to float the image of the small girl in a pool of time past. No more pink, no more party table.

I loved to swim. I learned to swim as a baby, or so I've been told. In another photo, now lost, I am a 4-year-old girl sitting—up straight, of course—on the swimming pool step at the Hollywood-style apartment building of my birthday party. There next to me is a rough and tough girl my age, a bull dyke these days before she was named as such. My knees are squeezed together, my hands are between my thighs, my shoulders are raised, and my hair is ponytailed. I'm smiling. I'm excited. It's summer and I'm 4 years old and I'm in the swimming pool. My shorthaired pal is leaning back, casually extending her arm on the hot summer poolside cement. Oh, how I loved to swim in the pool until my flesh puckered. Then I'd lie poolside with the hot California sun on my small back and colt legs with the steam heat of my wet belly simmering down between my thighs. The photograph is in black and white, so I could be wearing pink.

I am in the center of the marred and ghostly photo. The parameters of my face are gone to white so that a face becomes a face because of the hair on top and the slightly parted lips below and eyes so clear and defined that the pupils are visible, distinct from the irises. My eyes and mouth are asking a question without words. What does a 4-year-old ask a mother who constructs her family out of photographs?

The submissive gesture is there in my body—the one foot forward, toes curled and foot turned out, hands behind my back opening up that tiny girl body. My head without the contours of a face is no longer tilted down in a shy gesture; instead my eyes look directly into the lens of the camera. I was a curious child, but I didn't seek explanations for the peculiar events of my life. My panty shows. It is a white triangle between the shadow of thighs. I opened my small body for intruders. Amid the blotches and watery spots is a fingerprint on my chest. An adult print. A man's print big with carved swirls toward a center that becomes an eye-like nipple on my chest. Hands are guilty. Marked by touch and marking those they touch.

The photograph is faded but pink in my memory.

Passing Realities
Allie Lie

Allie Lie lives and—at the time of this writing—is unemployed in Cambridge, Mass. When not going on interviews, she enjoys volunteering at the New England regional office of the National Gay and Lesbian Task Force and hanging out with her two immensely entertaining boys.

Cambridge—Summer 1998

We leave the café on Massachusetts Avenue, my young sons, "J" and "A," and I. It's seasonably hot and humid. I wear flip-flops, khaki shorts, a sleeveless T-shirt, and a wide-brimmed straw hat. I am not "presenting." I've promised the boys I won't embarrass them. (Children are defenseless against attacks aimed at nonconformity. Adults—their mother, for instance—just have to deal with it.)

As we cross Mass Ave., we come to a small park-cum-island in the middle of the intersection. Two men sit on one of the benches, and their small dog, tethered to a red nylon leash, sits beneath the bench. A, my oldest, who has a fondness for animals that way surpasses any he'd have for humans, goes up and asks if he can pet the dog. J and I have walked past them and are on the other side of the park. I hear the man saying, "Sure"— I see him nod in my direction—"but you'd better ask your mother first."

After work she stops at a grocery store a block from her apartment.

She has been here many times, both *en femme* and not. Today, as with every working day, she is *en femme*. She goes to the freezer section, pulls out a frozen yogurt and takes it up to the checkout counter. The middle-aged man behind the counter is not particularly friendly. No one who works at the store is. Once she pays for the yogurt, she asks the checkout man where she can find a plastic spoon. He gestures over his shoulder with a thumb, "Over there...pal."

She finds the spoons, then walks over to one of the luncheon tables in the front of the store and sits. She begins slowly eating the yogurt, carving out small, hard-frozen spoonfuls from the top layer, working around the edges first. She holds the spoon upside down, puts it in her mouth, and sucks on it meditatively. As she does this, she overhears the sotto voce reprimand of the store manager behind her. Words like harassment, trouble, careful...

I am with the boys again, this time buying ice cream. The line at the counter has unwound itself into an amorphous crowd. No one seems to know who's next or who's helping whom. Someone has been summoned from the back of the store. A man appears and begins scanning the crowd. Our eyes meet. "Ma'am, what would you like?" J and A and I squeeze up to the counter. J takes my hand. "Dad, he called you..."

"Shush, I know."

I order two vanilla cones for J and myself. As usual, A takes more time deciding. J gets his cone, then I get mine. The cashier motions to A (who wears his hair long because he's terrified of change and, despite his adolescent male misogyny, appears enviably androgynous). "What kind of cone would she like?" A looks at the floor.

"He'll have a sugar cone, please."

At a different grocery store...

"I'd like to write a check. How much over the amount can I write it for?"

Shrug. "Do you have a card?"

"Yes."

Shrug again. "Fifty...?"

She writes the check and hands it to the cashier. The cash register jams—seems not to like what it's been told. The cashier looks at her apologetically, then summons help. A manager appears.

"Her total came to ____."
"And she wrote a check?"
"Yes. But he wrote it for $30 over the amount."
"Does he have a card?"
"Yes, she does."
"Well, she can only write it for 25 over the amount…"
"That's no problem," she says. "I'll just write another check."
The cashier is again apologetic. "Do you mind?"
"No," she says. "Not at all."

I am in the men's room of a restaurant. I have just washed my hands and looked in the mirror. This mirror is particularly unforgiving—thus I trust it. I am seldom happy with what I see. Reflective surfaces are to be avoided at all costs. The disparity between what I want to see and what actually greets me is too great. What I want to see: someone who could be Michelle Pfeiffer's female second cousin. What I see: longish, thinning hair; age lines (a.k.a. nasal labial folds); the faint, plucked remnants of beard; the wrong cheeks; the wrong lips. At times like this I think the course my life has taken is evidence of a delusional personality. I'm reminded of Nabokov's *Despair,* the story of a man who imagines that a stranger who looks not even remotely like him is his virtual twin.

This is why I am surprised when I turn to leave the restroom and see another man entering, noticing me, halting, then looking back to double-check the sign on the door.

Cambridge—Late Fall 1998

She leaves the elevator at the sixth floor and heads for the door marked "The Ass. of Tedium, Drudgery, and Objectified Labor." She is here for a job interview—a job she already knows she doesn't want, but after three months of uncompensated unemployment, a job that she needs like nobody's business. She is dressed in her only polyester power suit, in burgundy with matching jacket and skirt. She opens the door and walks to the receptionist's desk. "I'm here to see Mrs. Z."

"Take a seat, she'll be right with you."

She's had to pee for the last half hour. "Excuse me, may I please use the restroom first?"

The receptionist takes a key from her desk drawer and hands it to her. "Down at the end of the hall." She thanks the receptionist, exits the office and hurries to the room marked "W." She tries the lock. The door doesn't budge. She tries again. Still no success. The key ring is attached to a plastic badge. She turns the badge over and reads the words written in black indelible marking pen: "Men's Room."

Cambridge—Winter 1998–99

E and I have been separated for more than six months now. We'd been through couples counseling eight months before the separation. Eight months slogging through the muck of my midlife journey back and forth across the gender boundaries; eight months of soul searching (for both of us); dredging up all our fears, our needs; establishing who we are and what we are about. I volunteered everything I knew about myself and about the *condition* mental health practitioners choose to call *gender identity disorder*. I offered texts, testimonials, contacts for spouse and significant other support groups. She heard, but chose not to listen. The work failed. It was finally determined that (1) I couldn't live unless I established permanent residence in the land of the feminine, and (2) she couldn't live with me if I did.

Shortly after our separation, I transitioned to three-quarter time living as Allie. Very shortly after that I was fired from my job. I assured E that I'd continue to support her and the boys in any way I could; I borrowed money from my family and engaged in exhausting legal battles for unemployment benefits and for financial damages as the result of my unlawful firing. Through all this I remained committed to my newly found state of mental health, determined that I could face anything as Allie. I was also amply aware of the irony that, as hormones inexorably reduced Robert's potency, shrinking his gonads to the size of unripe May apples, Allie had more *balls* than Robert ever did.

Soon there were many people who knew me only as Allie, people who had never seen the vestiges of my past. The boys were introduced to her: J actually liked her; A would take some time. E, whenever we met, appeared as if she'd seen a ghost.

So now E and I are standing in her kitchen (formerly known as "ours"). We are discussing logistics: She will be going through a routine exam at a local hospital—nothing serious, but it will leave her groggy and in need of transportation home. Would I mind picking her up from the hospital? No, of course not. I want to do anything I can to help.

Good. E wants to say something else... What...? When you pick me up...? Yes...? Will you be wearing women's clothes?

The snow leaves only a small path on the sidewalk. I am heading back to my apartment after visiting the boys. I'm wearing clogs and a big wool hat but still not technically "presenting." I'm right behind a family of out-of-town parents and their college-age kids. The father is holding up the rear of the caravan. He senses me walking up behind him. The caravan is moving slowly, a herd of contented cows. The father turns to look at me, smiles, then moves to the side of the walkway. He yells to the others in front of him, "Wait, let this woman pass."

Western Pennsylvania—Circa Winter 1961: One Passing Retrograde Fantasy

"My daughter would like to play basketball."
"Sorry, the team isn't coed."
"Excuse me?"
"No girls. Only boys."
"My daughter is a boy."
A look of confusion...
"Go ahead, dear, show the man your penis."
"Well, ah...yes... But he can't play looking the way he does."
"How do you mean?"
"His hair. The pigtails. He can't play like that."
"Why not?"
"It'll affect his playing."
"Go ahead, dear, show the man..."
She dribbles the basketball a few times, then shoots from mid court. The ball whooshes through the net.
"That's fine...but...she still looks like a girl."
"Well, naturally... He *is* a girl."

Who Knows What Evil Lurks?
Lucas Dzmura

Lucas Dzmura is a writer, artist, and instructional systems designer. He is a fan of Rumi, studies the future of systems and software engineering, and would like to live in a co-housing community. On Io.

I was pushed out early from an unwilling womb, and a machine was my first nurturer; across its metallic hug and artificial respiration came the life-giving touch of my father's hand. I was no larger than a Barbie in his huge hand when his tears and my first drop of jaundiced urine mixed. The alchemy of that mixture produced a lifelong bond between father and a two-pound child destined for miracles in 1963. He was my connection to the world of light. I was its darkness, its subconscious.

When I reached the age of 4, Zach ran my finger under a lawn mower just to see what might happen, and Dad sewed it right back on. I mention this not to complain about traumas past but because it's a marker of a certain age. The only remaining scar is on my pinkie finger, not my spirit. And also it somewhat dramatically brings in the character of my brother and the slavish devotion of the miracle child; I served faithfully as his shadow until he went off to big kids' school. It would have been a lonesome childhood without him! He was "the boss of me," and I was his willing puppy. At big kids' school, though, he learned I was a shadow, and he closed the door on my life when he told me.

I aced every spelling bee and got warm-bellied with the praise of my female teachers. My blood boiled in neck-and-neck competition with the other boys in math bees. Sister Seraphia pulled me aside one day and said, "Don't compete with the boys. They don't like a shadow who wins. You'll never get a husband if you're smarter than men!" I had no guidance. If I was a shadow, then surely one day I must want a husband. Like the clever and accomplished shadow I was, I listened, and I taught myself sign language during math class. I heard the muffled noise of the world through a well-packed cotton tube of silence. I had to get glasses.

I was beaten every day at the bus stop by older children who must not have liked shadows. I turned the other cheek and I listened, like a good Catholic shadow. Shadows, I learned, can be seen in the daylight.

I spent high school entirely in the company of shadows and discovered that in the dimness we could ascertain our individual shapes, and find them wanting. I was not like the others—I found them beautiful.

From the nuns I learned silence; from my parents I learned silence; from children and beatings I learned silence. I learned my place. I learned my role as a shadow. I learned to whisper in the shadow ways. I learned to silence the whispers of my shadow heart. I was not made aware of any alternative. I saw the world of light, and I saw its darkness. I was not underprivileged. I was not denied or deprived.

In college I was treated like I might be substantial, but I knew only shadow ways and so continued.

In graduate school I was sick and bored, and I studied too hard. I met a man who was a terrorist from a foreign country. He seemed like any other man; he was a scientist and he killed people. So, sick and bored and unfocused, I slept with the terrorist, nearly died of a shadow sickness, with him lying on top of me in the hospital, crying. I was probed 13 times by male student doctors. They called it toxic shock. I wasn't surprised.

I wanted to have a meaningful life after I almost died, so I volunteered to help create, fund, and staff an AIDS residence for gay men. I discovered shadows more like me, gay shadows.

When my dad died I lost my link to the world of light and floated in a realm of shadows. I learned to circle around. I learned the names of the Mother Goddess, yet never understood nurturing or selflessness or the reason for the martyrdom so common among shadows. I learned therapy. I learned what it means to support and to be supported. I learned the strength and the weakness of a victim, shrill and desperate. I learned the shadow's way of healing. I became aware of myself as a shadow. As my awareness grew, so did my hatred and my anger. I learned to love other shadows.

I learned a name for what I feared. I knew the Enemy for the first time in my pacifist shadow lifetime. I hated Him. Went back through my life and had flashbacks of Him. Remembered victimizations that I, as a shadow, walked into with no defense or knowledge of a self to defend. Remembered how I cast Him away from me in the Church because he could not love shadows like he could love men. I pushed away the Brother God like my brother pushed me away. Learned to associate my characteristics with His evil opposite and love them too. Of course I came to love an ancient pagan God with horns and hooves!

One day I saw a shadow take off its clothes, and there was a man's penis underneath! I was so angry. I hated it, vilified it. It was every terror I had ever known, and it destroyed my trust and my sacred safety. I turned my back on it. For months I saw it on television, read it in books, dreamed. It was my doppelgänger.

I looked under my own clothing, and discovered that I was not a shadow! Perhaps there is no such thing as a shadow. Perhaps there are girl children and boy children, and shadow children?

If I am still a shadow, then a shadow of what? And what was that tenuous growing tube of light between my legs? Why was my vision choosing this moment to become focused? My hearing acute? Too many questions! Too much information! Too much truth! Too much to lose, and an Enemy to gain. Betrayal of everything I'd ever known. The contradiction of misogyny in what used to be a lesbian separatist!

Then I found a mountaintop, for I looked at the Enemy and He was me.

So I shouted from that mountain, in my strength, in my power, in the reality of my self: I am done with speaking soft preening words for the ruffled feathers of me—or of stifled shadows. I wish I had the chubby, lavender-dressed doll of my female childhood who said, "I'm afraid of noisy boys! My name is Shrinking Violet." I pulled her fabric lips off then, and protected her. Now I would finish the job and rip off her feathered head.

My voice has spoken loudly in defense of women-only space, and now, by some, I am considered the Enemy as I fight for the right to share that space. My voice, my voice, my female voice! My voice, my FTM voice, my masculine voice, my two-spirit voice! And one day, when that voice finally cracks in a long, postponed adolescence, my male voice. My *own* voice.

And when I say who knows what evil lurks in the hearts and minds of men, we both know the answer.

And find redemption in it.

My Woman Poppa
Joan Nestle

Joan Nestle, author, editor, once teacher, cofounder of the Lesbian Herstory Archives, is grateful to all those who have made it possible for the imagination and the body to know the power of gender liberation and recreation.

You work at a job that makes your back rock-hard strong; you work with men in a cavernous warehouse loading trucks while others sleep. Sometimes when you come to me, when my workday is just beginning, you fall asleep in my bed on your stomach, the sheet wrapped around your waist, the flaming unicorn on your right shoulder catching the morning sun.

I just stand and look at you, at your sleeping face and square, kind hands, my desire growing for you, for my woman poppa who plays the drums and knows all the words to "Lady in Red," who calls me sassafras mama—even when I am too far from the earth, who is not frightened off by my years or my illness.

My woman poppa who knows how to take me in her arms and lay me down, knows how to spread my thighs and then my lips, who knows how to catch the wetness and use it, who knows how to enter me so waves of strength rock us both.

My woman poppa who is not afraid of my moans or my nails but takes me and takes me until she reaches beyond the place of entry into the core of tears. Then as I come to her strength and woman fullness, she kisses away my legacy of pain. My cunt and heart and head are healed.

My woman poppa who does not want to be a man but who travels in "unwomanly" places and who does "unwomanly" work. Late into the New Jersey night, she maneuvers the forklift to load the thousands of pounds of aluminum into the hungry trucks that stand waiting for her. Dressed in the shiny tiredness of warehouse blue, with her company's name stitched in white across her pocket, she endures the bitter humor of her fellow workers, who are men. They laugh at Jews, at women, and—when the black workers are not present—at blacks. All the angers of their lives, all their dreams gone dead, bounce off the warehouse walls. My woman grits her teeth and says when the rape jokes come, "Don't talk that shit around me."

When she comes home to me, I must caress the parts of her that have been worn thin from trying to do her work in a man's world. She likes her work, likes the challenge of the machines and the quietness of the night, likes her body moving into power.

My woman poppa is 13 years younger than I am, but she is wise in her woman-loving ways. Breasts and ass get her hot, that wonderful hot which is a heard and spoken desire. I make her hot, and I like that. I like her sweat and her tattoos. I like her courtliness and her disdain of the boys. I mother her and wife her and slut her, and together we are learning to be comrades.

She likes me to wear a black slip to bed, to wear dangling earrings and black stockings with sling-back heels when we play. She likes my perfume and lipstick and nail polish. I enjoy these slashes of color, the sweetened place in my neck where she will bury her head when she is moving on me.

I sometimes sit on her, my cunt open on her round belly, my breasts hanging over her, my nipples grazing her lips. I forbid her to touch me and continue to rock on her, my wetness smearing her belly. She begins to moan and curves her body upward, straining at the restrictions.

"Please baby, please," my woman poppa begs. "Please let me fuck you." Then suddenly, when she has had enough, she smiles, opens her eyes, and says, "You have played enough." Using the power she has had all along, she throws me from my throne.

Sometimes she lies in bed wearing her cock under the covers. I can see its outline under the pink spread. I just stand in my slip watching her, her eyes getting heavy. Then I sit alongside her, on the edge of the bed, telling her what a wonderful cock she has, as I run my hand down her belly until I reach her lavender hardness. I suck her nipples and slowly stroke her, tugging at the cock so she can feel it through the leather triangle that holds it in place.

"Let me suck you," I say, my face close to hers, my breasts spilling out on hers. "Let me take your cock in my mouth and show you what I can do." She nods, almost as if her head were too heavy to move.

Oh, my darling, this play is real. I do long to suck you, to take your courage into my mouth, both cunt, your flesh, and cock, your dream, deep into my mouth, and I do. I throw back the covers and bend over her carefully so she can see my red lips as I move on her. I give her the best I can, licking the lavender cock its whole length and slowly tangoing at the tip, circling the tip with my tongue. Then I take her fully into my mouth, into my throat. She moans, moves, tries to watch but cannot as the image overpowers her. When I have done all that I can, I bend the wet cock up on her belly and sit on her so I can feel it pressing against my cunt. I rock on her until she is ready, and then she reaches down and slips the cock into me. Her eyes are open now, wonderfully clear and sharp. She slips her arms down low around my waist so I am held tight against her. Very slowly, she starts to move her hips upward in short strong thrusts. I am held on my pleasure by her powerful arms; I can do nothing but move and take and feel. When she knows I have settled in, she moves quicker and quicker, her breath coming in short, hard gasps. But I hear the words "Oh, baby, you are so good to fuck."

I forget everything but her movements. I fall over her, my head on the pillow above her. I hear sounds, moans, shouted words, know my fists are pounding the bed, but I am unaware of forming words or lifting my arms. I ride and ride harder and faster, encircled by her arms, by her gift.

"Give it all to me, let it all go," I know she is saying. I hear a voice answering, "you you you you" and I am pounding the bed, her arms, anything I can reach. How dare you do this to me, how dare you push me beyond my daily voice, my daily body, my daily fears? I am chanting; we are dancing. We have broken through.

Then it is over. We return, and gently she lifts me off her belly. I slide down her body, rest, and then release her from the leather. We sleep.

Yes, my woman poppa knows how to move me, but she knows many other things as well. She knows she will not be shamed; she knows her body carries complicated messages. She knows that breast and cock and cunt are shaped by dreams. My woman poppa, my dusty sparrow—how special you are.

A Fem's Diary
Joan Nestle

The snow falls outside the high, small windows of our little apartment atop an old Provincetown gray-shingled house. We see it mix with the seagulls and the tops of the bare trees and then float past us to a lower place we do not see. I have asked her to dress for me, and she comes out of the bathroom in her lavender negligee with a lace jacket thrown over her shoulders. Her hair is down in full life, spreading out around her face. She has put on deep red lipstick; her eyes glisten with touches of color. Perfumes reach me first, and I tighten with desire. She is smiling, her taunting smile, her knowing smile that denies her 28 years. When she is this way, so splendid in her largeness and beauty, I feel my years drop away. I am younger, far younger, than this woman who has the knowledge of body painting, of how to hold her long legs so the gown reaches mid thigh but no higher.

I ask her to lie down on the couch, and I get a pillow for the back of her head so she will be comfortable. As she places herself on the couch, the jacket opens and her full breasts are exposed to me. I have already left my mark on one of them, a large brown mark left by my teeth and my relentless mouth that has such need of her. I stay at the opposite end of the couch from her, resting my head on her knee, one of her legs stretched out alongside of me. She slowly starts caressing her breast, fingering her nipples, daring me to touch her. She pushes my hand away every time I try. I learn to wait, but waiting is also pleasure because I have her legs, her smooth calf and her thighs to caress and to run my lips over, and the smell of her powder and her sex as I push my head into her lap. She laughs at me, at my adoration, as she rumples my hair. She laughs at me as I grip her full, gowned body in my woman's hands.

Then I can no longer play. I push her hands away and she gives me her breasts. I find her under the gown and raise her legs up over my shoulders. My fingers find her open and I push into her, watching her face all the time, the heaving of her breasts. I am fully clothed but naked in my want, in my imagination, in my need to be her lover. I grasp the cock I have chosen, the biggest, the longest one that will give her the most pleasure, and while her legs are on my shoulders, I enter her with it, first slowly and deeply and then quicker and harder, my body behind each thrust. Her legs are now bent, her knees almost on her breasts. She is moving and moaning, holding me to her—and then as if her body were mine, I sense the tiredness of her legs and pull out. I let her legs drop and she smiles, "Thank you." I lie over her, my face buried in her neck.

She starts to touch herself, almost as if she is afraid I will not know her need. But I do. I spend long minutes, long, wonderful moments buried in her cunt, my cheeks caressed by her hanging gown, sucking her into me, always smelling the perfume of her body, of her anointing.

Later I will play old whore to her younger girl. I will wear my black slip and stockings and she will wear her white undershirt with a little ribbon over her breasts. And after I have taught this woman what she wants to know, the pleasure of ass fucking, she will plead for the right to touch me, and then my own fem need will come flooding back, and she will hold me in her arms, saying quietly, "Joan, I want to fuck you," and all her perfume will be part of her strength as she enters me with her long fingers dipped in red, not riding me but pushing me to let go. "Fuck my fingers, fuck my fingers," she urges.

To me, she appears as nothing other than a woman, but in my mind's passion, I have been boy, older man, aging whore, woman. I am grateful for the height of our windows, that the only witnesses to our moments are the clouds and falling snow, not because of shame but because they speak of dreams, of certainties loosened from their moorings, dreams of desire and touch that we have shared. I have held cocks and a woman who reminded me of my mother dressed for her lover, and

I have been her lover. I have taken my own womanness and used it as a teacher for this beautiful and caring woman.

After J. leaves, the sadness descends. I read the papers every day in this hiding-away place. I mourn for D., have nightmares of screaming at her. I wonder what worth I am to my students. Perhaps all the fucking, all the nuances are hopeless. Governments with their pale men in suits kill and flaunt and designate despair. Where could such a shifting exchange between two women, one 20 years older than the other, have meaning other than among the clouds of a village at the edge of the sea?

I Walked Into the Oaks Club
Chino Lee Chung

Chino Lee Chung is a triple Leo, TG, and firefighter from San Francisco. Involved in a fun and passionate relationship with Maya, Chino lives among a wonderful queer Asian Pacific Islander and TG community who defy the static notions of gender and racial identity.

I walked into the Oaks Club wearing my striped shirt, fresh from the dry cleaners, my favorite old gray jeans, and freshly shined brown boots. The security guard returned my nod. A crisp, clean movement that reminded me of a military academy. All that was missing was the bright white gloves on his dark brown hands.

Dull voices buzzed as I walked farther into the club. I squinted at the fluorescent lights. My nostrils burned from the thick cloud of cigarette smoke. In the pit, the green felt tables lined up like brown egg cartons with the players' heads as rows of multicolored eggs.

"Two-four stud," I said to the floorman. She had orange hair and wore orange-colored glasses that made her eyes look really big.

"Name?" she studied her board, erasing and adding names.

"Nanren," I stood on my tiptoes to see. Four names on the board already.

"Nanren?" she looked up at me. "Is that your first or last name?"

"Last." I pushed my thick black glasses up on my nose.

"What does it mean?"

"It means 'man' in Cantonese."

The floorman looked at my face closely. She studied my eyes, and then her gaze moved down my neck, finally stopping at my shirt pockets.

My face flushed red-hot. I shifted my body so she couldn't stare at my chest.

"What's your first name?" she asked.

I let out a long sigh and rubbed my eyes. "How about Lee?"

"I see lots of Orientals who take on American names. But Lee's not for you. It's too common. You look more like a Jimmy or a Lester to me. You know, a girlfriend of mine once told me there were really only about 100 surnames in Chinese, and all *those* people use the same names over and over."

"Hmm." I kept my voice monotone. A bitter taste started in my mouth, like after eating Chinese melon.

She looked down at me from her podium. "Imagine all those *people* flocking to America on those little boats. And they all have the same names. It's a crying shame." She jerked her head back and forth in quick, tense motions, and it was the first time I noticed the deeply etched lines that cut up her face and how vivid they were around her lips and in between her eyes. She picked up a thick black marker then wrote my name down on the white board.

"Hi-ya-a-a!" an Asian man exclaimed from one of the Pai Gow tables in the pit.

He waved his arms and stomped his feet. I walked over and squeezed in next to him. The woman dealer sat at the middle of the table and a crowd of people stood behind every chair. The old guy had a great hand, a pair of 10s on top and three kings and two jacks on the bottom. He pointed to the dealer's hand. The dealer had a pair of aces on top and four queens on the bottom. The dealer looked up at the old guy, opened her arms wide, shrugged her shoulders, and tipped her head apologetically.

The old guy looked over at his buddy and spoke in Cantonese, "I had big money riding on that hand. I saw those three kings and I knew I had it in the bank. Then the white devil came up with the queens. It's not right. Kings are always superior over queens." He turned toward me. His black hair was pasted to his forehead, and there were white, powdery dandruff flakes on his dark blue polyester jacket.

I tightened up the back of my throat, relaxed my tongue and said in my best Cantonese, "I think kings should always dominate."

"English only," the dealer said.

"Let's go, let's go," he said in English and smiled at me. The spaces between his teeth were green.

I walked over to the seven-card stud tables to watch the action. There I recognized a guy named Abdo. He looked like he had been there all night. The whites of his eyes were a bright red, with dark sagging slices underneath, and the top of his head glistened as he rubbed it back and forth with his open hand.

The loudspeaker crackled, "Nan, two-four stud. Nanren, you want two-four stud?"

The chair was still warm from the last guy. A woman with long brown hair sat to my left. She reached up and pushed her hair behind her shoulders. It brushed my neck when it fell into place. I looked over at her and smiled. She smiled back.

I looked up at the dealer. Arnold, one of my favorites. He dealt so fast that every card clicked when it left his fingertips and his biceps bulged through his thin white shirt. He smiled his bright white smile. "How's it?"

"Good. I'm feeling lucky today."

Arnold nodded. "Cool. What would you like me to call you today?"

"Nan. What *else?*"

Arnold was my dealer the first time I walked into the Oaks Club a couple of years ago. I wasn't sure what the rules of the game were, so I kept quiet and watched the other players. I was just starting to figure out how to bet when the guy next to me poked me in the side and said, "What are you stupid, buddy? I told you twice that you have to bet $4, not $2." He was so close I could smell his sour Budweiser breath and see the dark, stubbly shadow on his jaw. I felt the challenge in his hard, tense body.

"Hey, man, I'm just here to play poker." I shrugged my shoulders and looked up at Arnold.

"Yeah, let's just play poker," Arnold said. "I don't want any trouble at this table." He looked directly at the Budweiser man.

"Faggot," the Budweiser man said before he got up and left.

I felt nauseated. I realized I had been holding my breath, so I cleared my throat and said, "Hey, man, thanks. It was getting a little tense there."

"Yeah, that guy's been saying obnoxious things all night." Arnold brought his thumb to his lips and tipped it up like a shot glass. "Good riddance to him." He snubbed his nose in the guy's direction and gave me a nod and a half smile. I remembered that moment like it was yesterday.

Now Arnold gave me that same nod, and the left side of his mouth went up in his half-smile. "Do you want a hand now?" he asked.

"Sure, deal me a good one too." I sneaked a look at the woman next to me. She was sitting on the edge of the chair with her back perfectly straight. I could smell her musky perfume.

Arnold dealt three cards. None of them matched, so I threw them in the muck. The guy next to me was wearing a bright red 49ers hat. It stood out against his dark skin. He ended up with a diamond flush.

I looked at him. "Did you have it all along?"

"Yeah, I felt it coming when the sixth card dropped and, man, there it was, my ace high flush. The name's Dwight." He put out his hand.

"Hey, nice ta meet ya." I grabbed his hand and we shook for a long time. He had smooth chocolate-brown hands and a nice firm handshake. "The name's Nan."

Arnold massaged the pile of blue chips and pushed it over to him.

"Nice hand," I said. "And nice pot too."

"It's my lucky night. I'm gonna ante for everybody." Dwight put $2 in the middle of the table and looked my way. "This here is a friendly game." He smiled. His teeth were white and perfectly straight.

Arnold scooped up the cards, shuffled them real fast, cut them, and dealt them out. His stiff black bangs shot forward every time he flicked a card toward a player.

"Two of clubs bet."

Dwight put down $1. I had three spades and bet a dollar too. Arnold flicked another set of cards at us and a diamond fell in front of me. I watched as the woman next to me folded.

"Don't have anything, huh?"

"I don't think so. I don't feel too lucky tonight," she said.

"It can change. I'm rooting for you," I said.

The only person left in was Abdo. His eyes looked glazed and vacant as he raised $4. Everybody looked at his cards; he had a three and a nine showing, unsuited.

I turned to Dwight. "Doesn't look like he has much, maybe a pocket pair."

"Yeah, he's been betting that way all along. What he must have in his pocket is a whole lot of money."

Arnold flicked an ace toward Abdo, who was looking at the woman next to me. "Hey, thanks for folding. I got my card," his words were trembling as he spoke. "You're a sweetheart. Are you married?"

The table was silent for a long moment. Everybody turned toward our end of the table. The woman turned her head slowly and nodded with a slight movement. "Yeah…" Her voice trailed off until it disappeared.

I looked down at her hands. Her fingers were bare.

"Ace bets," Arnold said.

Abdo put down four dollars. The woman looked toward my hand. I showed her my three spades and shrugged my shoulders.

"I'm sending you my luck," she said.

I raised my head in surprise. She was really pretty. I wondered why she'd talk to me. I was glad she was looking at my cards and not my face. "Thanks," I said. "I'm Nan. What's your name, if you don't mind me asking?"

"Alex." She shifted in her seat and her knee brushed my leg. It sent a shiver up my spine. "Do you come here often?" she asked.

"Yeah, probably a little too often." I smoothed down the short black hairs on the back of my neck. Sometimes they stick out like a cowlick and nothing will keep them in place.

"This is my first time," said Alex. Her dark brown eyes were large as she looked directly into mine. "I used to play poker with my dad when I was growing up, but I've never been in a card club before."

I wanted to ask her why she was here alone, but I felt too shy. I took a long swig of cold seltzer water. "Do you like it here?"

"I don't know. I'm not doing too good. I've already lost $20."

"Well, if that's all you lose tonight, you're doing *real* good."

Alex smiled.

Arnold dealt another card. That gave me four spades. I raised $4. Abdo stayed in. Arnold threw me the last spade, a queen. I showed my hand to Alex. She studied it for a while, her lips moving as she counted. I placed a bet. Arnold dealt the last card down. I didn't look at it and I checked. I heard the other players talking.

"She's got him beat," said Abdo.

"Who's she?" asked Dwight.

"Her." Abdo pointed at me.

Dwight looked up at me. I felt my stomach ball up and tighten in my throat. "Why are you calling him 'her'?"

"I've sat at the table with 'her' before," said Abdo.

Alex's long hair swished to her other side as she looked up at me. I tried not to look at her. I relaxed my lower jaw and breathed through my mouth. I put on my poker face. The stakes were high.

Dwight cleared his throat and wiped his lips with the back of his hand. He leaned closer to me, and I could feel his breath on my cheek as he studied my face. I shifted my chair to pull away. "Hey, Nan. Say, why are they calling you 'she'?"

Arnold stopped shuffling the deck. Everything was still.

I shrugged my shoulders and looked straight into Dwight's eyes. "I wonder that myself," I said. "Maybe it's my fine Asian skin makes me look girly." I was using my lowest-timbre voice from deep in my throat.

Dwight and Abdo laughed.

I softened my shoulders, then looked over at Alex. She was looking off into the distance. I followed the path of her eyes. She was staring at an empty space on the wall in between the men's restroom and the cigarette machine.

"I'll bet," said Abdo, and he put down $4.

The whole table turned back to the game. Little else mattered in this big room except this moment—the cards, the bet, a momentary brush of luck, a heavy sigh from your opponent. I liked the way we could move on so fast.

"I'll raise," I said. I took a stack of eight chips, stood them up, and tipped them over so they fell like dominoes into the pot.

Abdo picked up his hole cards, brought them up real close to his face, and studied them for a long time. Beads of sweat shimmered on his forehead. I held my breath. Then he looked at my cards, at his cards, back at my cards, and put $4 more down.

"First one over wins," proclaimed Arnold.

I showed my spade flush. Abdo turned all his cards over and pushed them toward Arnold.

"Ante up," said Arnold as he pushed the pile of chips toward me.

I put both my arms out and scooped up the blue and green chips. I threw $2 into the middle of the table. "I'll ante for everybody to keep the table tradition."

Arnold shuffled the deck and dealt them again. He gave Alex the lowest card, and she bet. She had about $20. The pot kept getting raised. I watched as her pile got smaller and smaller until there were no chips left in front of her. She reached down to call the last bet. I put my hand on top of hers.

Alex looked up at me. Her lower lip was quivering. She showed me her cards, two aces in the hole. I looked around the table. Dwight was the only one left in.

"You gotta bet it," I whispered. "Dwight may only have that pair of threes showing on the table. I think he has a tendency to bluff."

She threw in her last $2. "All in," she said.

"Good luck," I said and squeezed her shoulder.

Alex tipped her head in my direction.

Arnold dealt the last card.

Dwight turned his cards up. He had a pair of threes and a pair of sixes. Alex showed her aces.

"I'm sorry," said Dwight. He winked at Alex.

She looked at me. "I had the aces from the beginning." She looked down at the empty space in front of her, took her wallet out of her purse, started to open it, and then put it back.

Dwight took a stack of chips from his pile and slid them over toward Alex. "I think *you* should have won that game."

Alex turned to Dwight. "Thanks anyway," she said.

"I really wouldn't be offering if I didn't think you deserved it," said Dwight. "I got that other pair on the river. You had me beat until the last card."

"Well, let me think about it while I use the ladies' room." She smiled at Dwight.

Dwight's eyes stayed on her until she disappeared around the corner. I followed.

She seemed to be waiting for me outside the bathroom doors.

I said, "Sorry about those pocket aces, but your instincts were right." I looked down at the floor and moved the carpet around with the toe of my boot. "Say, are you gonna take that money from Dwight?"

"I don't know... Do you think I should?"

I looked up and shrugged my shoulders.

"I think somebody's trying to tell me something, like it's time to go home." She winked at me.

I wiped my cold, sweaty hands on my jeans. I could feel her eyes on my face. I wondered if she knew and if she'd still want me. I looked back down, there was a worn path leading straight up to the men's room.

"Are you all right?" she asked.

"Yeah, I'm OK. I just gotta go." I crossed my legs and squeezed them tight together.

She smiled. "Well, OK, it was nice meeting you." She looked at me, waiting.

A young Chinese guy with spiky hair walked toward the men's room. I looked at the women's bathroom, then back at Alex. She watched me closely.

"Nice meeting you too." I stepped toward her so she could see my face closer.

Then I followed the Chinese guy into the men's room.

Transie

Ethan Zimmerman

Ethan Zimmerman is a binational, multigendered transfag attracted to boys of both sexes. His fiction has appeared in Queer View Mirror 2, Myths, Beginnings, Awakening the Virgin, *and* Batteries Not Included.

A bar conversation:

> Drunk: Hey, what the hell are you anyway?
> Me: A tranny.
> D: What's a transie?
> Me: I said tranny.
> D: A transie?
> M: Right, I'm a cross between a pansy and a transexual.

Things people say:

Are you a he or a she? Are you a girl or a boy? You're a he/she, aren't you? What sex are you? How can you be a faggot? You must be confused. Why don't you like women? You must hate your own body. Why do you want to get your tits cut off? It sounds awfully painful. It must cost a lot of money. Why don't you just go to therapy? If you like men, then why aren't you straight? Excuse me, ladies, you're in the wrong bathroom. Can I help you, ma'am? He, she, it, or whatever you are. You're still a girl to me. You'll always be a girl on the inside. You don't really look much like a guy. Have you started hormones? Why don't you take hormones? You should take hormones before surgery. You should definitely take hormones after surgery. You haven't started transitioning yet, have you? I like your old name better. Yeah, right, you're a fag. You have to have a dick to be a fag. Fags will never ask you out. What kind of plumbing do you have? Does your boyfriend have a penis? I don't care what sex you are. It would be freaky dating you. You look kind of like my brother. Is this official now? Can I see your scars after you have surgery? You'll look a lot better after it's over. But you look OK now. What does your driver's license say? Does your mother know she has a son now? Are you going to grow a beard? But your voice is still so high. I've never thought of you as a girl anyway. I'll love you no matter what sex you are.

Things they don't say:

"She" doesn't know what she's doing. She's just being trendy. It's just a phase. She must hate women. She was such a pretty girl. Why does she want to alienate herself like this? Anything to be different. I hate that she's doing this to her mother. So she's a he now, I suppose. But she's so feminine—how could she be a boy? Being a tomboy is one thing, but this is something else. This time she's gone too far. I don't think she should be allowed on womyn-only land. I'm so angry with her for making this decision. She should just stay a she. I don't get her. I don't get this whole transexual thing. Didn't she used to be a model? Does she like to be fucked? It must suck to hate your own body. She does hate her body, doesn't she? She doesn't know what gender she is. Who's going to want to date her now? I'm glad I'm not that fucked up.

Things I say to myself:

What will my mother think? Was I born this way? Why do I like to suck dick so much? How come I never liked being a lesbian? Why am I less angry now that I've figured out who I really am? Did my father abuse me as a child? Have I always felt this way? How do I feel? Am I feeling anything yet? Do I deserve to be here? Why are people so afraid of me? Sometimes I wish I were dead. No one will ever understand me. Thank God I found other people like me. I can't wait until I get chest surgery. Will I ever want to get bottom surgery? I guess I can't go to the Michigan Womyn's Music Festival anymore. Can I still have sex with boy-dykes and call myself a fag? Will I get caught if I try to give a guy a blow job in a public restroom? Is it freaky in this body or what? I like being fucked in the cunt, so I must not be a real transexual. The Benjamin Standards suck. It's great that I am figuring all this stuff out. I'm tired of thinking about all this stuff. How come my only dating options are straight men who see me as a girl and fags who don't quite see me as a boy? If I had a real dick, I'd be happy. If I had a real dick, I'd be a fag who is sometimes sad.

Things I tell people:

Don't worry, I'm still the same on the inside. It's not catching. I don't really feel like a man. I don't really feel like a woman. Will you please refer to me as he? It makes me feel a lot better. I'm sorry this is so hard for you. I still love you. I've always felt this way. I've never felt this way before. I really need your support. I can't wait for you to touch my chest after surgery. I can't take my shirt off during sex. What do you mean, I haven't started transitioning yet? My new name does so fit me. Thanks for coming to my naming party. You're cute, wanna dance? I'm just a different kind of fag. I love my new name too. My dick comes in all sizes. Yes, my boyfriend has a dick, and it's pointing at me. No, I didn't see the Sally Jessy Raphael show yesterday. Don't worry, honey, you're in the right washroom. The binary gender system sucks. If I wanted augmentation I wouldn't need a damn letter from a behavioral scientist. I don't want to be a man; I just want to feel more like me. But I don't enjoy sleeping with femmes. I don't think I was abused as a child. What does that have to do with it anyway? Everything.

How I feel:

Happy that my world is making more sense every day, crazy because I'm sure at least once a day that no one else could possibly understand how I feel, disjointed, excited about my new chest, angry that the world can be such a shitty place to people who don't fit in, confused, scared, sexy, freakish, relieved, lucky to have my trans community, thankful to modern medicine, pissed off at being born in the wrong body, scared to do hormones, glad I have a boyfriend who is transgendered like me, afraid that someone will try to kill one of us one day, afraid to travel alone, to use public restrooms, to smile at the wrong person, to let myself be afraid, anxious to be free of the bits of flesh that sit on my male chest, afraid that it will hurt my mother when she finds out she has a son and not a daughter, grateful that I've met my brother Marcel, scared that I've made the wrong decision, guilty that I don't mind the plumbing that I have, sad that the world hates us and won't even try to see who we are, horny when I think about fucking men, especially daddy figures, especially Henry Rollins, especially that cute older fag who cruises me at my work, and especially other trannies like my boy Jackson. Like I did when I was 10 years old.

How I survive:

By writing and dancing, by talking to people who get it, by screaming into my pillow, by crying when I can't take it anymore, by reading reaffirming words by other gender warriors, by fantasizing that I have a huge dick, a flat chest, and a deep voice, by reminding myself that I felt like a boy as a child and it didn't feel freaky or weird, by spending time with brother Marcel, by kissing my boy on his flat chest and telling him how sexy he is, by telling the truth, by imagining how sexy I'm going to feel after chest surgery, by listening to other people's stories, by not taking on other people's bullshit, by calling people on their prejudices, by keeping a sense of humor, by hugging my cat who has loved me through any gender expression, by running and feeling my boy body move, by honoring other people's gender expressions, by learning when to be open and when not to, by being in my body even when I feel as though it has betrayed me, by attending the womyn's festival anyway—no matter what they think about male privilege, by believing my friends when they tell me they love me, by trying to love the girl parts of me I can't get rid of. By being me.

Story of a Preadolescent Drag King
L. Maurer

L. Maurer set out on a gender journey years ago with little more than a compass and a box of crayons. Today, Maurer is a sexuality educator and activist in upstate New York, and that journey is still unfolding.

I had watched that bike for months in Pulver's Store window downtown. Shiny orange frame with a top tube (a boy's bike), gleaming pedals, those newfangled racing-style handlebars, 10-speeds—and the only thing standing between me and that bike was my fifth-grade teacher and my gender identity.

This masterpiece of biking technology would surely bring hours of fun and freedom to its eventual owner. How I yearned for that bike! However, there was much more responsibility resting on that bike than merely my hopes and dreams. That shiny new bike was also the key component in my parents' elaborate plan to keep me from failing the fifth grade.

The problems began almost immediately on the first day of school. Mrs. Kay, well-known and respected for the discipline and high academic achievement her fifth-grade pupils displayed, introduced herself to the class. Dressed in my best Toughskins jeans and happy-face-emblazoned T-shirt, I was eager to please. Upon completing this last year of elementary school, I would be moving up to junior high.

"You—little boy in the last row—you must be in the wrong classroom," said Mrs. Kay. The class giggled.

"No ma'am," I stammered. "I'm in the right place."

"My roster indicates 14 boys and 14 girls—try down the hall, Mr. King's room. Oh and when you get there, please direct our last pupil down to our room. Poor thing, she must be lost."

"Um, Mrs. Kay...I really think I'm supposed to be here."

"Go on, go!" More giggles from my classmates. It felt like an eternity as I sat at my desk, trying to figure out what to do. The teacher continued staring at me, amazed at my apparent insubordination. "I asked you to go down the hall and retrieve our little lost girl. Is there a problem, Mr.—Mr—."

"Mrs. Kay," I blurted out, "I'm a girl."

Mrs. Kay's mouth fell open. Her face turned the same color as the red marking pen that fell from her hand, and we all, the class of room 41K, watched in stunned silence, waiting for whatever would come next.

"How was school today?" asked my mother as I climbed into the car. *Well, the whole class laughed at me, and Mrs. Kay's head nearly exploded,* was what I thought.

What I said was, "Uh, fine."

"I've heard Mrs. Kay's a unique teacher," my mom continued.

"Yeah, she gave a pop math quiz on the first day of school! Nobody was too happy about that, but I did fine," I said, deciding not to relay any of the other unusual events of my first day as a fifth-grader.

The weeks flew by, autumn changed to winter, and heavy ski sweaters, overalls, and galoshes slowly replaced my T-shirts and jeans. Report card day—I never really dreaded it as some of my friends did. Just another day like any other, or so I thought. In teacher's red ink, my report card envelope read: "Parents—Please call for a conference. Mrs. Kay." Conference? In the past, "conferences" were brief chats my parents had upon bumping into my teachers at the grocery store or the library. "Yes, she's bright, works hard, no trouble at all, and loves learning. Wish I could have 15 more of her in my class" was the general gist of these impromptu progress reports.

My parents called me into the living room, grave looks on their faces. No words were spoken. My father simply pointed to the big red F in penmanship. Penmanship? The way I write? There must have been some mistake; although clearly not a calligrapher, I had landed in the fifth grade without any previous mention of substandard penmanship. What was this all about?

I stayed home that evening watching *Mission: Impossible* on television. Mom and Dad made the dreaded pilgrimage to the parent-teacher conference. Mrs. Kay, in no uncertain terms, deemed my handwriting atrocious and disgraceful. "A girl must be schooled in the proper way to write, the proper way for a lady," Mrs. Kay stated as the rationale for this penmanship crusade. "It's for her own good. Her sloppy habits must be broken." Mrs. Kay continued to explain the situation to my stunned parents. "I'm prepared to help her break those habits—even if it takes a drop in all her other grades to add a little motivation."

My parents left this conference shaking their heads, and were still shaking them when they arrived home. "Well?" I asked. "What's up?"

They explained the conversation in great detail, as if they had to hear it again themselves in an attempt to determine if it made any sense at all the second time around. They ended with "She's a little…um…different. Let's just go on as if this never happened. Just keep your subject grades up and try to smile a little more in class. You'll catch more flies with honey than vinegar." My mother often used this cryptic phrase when she wasn't exactly sure what to make of a situation.

Smile more? OK, sure. Mom and Dad still seemed filled with utter disbelief yet not concerned enough to do anything, so I would just put this whole unusual episode out of my mind and concentrate on my schoolwork.

Soon afterward, though, it began. A spelling test handed back—although I had spelled every word correctly, it was marked C in Mrs. Kay's red pen. When I bolted up to her desk for an explanation, she grimly stated that she would continue to reduce my actual marks two letter grades until my handwriting improved. I was in shock. This was not fair! Surely my achievement in academic subjects could not be affected by her ideas about my penmanship!

The principal's response to my parents' angry visit the next morning was "I'm sorry, but I don't believe in meddling in the classroom decisions of our teachers. You'll have to work this out with Mrs. Kay directly."

Another family conference in the living room, this time much more anxious. "We know this isn't fair, but there's nothing more we can do. Please, take Mrs. Kay seriously. Listen to what she has to say about your penmanship. We'll practice at home, and she's agreed to tutor you during recess and after school."

"No way! I'm almost 11 years old, and I have to sit with the teacher during recess to be tutored in penmanship? Forget it!"

"It's only until the end of the school year, honey. Please. If things go on as they are, you'll fail the fifth grade over your penmanship."

"I won't, I won't, I won't!" My tantrum didn't last as long as the time I would later spend pondering this whole strange situation. I soon decided to embark upon some scientific inquiry.

I pressured my best friend: "Lemme see your homework, Arthur!"

"Why? You know you probably got all the answers right. Why do you wanna see mine?"

"Just shut up and lemme see!" His handwriting was nearly illegible. I could barely even discern his name at the top of the page. Armed with this baseline, I waited. As the graded homework papers came back to us, I held my breath. Arthur's paper: A-; he had worked two math problems incorrectly. Mine: C-; poor penmanship again, although all my answers were correct.

Meanwhile, I had also given up my reign as four-in-a-square champion at recess to do penmanship prison time with Mrs. Kay. She had borrowed a *Palmer Method Cursive Workbook for Beginning Students* from the first-grade classroom. It appeared I was incorrigible and needed to start from square one, unlearning all the bad handwriting habits that neither my parents nor I were aware that I had.

"Slowly, carefully form each letter," she coached. "Try to make them more soft and ladylike." When I balked, she brought in wide-lined paper, the kind with the big dotted line down the middle of each wide green row that the kindergartners used when they first began learning to write their names. "If you insist on writing like a kindergartner, you'll be treated like one," she simply stated.

My parents tried another approach—desperate times call for desperate measures. Remember Pulver's Store window, with the gleaming boy's 10-speed racing bike? It was offered up as a bribe—if only I could raise my handwriting grade to an A, that bike would be mine. I already had a bike, one I had received as a gift from my grandparents for a long-ago birthday, one that suited my need for speed and daredevil stunts but not my preferred expression of my personality. I was constantly embarrassed when people saw me on it. My mom and dad knew how I loved to ride and also knew how much I disliked its appearance.

It was hot pink, with multicolored tassels hanging from the handle grips. I held on to the big, wide, rusting handlebars and sat on a long banana seat, with bright orange, pink, and yellow flowers adorning its vinyl cover. Coaster brakes, three speeds—one was called "neutral" and disengaged the pedals entirely. A girl's bike. A girl's bike through and through. I spent endless hours riding it up and down the driveway, and up and down the street, releasing all the anger I had toward Mrs. Kay and this ridiculous handwriting crusade through my pedaling. And as I pedaled away the anger and frustration, I daydreamed I was actually riding that shiny new boy's racing bike.

Although I now had all the motivation I needed, my penmanship was going nowhere. My artificially deflated grades were taking a toll. These lowered marks, combined with any more penmanship F report card grades, would cause me to be left back to repeat fifth grade (and, most likely, Mrs. Kay's class and our own private penmanship mini penal colony).

I played my teacher's words over and over in my head, searching for some meaning I had missed. Surely this could not truly be about penmanship, and besides, mine was no worse than that of my best friends, Arthur, Mike, and John.

"Try to make them more ladylike," echoed in my mind, suddenly transposed over my memory of that first horrible day in school, the day Mrs. Kay mistook me for a boy.

This was crazy! But I had to see if it was true. I swallowed my pride—and a few tears—and in a flower-print polyester jumper and Peter Pan–collared blouse, both borrowed from my mother's closet (at barely 11 years old, I was already her height and size, and I hoped to go on to become tall enough to become a professional basketball player someday...but that's another story), I reported for penmanship tutoring.

"Well, what a nice young lady you are today! I almost didn't recognize you!" (*Just a coincidence,* I thought.) "You'll be able to pay more attention to your letters, won't you? (*No, this cannot be happening...*) "Now, as you practice writing these vowels, think beautiful, flowery, and frilly, just like your dress!" (*Bingo!*)

My sleuthing had, sadly, paid off.

The realization hit me hard. Mrs. Kay wanted me to write more like a girl. But I loved my natural handwriting. I had practiced it over the years, modeling it on the clean, efficient pen strokes of my father. I had spent weeks perfecting my signature so that my signed last name appeared indistinguishable from his. And although I had no real concept of this at the time, I identified with my handwriting. It was an expression of my innermost self, the self that loved rough-and-tumble play, splashing in puddles, wearing "boy" clothes, and being mistaken for a boy.

The next day I donned a long muumuu type dress (again, borrowed from my mom). "Now you're serious about improving your penmanship, aren't you?" Mrs. Kay greeted me that morning. Although I gritted my teeth as I clutched the thick beginner's pencil she had sentenced me to in her ongoing attempts to shame me into writing in a manner more in accordance with her wishes, Mrs. Kay lavished praise on my efforts. She even ended our tutoring session 10 minutes early. *Great,* I thought, *still time to get out on the playground!*

"Because of your efforts, you can use your extra time to help prepare snacks for the class," she said, as she pressed a box of powdered hot chocolate and a measuring spoon into my hands. "The boys will be cold and tired when they come in from recess—we can warm them up with some cocoa." She wrapped an apron around me. "And the girls will all be so jealous that you're the teacher's helper today."

But I didn't want to make the other girls jealous. And I didn't care about warming up the boys or feminizing my penmanship or appearance. I just wanted to be me.

My parents offered all the support they could, although I did not share with them the insidious gender plot I suspected was unfolding in my classroom. "Whatever you're doing, keep it up! Mrs. Kay called today to say how proud she is of your progress. Remember, all your work and patience will be rewarded when you ride that new bike home!"

For the next four months I forced all the feelings, beliefs, and ideas that truly made up the core of my being down to the pit of my stomach. Forced smiles and bright floral print jumpers became the uniform I hid behind. By now my appearance was drawing daily giggles from my schoolmates, as if they sensed that something was very wrong with my newly adopted persona. Although I had always endured some taunting and teasing about my tomboyish mannerisms, now it was as if my fellow students were aware of the gender dissonance between the person they had known as me and the new appearance I had put on to try to hide my true self. I was an 11-year-old in drag—a kid for whom biological sex and gender identity did not agree, now desperately trying to "fit" into my teacher's neatly ordered idea (and ideal) of the binary gender box. Every evening I tried to muster enough emotional strength to go hunting in my mother's closet again, hunting for the outfit that would finally earn my penmanship—or "gendership"—an A from Mrs. Kay once and for all. If only I could convince her of how feminine I had become, I could end this elaborate charade.

I had even begun dotting my i's with large circles, sunshines, and—in one of my most cynical moments—caricatures of the flowery designs on my clothing. To my horror, Mrs. Kay loved these new handwriting flourishes and encouraged me to develop them further. "Someday this lovely creativity will land you a fine husband," she told me.

I was also now charged with many new tasks, as my mother's all-powerful polyester wardrobe mysteriously assisted my meteoric rise from class scapegoat to teacher's pet. It seemed that for each new "girl" accessory I added to my appearance, I was assigned a correspondingly higher level of feminine responsibility. The week I added a barrette to my hair, Mrs. Kay assigned me to supervising the boys as they clapped blackboard erasers (a highly coveted task among the boys) and emptied the trash.

"Boys," she stated in a matter of fact way, "neither know nor care much about cleanliness. You are to supervise them to be sure they get these chores done in a satisfactory manner." Although I had to bite my tongue to avoid making some smart-aleck response, blackboard eraser duty was not too bad. Resourceful as I was, once outside I paid each boy a quarter in exchange for letting me clap the erasers myself, as they went behind the school to steal a few puffs on a cigarette.

Every few days, my parents would make sure I somehow went past that new bike in the store window, and, although it seemed an eternity to me, those days strung together into weeks and months, and soon it was spring. Instead of cutoffs and tank tops, however, my wardrobe transition this season was from corduroy skirts to lighter-weight, lace-trimmed frocks. Since I was still confined to the classroom at lunchtime, I remember little of those first sunny, warm days when the snow finally melted, along with the need for bulky snowsuits, boots, and mittens on the playground.

Mrs. Kay, apparently satisfied that my gender reeducation had been completed, awarded me an A in penmanship on my final report card that year. My parents took me directly to Pulver's Store that afternoon, and I rode home on my shiny 10-speed reward for having responded appropriately to Mrs. Kay's efforts. How ironic that my reward for acting more like a girl was the quintessential boy's bike.

The summer between fifth grade and junior high was a busy one, spent unlearning the Palmer Method of penmanship and rediscovering my own natural style. There were also clothes to be neatly put back in Mom's closet and barrettes to be given away to girlfriends and my little brother's play dress-up box. And of course there were plenty of bike races and daredevil stunts to amaze my friends with as I easily slipped back into the role of being "just one of the boys."

My parents still sigh and chuckle a little when reminded of this odd episode from my elementary school career. I do too. That boy's 10-speed bicycle is still in my garage today, and I take it on a spin around the neighborhood about once a year—to remember the fifth grade and the bittersweet beginning of my gender consciousness. And to forget it as well. As I pedal into the breeze, I celebrate being me, a grown-up gender rebel with gloriously slanted, steady, distinctive, slightly illegible penmanship.

Two Women
Loree Cook-Daniels

Loree Cook-Daniels is a GG (genetic girl) in her fifth decade. The widow of one FTM, she is now the partner of another. She, her GB son, and her partner live in Milwaukee. She owns WordBridges, a freelance writing and conflict resolution consulting firm.

Let's talk about two women. One we'll call Susie Suburb. Raised in a middle-class, segregated neighborhood in a medium-sized Northern California town. Her blond, blue-eyed little-girl good looks and personality began paying off early. She was exactly 6 years old when she became her elementary school's Queen of the May.

By 17 she was valedictorian of her high school class; by 22 the top departmental honoree at her state university graduation. She won a nationwide competition for a prestigious public policy fellowship at age 24 and moved to Washington, D.C. There she got married, earned her master's degree, bought a house in the suburbs, and became a mother—in that order. She's now active in her child's day care center's parent advisory board, works part-time for a national professional association, and spends the rest of her time on her family and her favorite pastimes, reading and writing.

Can you picture her? I thought so. That's Susie.

The woman we'll call Rosie Radical also showed her colors early. An organizer from the get-go, by the age of 13 she was heading an activist girls group that eventually managed to change the school's dress code so girls could wear pants. By 17 she was the only out lesbian active in the town's women's center. She cofounded a gay people's association at 18 and moved to San Francisco at 20 to enroll in the country's most radical women's studies program. At 21 she was cochair of the San Francisco committee for the very first march on Washington for lesbian and gay rights.

In order to finally cut the ties to an ambivalent relationship she'd been unable to end, Rosie moved across country and became one of the first out lesbians ever to work for Congress. She and her new lover, a black butch, reveled in pushing the envelope, holding a public commitment ceremony long before such events were commonplace, becoming the first lesbians they'd ever heard of who legally hyphenated their names, buying a house together (and then talking about the experience in a nationally prominent, straight newspaper), and finally becoming parents together. Rosie now juggles three part-time jobs, is seeing her 15th therapist, is active in an interracial lesbian couples group, and writes a monthly column for the local lesbian and gay newspaper.

So much for Rosie.

Susie Suburb and Rosie Radical. Chances are you know one of them, or at least a woman just like her.

Or do you? How would you react if I told you that Susie and Rosie are the same woman? If I said that Susie became a mother when her lesbian partner gave birth, that Rosie became a wife after her lesbian lover became a man, what would you think? How about the heterosexual wife and mother who was the only lesbian "father" in her spouse's childbirth class? How would your mind wrap around the lesbian columnist who is on her husband's health insurance?

Do you know how to make sense of such a woman?

Does she?

Affronting Reason
Cheryl Chase

Cheryl Chase founded the Intersex Society of North America, and pro-
duced the video Hermaphrodites Speak! *Her work has been covered in*
The New York Times *and* Newsweek *and on* NBC's Dateline *and*
National Public Radio's Fresh Air *and* All Things Considered.

"It seems that your parents weren't sure for a time whether you were a
girl or a boy," Dr. Christen explained as she handed me three fuzzy pho-
tostats. I was 21 years old and had asked her to help me obtain records
of a hospitalization that occurred when I was 1½. I was desperate to
obtain the complete records, to determine who had surgically removed
my clitoris, and why.

"Diagnosis: true hermaphrodite. Operation: clitorectomy." The hospital records showed Charlie admitted, age 18 months. His typewritten
name had been crudely crossed out and "Cheryl" scribbled over it.

Though I recall clearly the scene of Dr. Christen handing me the
records, dismissing me from her office, I can recall nothing of my emotional reaction. How is it possible that I could be a *hermaphrodite*? The
hermaphrodite is a mythological creature. I am a woman, a lesbian,
though I lack a clitoris and inner labia. What did my genitals look like
before the surgery? Was I born with a penis?

Fifteen years of emotional numbness passed before I was able to seek out the answers to these and many other questions. Then, four years ago, extreme emotional turmoil and suicidal despair arrived suddenly, threatening to crush me. *It's not possible,* I thought. *This cannot be anyone's story, much less mine. I don't want it. Yet it* is *mine.* I mark that time as the beginning of my coming-out as a political intersexual, an "avowed" intersexual, to borrow an epithet that until recently adhered to homosexuals who refused to stay invisible.

The story of my childhood is a lie. I know now that after the clitorectomy my parents followed the physicians' advice, and discarded every scrap of evidence that Charlie had ever existed. They replaced all of the blue baby clothing with pink, discarded photos, birthday cards. When I look at grandparents, aunts, and uncles, I am aware that they must know how one day Charlie ceased to exist in my family, and Cheryl was there in his place.

The medical establishment uses the terms *hermaphrodite* and *intersexual* to refer to us. The word *hermaphrodite,* with its strong mythological associations, reinforces the notion that hermaphroditism is a fantasy, not your neighbor, not your friend, not your teacher, and especially not your baby. And because it falsely implies that one individual possesses two sets of genitals, it allows my clitoris to be labeled as a penis, and the clitorectomy performed on me to be justified as "reconstructive surgery." For these reasons I prefer the term *intersexual.*

Kira Triea, one of many who has joined me in speaking openly about her intersexuality, also feels strongly about this point. "It irks me so when I am trying to explain to someone who I am, what my experience has been, and they begin to quote Ovid to me." For Kira (an intersexual who was assigned male at birth and raised as a boy but began to menstruate through her penis at puberty and now lives as a lesbian-identified woman), hermaphroditism is a real presence in her life every day. She need not look to poetry penned in Latin two millennia ago.

At the beginning of my process of coming out as intersexual, I chose to examine again the three pages of medical records I had set aside for 15 years. The word *hermaphrodite* was horribly wounding and drove me to the brink of suicide. I thought back to my earlier process of coming out as a lesbian. The way out of this pain was to reclaim the stigmatized label, to manufacture a positive acceptance of it. This second coming out was far more painful and difficult. As a teenager recognizing my attraction to women, I visited the library, stealthily examined Del Martin and Phyllis Lyon's *Lesbian/Woman* and Radclyffe Hall's *The Well of Loneliness*. I learned that other lesbians existed, that they somehow managed to live and to love women. Somehow I would find them. There was a community where my lesbianism would be understood, would be welcomed. No such help was available to reclaim my intersexuality. The only images I found were pathologized case histories in medical texts and journals, close-ups of genitals being poked, prodded, measured, sliced, and sutured—full body shots with the eyes blacked out.

For many months I struggled to reclaim the label *hermaphrodite*. I knew that I had been mutilated by the clitorectomy, deprived of the sexual experience most people, male and female, take for granted. What would my life be had I been allowed to keep my genitals intact? *No,* I thought, *I don't wish to have a penis between my legs, for my body to look like a man's body. I could never relate sexually to a woman as a man.*

"Never mind. Just don't think about it," was the advice of the few people to whom I spoke, including two female therapists. "You look like a woman."

There is a powerful resistance to thinking about intersexuality. Because they look at me and make a female attribution, most people find it impossible to imagine that my experience and my history are not female. The resistance to thinking about what my sexual experience might be is even more profound. Most people, including the two therapists mentioned above, are paralyzed by the general prohibition on explicit sex talk. But sex radicals and activists are little better. They assume I am having "vaginal orgasms" or even "full body orgasms." If I persist in asserting my sexual dysfunction, many patronize me. "I am completely confident that you will learn how to orgasm," one man told me, then continued his explanation of how male circumcision was just as damaging as clitorectomy—my experience to the contrary.

What is most infuriating is to read popular media denunciations of African female genital mutilation as barbaric abuses of human rights, which fail to mention that intersexed children's clitorises are removed every day in the United States. Such writers occasionally note that clitorectomy has been practiced in the United States but always hurry to assure the reader that the practice ended by the 1930s. Letters to these authors receive no reply. Letters to editors pointing out the inaccuracy are not published.

In 1996 Congress passed H.R. 3610, prohibiting "the removal or infibulation (or both) of the whole or part of the clitoris, the labia minor, or the labia major." However, the next paragraph specifically excludes from prohibition these operations if they are performed by a licensed medical practitioner who deems them necessary. As early as 1993, Brown University professor of medical science Anne Fausto-Sterling had joined intersexuals to ask Congresswoman Pat Schroeder, in drafting the prohibition, not to neglect genital surgery performed on intersexed infants. Schroeder's office made no reply. Newspaper accounts in 1996 lauded the bill's passage as an end to clitorectomy in the United States.

It took months for me to obtain the rest of my medical records. I learned that I had been born not with a penis but with intersexed genitals: a typical vagina and outer labia, female urethra, and a very large clitoris. Mind you, "large" and "small," as applied to intersexed genitals, are judgments that exist in the eye of the beholder. From my birth until the surgery, while I was Charlie, my parents and doctors considered my penis to be very small and with the urethra in the "wrong" position.

My parents were so traumatized by the appearance of my genitals that they allowed no one to see them: no baby-sitters, no helpful grandmother or aunt. Then, at the very moment the intersex specialist physicians pronounced my "true sex" as female, my clitoris was suddenly monstrously large. All this occurred without any change in the actual size or appearance of the appendage between my legs.

Being intersexed is humanly possible but (in our culture) socially unthinkable. In modern industrial cultures, when a child is born the experts present, whether midwives or physicians, assign a sex based on the appearance of the infant's genitals. They are required—both legally and by social norms—to assign the child as either male or female. Were parents to tell inquiring friends and relatives that their newborn's sex was "hermaphrodite," they would be greeted with disbelief. Should the parents persist in labeling their child "hermaphrodite" rather than "male or female with congenital deformity requiring surgical repair," their sanity would be questioned.

Thus, intersexed children are always assigned either male or female. In making these sex assignments, specialist physicians are generally consulted. The assignment may not be made for several days, and it is sometimes changed, as was done with me. In fact, there are documented cases in which the sex assignment has been changed (without soliciting the opinion of—or even *informing* the child) as many as three times.[1]

Most people take for granted, even assume as "scientific fact," that there are two, and only two, sexes. In reality, about one in 2000 infants is born with an anatomy that refuses to conform to our preconceptions of male and female. Few outside the medical profession are even aware of our existence. I now know that hundreds of thousands of people in this country alone share my experience, and we are organizing ourselves through the Intersex Society of North America.[2] My ability to embrace the term *hermaphrodite,* however halting and uncertain at first, has grown in depth, conviction, and pride as I have met other intersexuals. Together we have shared our stories, our lives, and our anger.

Struggling to understand why society so utterly denies the phenomenon of intersexuality, I read widely in such diverse fields as philosophy, history, psychology, and ethnography. I was excited to discover that in recent years a number of scholars have begun to examine the ways in which sex and gender are socially constructed. These and related works constitute a recognition that the paradigms of previous investigators have caused them to overlook information about nonreproductive sexual conduct, practices, and categories. Data at odds with their culturally determined, heterosexist, dimorphic point of view were ignored because they could not be accounted for.

Americans are apt to express disbelief when confronted with evidence of intersexuality. Modern Western culture is the first to rely on technology to enforce gender dichotomy. Since the 1950s or so, surgical and hormonal means have been used to erase the evidence from intersexed infants' bodies. Medical literature speaks with one voice of the necessity of this practice, even as it concedes that it may damage sexual function. Silence has been considered evidence of patient satisfaction.

For over 40 years some form of clitorectomy or clitoroplasty has been used to treat little girls with adrenogenital syndrome (one of dozens of reasons why an infant may be born intersexed). The only indication for performing this surgery has been to improve the body image of these children so that they feel "more normal...."

Not one has complained of the loss of sensation even when the entire clitoris was removed.... The clitoris is clearly not necessary for orgasm.

(Edgerton 1993, 956).[3]

What are genitals for? *My* genitals are for *my* pleasure. In a sex-repressive culture with a heavy investment in the fiction of sexual dichotomy, infant genitals are for discriminating male from female infants. It is very difficult to get parents or even physicians to consider the infant as a future adult sexual being. Medical intersex specialists, however, pride themselves on being able to do just that.

For intersex specialists, male genitals are for active penetration and pleasure, while female genitals are for passive penetration and reproduction: Men have sex, women have babies. Asked why standard practice assigns 90% of intersexed infants as females (and surgically enforces the assignment by trimming or removing the clitoris), one prominent surgical specialist reasoned, "You can make a hole, but you can't build a pole." (Hendricks 1993, 15).

Notice how John Gearhart, a noted specialist in genital surgery for intersexed children, evades questioning about orgasmic function following presentation of his paper on additional surgeries for repair of vaginas surgically constructed in intersexed infants. (Dr. Frank, in attendance at the presentation, shares a professional interest in such surgery. The discussion was published in the *Journal of Urology* along with the paper.)

Dr. Frank: How do you define successful intercourse? How many of these girls actually have an orgasm, for example? How many of these had a clitorectomy, how many a clitoroplasty, and did it make a difference to orgasm?

Dr. Gearhart: Interviews with the families were performed by a female pediatric surgeon who is kind and caring and who I think got the maximum information from these patients. Adequate intercourse was defined as successful vaginal penetration.... (Bailez et al. 1992, 1140).

Dr. Gearheart has since condemned outspoken intersexed adults as "zealots" (Angier 1996) and minimized reports by former patients of damaged sexual function after clitoral surgery because "some women who have never had surgery are anorgasmic." (Chase 1996, 1140).

Intersex specialists often stress the importance of a heterosexual outcome for the intersexed children consigned to their care. For instance, Slijper et al. state, "Parents will feel reassured when they know that their daughter can develop heterosexually just like other children." (Slijper et al. 1994, 15). Dr. Y, a prominent surgeon in the field of intersexuality, agreed to be interviewed by Ellen Lee only under condition of anonymity. He asserts that the ultimate measure of success for sex assignment of intersexed children is the "effectiveness of intercourse" they achieve as adults. (Lee 1994, 60). Intersexuals assigned female who choose women as sexual partners and those assigned male who choose men as sexual partners must then represent failures of treatment in the eyes of our parents and of intersex specialists. Indeed, my mother's reaction on learning that I was sexual with women was to reveal to my siblings—but not to me—my hermaphroditism and history of sex change and to regret that she had allowed physicians to assign me female rather than male.

My mother and father took me into their room one day to share a secret with me. I was 10 years old, still utterly ignorant about sexual matters. "When you were a baby, you were sick," they explained. "Your clitoris was too big. It was *enlarged*." The way they spoke the word *enlarged*, it was clear that it was being given some special, out-of-the-ordinary meaning. "You had to go into the hospital, and it was removed."

"What is a clitoris?" I asked.

"A clitoris is a part of a girl that would have been a penis if she had been a boy. Yours was enlarged, so it had to be removed. Now everything is fine. But don't ever tell anyone about this."

Who am I? I look at my body. It *looks* female. Yet I have always harbored a secret doubt. I remember myself as a withdrawn, depressed adolescent, trying to steal a glance of a woman's genitals. Do hers look like mine? I had never seen a naked woman up close. I had no idea that my genitals were missing parts. In fact, one cannot discern the difference between my genitals and those of any other woman without parting the outer labia. I do recall learning from a book about masturbation. Try as I might, I could not locate a focus of pleasurable sensation in my genitals, couldn't accomplish the trick I had read about. I wasn't able to associate this failure with the secret about the enlarged clitoris that had been removed. I simply couldn't take in that such an irreversible harm had been done to me—and by adults who were responsible for my well-being. I often woke from a nightmare in which my life was in danger, my gender in question, and my genitals were somehow horribly deformed, spilling out of me like visceral organs. It wasn't until I became a young adult that I was able to make the connection between the removal of my clitoris and my feeble sexual response, my inability to experience orgasm.

Who am I? I now assert both my femininity and my intersexuality, my "not female"-ness. This is not a paradox; the fact that my gender has been problematized is the source of my intersexual identity. Most people have never struggled with their gender, are at a loss to answer the question, "How do you know you are a woman (a man)?"

I have been unable to experience myself as totally female. Although my body passes for female, women's clothing does not fit me. The shoulders are too narrow, the sleeves too short. Most women's gloves won't go on my hands or women's shoes on my feet. For most women, that wouldn't be more than an inconvenience. But when clothing doesn't fit, I am reminded of my history.

Of course, men's clothing doesn't fit me either. The straight lines leave no room for my large breasts or broad hips. Still, I experience something about the way that I work and move in the world as relatively masculine. And when a man expresses an intimate attraction to me, I often suspect he is wrestling with a conflicted homosexual orientation, attracted to a masculine part of me, but my feminine appearance renders his attraction safely heterosexual.

As a woman, I am less than whole. I have a secret past. I lack important parts of my genitals and sexual response. When a lover puts her hand to my genitals for the first time, the lack is immediately obvious to her. Finally, I simply do not feel myself a woman (even less a man). But the hermaphrodite identity was too monstrous, too Other, too freakish for me to easily embrace. A medical anomaly, patched up as best as the surgeons could manage. I had an article from a medical journal stating that only 12 "true hermaphrodites" (the label applied to me by my medical records) had *ever* been recorded. (Morris 1957, 540).

Who benefits from this medical erasure and social silencing? Certainly no intersexed children. I have been mutilated, left to wonder and to search for the truth in utter silence and isolation. At first I was vexed by the question of identity. My earlier experience of coming out as a lesbian helped me to see the solution to my predicament. The terms *homosexual* and *lesbian*, like the term *intersex*, were inventions of medical discourse, used to pathologize disapproved sexualities. I decided to proudly assert my identity, to insist that the medical construction of intersexuality as disease is oppression, not science. I decided to find others who share my experience, others who would speak out with me. A community can provide emotional and logistical support for its members and mount a much more powerful resistance than individuals acting alone.

It wasn't easy to overcome my feelings of intense shame. I remember furtively using the printer, copier, and fax machine at the office, my heart pounding with the fear that someone would see the documents I was working with—medical records, articles from medical journals, a journal of my emotional progress. I still believed that intersexuality was so rare I might never find another whose experience was similar to mine.

Alice Walker had just published *Possessing the Secret of Joy,* a novel that focused Western attention on the African cultural rite euphemistically referred to as female circumcision. I thrilled to read how the elderly midwife, whose long life had been spent performing clitorectomies, castigated her former victim for suggesting clitorectomy might be justified for hermaphrodites, if not for females. "It's all normal, as far as that goes," says M'lissa. "You didn't make it, so who are you to judge?" I located and spoke with African women who had been mutilated in this way, now organizing in the United States against the practices of their homelands. The examples of these brave people helped me to deal with my shame.

I began to speak, at first indiscriminately, with friends and acquaintances about what had been done to me. Within a year I had turned up half a dozen other intersexuals, most of them also genitally mutilated: two living with their atypical genitals intact; a woman clitorectomized during her teens who knew from masturbation that her clitoris was the focus of sexual pleasure but was unable to express this or otherwise resist the pressure of parents and doctors; a child who had been clitorectomized just two years previously; a woman who was grateful to her mother for resisting years of medical pressure to remove her daughter's large clitoris; a man who had been raised as a girl and who switched to living as a man (with intact intersexed genitals) after he developed a masculine body; a man whose penis had been severely damaged by repeated surgeries to "correct" the position of his urethral meatus; a man who had discovered that the childhood surgery no one would explain to him had actually been to remove his uterus and single ovary. None of these people had ever spoken to another intersexual.

Surgeons assert that the reason they fail to provide us with counseling is that they cannot locate mental health professionals with experience in dealing with intersexuality (Lee 1994). Yet surgeons perpetuate this situation by mutilating, traumatizing, stigmatizing, and silencing us, their intersexed patients. We grow up with so much shame that as adults we are not able to discuss our experience openly, and the phenomenon of intersexuality remains invisible. Indeed, as recently as 1996, one entrant in a medical ethics contest won a cash prize for her essay encouraging physicians to lie to their intersexed patients in order to prevent them from knowing their diagnoses (Natarajan 1996). In adulthood, many who were treated as children by medical intersex specialists feel so betrayed that they shun all medical care.

What do I see when I look in the mirror? A female body, though scarred and missing some important genital parts. When I interact in daily life with others, though, I experience a strange sort of bodily dissociation; my perception of myself is as a disembodied entity, without sex or gender. I view healing this split as an important element of personal growth that will allow me to reclaim my sexuality and to be more effective as an intersex advocate. My body is not female; it is intersexed. Nonconsensual surgery cannot erase intersexuality and produce whole males and females; it produces emotionally abused and sexually dysfunctional intersexuals. If I label my postsurgical anatomy *female,* I ascribe to surgeons the power to create a *woman* by removing body parts. I accede to their agenda of "woman as lack." I collaborate in the prohibition of my intersexual identity. Kessler quotes an endocrinologist who specializes in treating intersexed infants: "In the absence of maleness, you have femaleness.... It's really the basic design" (Kessler 1990, 15).

Must things be this way? In all cultures, at all times? Anthropologist Clifford Geertz contrasted the conceptualization of intersexuals by the Navajo and the Kenyan Pokit ("a product, if a somewhat unusual product, of the normal course of things") with the American attitude. "Americans...regard femaleness and maleness as exhausting the natural categories in which persons can conceivably come: what falls between is a darkness, an offense against reason" (Geertz 1984, 85). The time has come for intersexuals to denounce our treatment as abuse, to embrace and openly assert our identities as intersexuals, to intentionally affront the sort of reasoning that requires us to be mutilated and silenced.

Even before intersexuals began to speak out, there were a few strings of awareness that something fishy was up at the boundaries of the sexes. In 1980, Ruth Hubbard and Patricia Farnes pointed out that the practice of clitorectomy was not limited to the Third World but also occurs "right here in the United States, where it is used as part of a procedure to 'repair' by 'plastic surgery' so-called genital ambiguities" (Farnes and Hubbard 1980). Reacting to intersex specialist John Money's explanation to a 3-year-old girl that clitorectomy "will make her look like all other girls," Anne Fausto-Sterling wryly noted, "If the surgery results in genitalia that look like those shown in [Money's] book, then [he is] in need of an anatomy lesson!" (Fausto-Sterling 1985, 138). Five years later, Suzanne Kessler, whose work has been influential in motivating the current discourse on gender as a social construction, interviewed physicians who specialize in managing intersexed children. She concluded that genital ambiguity is treated with surgery "not because it is threatening to the infant, but because it is threatening to the infant's culture" (Kessler 1990, 25). Finally, Fausto-Sterling suggested that genital surgery should not be imposed on intersexed infants (Fausto-Sterling 1993).

A letter to the editor in which I responded to Fausto-Sterling's article, announcing the formation of the Intersex Society of North America, brought emotional responses from other intersexuals. One, Morgan Holmes, has completed an extended analysis of the reasons why medical technology has been used to erase intersexuality in general, and from her own body in particular (Holmes 1994). Until she contacted me, Holmes had shared her experience of intersexuality with no one. The only other intersexual in her universe was Herculine Barbin, the 19th-century French hermaphrodite whose journals were edited and published by Michel Foucault. Barbin's life ended in suicide. By 1996, ISNA had grown to include more than 150 intersexuals throughout the United States and Canada, and several in Europe, Australia, and New Zealand.

In Britain as well, intersexuals have begun to speak out against the extreme secrecy, shame, and freakishness surrounding their condition. The British movement was given a boost when the respected British Medical Journal carried an exchange that led to the publication of an address for a support group.

Mine was a dark secret kept from all outside the medical profession (family included), but this is not an option because it both
increases the feelings of freakishness and reinforces the isolation
(Anonymous, 1994b).

It's not that my gynecologist told me the truth that angers me
(I'd used medical libraries to reach a diagnosis anyway), but that
neither I nor my parents were offered any psychological support
but were left to flounder in our separate feelings of shame and
taboo (Anonymous, 1994a).

Both writers have androgen insensitivity syndrome. During gesta-
tion, their XY sex chromosomes caused them to have testes, and their
testes produced testosterone. But because their cells were incapable of
responding to testosterone, they were born with genitals of typical
female appearance—but with a short vagina and no cervix or uterus.
Raised as girls, with bodies that develop many adult female characteristics at puberty, women with AIS are often traumatized to read in
medical records or texts that they are "genetic males" and "male
pseudohermaphrodites." The publication of these letters led to a swell
of visibility and participation in Britain's AIS Support Group, which by
1996 had chapters in the United States, Canada, the Netherlands,
Germany, and Australia.

In Germany intersexuals have formed the Workgroup on Violence in
Pediatrics and Gynecology for mutual support and in opposition of
medical abuse. In Japan intersexuals have formed Hijra Nippon, with a
similar agenda. In the United States, HELP and the Ambiguous
Genitalia Support Network were separately founded by mothers who
opposed the drastic surgical interventions and secrecy that medical specialists recommended for their intersexed children. One of these
women has a suit pending against physicians who removed her son's
testes against her stated wishes.

Some intersexuals whose bodies resemble mine have an XX, some
an XY karyotype; others have a mosaic karyotype, which differs from
cell to cell. There is no possible way to discern my karyotype without
sending a tissue sample to a laboratory. If the result were XX, should
this information bolster my identity as a female? As a lesbian? If XY,
should I reconceptualize myself as a heterosexual man? It is ludicrous

that knowledge of the result of a laboratory test in which cell nuclei are stained and photographed under a microscope should determine the perception of anyone's sex or gender.

The International Olympic Committee has learned this the hard way. Since the IOC began to karyotype women in 1968, one in 500 female athletes tested have been rejected due to unusual chromosomes; in some cases the decision was made only after the event, and the woman was stripped of her title and barred from future competition. To this writer's knowledge, only one person treated in this way has thus far been willing to speak openly about her experience. When meet officials presented Maria Patino with the news that she was "genetically male," they advised her to fake an injury and leave quietly (Pool 1994).

When I first began to seek out other intersexuals, I expected and wanted to find people whose experiences exactly matched mine. What I have discovered is that, in one sense, we are very different: The range of personalities, politics, and anatomies in our nascent intersexual movement is broad. Some of us live as women, some as men, some as open intersexuals. Many of us are homosexual, as that term is narrowly understood in terms of the social gender roles of the partners. Some of us have never been sexual. But in another sense, our experiences are surprisingly coherent: Those of us who have been subjected to medical intervention and invisibility share our experience of it as abuse.

I claim lesbian identity because women who feel desire for me experience that desire as lesbian, because I feel most female when being sexual, and because I feel desire for women as I do not for men. Many intersexuals share my sense of queer identity, even those who do not share this homosexual identity. One, assigned female at birth and lucky enough to escape genital surgery through a fluke, has said that she has enjoyed sex with both women and men but never with another intersexual. "I'm a heterosexual in the truest sense of the word" (Angier 1996, E14).

Healing is a process without end. The feeling of being utterly alone may be the most damaging part of what has been done to us. My work as an activist, listening to, counseling, and connecting other intersexuals, and working to save children born every day from having to repeat our suffering, has been an important part of my own healing, of feeling less overwhelmed by grief and rage.

Notes

1. Money describes a child who was assigned male at birth, female a few days later, male at age 3 weeks, and female at age $4\frac{1}{2}$. She was clitorectomized in conjunction with the final sex change. Her history of sex reassignments was kept secret from her, tabooed from family discussion although she recalled it in dreams (Money 1991, 239).

2. Intersex Society of North America, P.O. Box 31791, San Francisco, CA 94131. E-mail info@isna.org. http://www.isna.org.

3. Although this statement was written in connection with an article about "clitoroplasty without loss of sensitivity," the authors provide no evidence that this standard procedure, which removes nearly the entire clitoris and relocates the remainder, leaves sexual sensation intact. On the other hand, Morgan Holmes, who was subjected to it as a child, characterizes it as a "partial clitorectomy" (Holmes 1994). Another woman, who had the procedure performed as an adult and is able to contrast her sexual experience before and after the surgery, calls it "incredibly desensitizing" (Chase 1994).

References Cited

Angier, Natalie. 1996. Intersexual Healing: An Anomaly Finds a Group. *The New York Times*, February 4, E14.

Anonymous. 1994a. Be open and honest with sufferers. *BMJ (British Medical Journal)* 308 (April 16): 1041–1042.

Anonymous. 1994b. Once a Dark Secret. *BMJ (British Medical Journal)* 308 (February 19): 542.

Bailez, M. M., John P. Gearhart, Claude Migeon, and John Rock. 1992. Vaginal reconstruction after initial construction of the external genitalia in girls with salt-wasting adrenal hyperplasia. *Journal of Urology*, 148: 680–684.

Berlin, Meyer, and Shlomo, Josef Zevin. 1974. *Encyclopedia Talmudica*, 1: 386–389. Jerusalem: Phillip Feldheim.

Butler, Judith. 1990. *Gender Trouble: Feminism and the Subversion of Identity.* New York: Routledge.

Chase, Cheryl. 1993. Letters From Readers. *The Sciences*, July-August, 3.

Chase, Cheryl. 1994. Winged labia: Deformity or gift? *Hermaphrodites With Attitude*, Winter 1994, 3.

Chase, Cheryl. 1996. Re: Measurement of Evoked Potentials during Feminizing Genitoplasty: Techniques and Applications (letter). *Journal of Urology*, 156 (3): 1139–1140.

Conte, Felix A. and Melvin M. Grumbach. 1989. Pathogenesis, classification, diagnosis, and treatment of anomalies of sex. In *Endocrinology*, ed. Leslie J. De Groot: 1810–1847. Philadelphia: Saunders.

Edgerton, Milton T. 1993. Discussion: Clitoroplasty for Clitoromegaly due to Adrenogenital Syndrome without Loss of Sensitivity (by Nobuyuki Sagehashi).

Plastic and Reconstructive Surgery, 91 (5): 956.

Edgerton, Robert B. 1964. Pokot intersexuality: An east African example of the resolution of sexual incongruity. *American Anthropologist,* 66 (6): 1288–1299.

Emans, S., Jean Herriot, and Donald Peter Goldstein. 1990. *Pediatric and Adolescent Gynecology.* Boston: Little, Brown and Company.

Farnes, Patricia, M.D. and Ruth Hubbard. 1980. Letter to the editor. *Ms.,* April, 9–10.

Fausto-Sterling, Anne. 1985. *Myths of Gender: Biological Theories about Women and Men.* New York: Basic Books.

Fausto-Sterling, Anne. 1993. The Five Sexes: Why Male and Female Are Not Enough. *The Sciences,* 33 (2): 20–25.

Foucault, Michel. 1980a. *Herculine Barbin, Being the Recently Discovered Memoirs of a 19th-Century Hermaphrodite.* Translated by Richard McDougall. New York: Colophon.

Foucault, Michel. 1980b. *The History of Sexuality, Volume I: An Introduction.* Translated by Robert Hurley. New York: Viking.

Furth, Charlotte. 1993. Androgynous males and deficient females: Biology and gender boundaries in 16th- and 17th-century China. In *The Lesbian and Gay Studies Reader,* ed. Henry Abelove, Michéle Aina Barale, and David M. Halperin: 479–497. New York: Routledge.

Geertz, Clifford. 1984. *Local Knowledge.* New York: Basic Books.

Hendricks, Melissa. 1993. Is it a Boy or a Girl? *Johns Hopkins Magazine,* November, 10–16.

Herdt, Gilbert. 1994. Mistaken Sex: Culture, Biology, and the Third Sex in New Guinea. In *Third Sex, Third Gender: Beyond Sexual Dimorphism in Culture and History,* ed. Gilbert Herdt: 419–446. New York: Zone Books.

Holmes, Morgan. 1994. Medical Politics and Cultural Imperatives: Intersexuality Beyond Pathology and Erasure. Master's thesis, York University.

Kessler, Suzanne. 1990. The Medical Construction of Gender: Case Management of Intersexual Infants. *Signs: Journal of Women in Culture and Society,* 16 (1): 3–26.

Kessler, Suzanne J. and Wendy McKenna. 1978. *Gender: An Ethnomethodological Approach.* New York: John Wiley and Sons.

Laqueur, Thomas. 1990. *Making Sex: Body and Gender from the Greeks to Freud.* Cambridge: Harvard University Press.

Lee, Ellen Hyun-Ju. 1994. Producing Sex: An Interdisciplinary Perspective on Sex Assignment Decisions for Intersexuals. Senior thesis, Brown University.

Money, John. 1991. *Biographies of Gender and Hermaphroditism in Paired Comparisons.* Edited by John Money and H. Musaph. Clinical Supplement to the Handbook of Sexology. New York: Elsevier.

Morris, John McL. 1957. Intersexuality. *Journal of the American Medical Association,* 163 (7): 538–542.

Nanda, Serena. 1994. Hijras: An Alternative Sex and Gender Role in India. In *Third Sex, Third Gender: Beyond Sexual Dimorphism in Culture and History,* ed. Gilbert Herdt: 373–418. New York: Zone Books.

Natarajan, Anita. 1996. Medical Ethics and Truth-Telling in the Case of Androgen

Insensitivity Syndrome. *Canadian Medical Association Journal,* 154: 568–570.

Pool, Robert E. 1994. *Eve's Rib: The Biological Roots of Sex Differences.* New York: Crown Publishers.

Roscoe, Will. 1991. *The Zuni Man-Woman.* Albuquerque: University of New Mexico Press.

Slijper, Froukje M.E., S.L.S. Drop, J.C. Molenaar, and R.J. Scholtmeijer. 1994. Neonates With Abnormal Genital Development Assigned the Female Sex: Parent Counseling. *Journal of Sex Education and Therapy,* 20 (1): 9–17.

Vance, Carol S. 1991. Anthropology Rediscovers Sexuality: A Theoretical Comment. *Social Science and Medicine,* 33.

Walker, Alice. 1992. *Possessing the Secret of Joy.* New York: Simon and Schuster.

A Safe Trip Home
Dawn Dougherty

Dawn Dougherty is a writer and consultant living in Boston. Her work has appeared in Bay Windows, Sojourner, Paramour, Lesbian Short Fiction, *and* Best Lesbian Erotica. *She has long red nails and loves to belly-dance.*

My lover came back from grocery shopping and said she'd been called a bull dyke in the parking lot. Apparently she beat some guy to a spot and he yelled at her through his open window. She had a smile on her face as she told the story. We both knew that his attempt to insult her was actually a source of pride because my lover clearly is a bull dyke. He was merely stating the obvious. It's like screaming "Trees!" at a forest.

The next week we were driving home from Easter dinner with her parents. I had the seat reclined and was dozing off when we stopped at a light. I heard a car beep behind us.

"Is he beeping at us?" I asked, assuming correctly that it was a man. I looked up in time to see my lover flip him off.

"What are you doing that for?" I asked nervously as I sat up. Before she got a chance to answer he had pulled up beside us.

"You fucking faggot!" he screamed. The veins in his neck bulged as he swerved and nearly hit the side of our car. "You fucking faggot...I wasn't honking at you. You goddamn fucking faggot!"

I was stunned and looked from this maniac to my lover and back again. I was terrified he was going to hit our car or get out and come after us. But the whole time I wondered if he actually thought she was a gay man or if it was just a matter of semantics; maybe "you fucking dyke" didn't hold the same sting for him. Then, as quickly as he had pulled up, he cut us off in traffic and made an illegal left turn into a porn shop a half-mile down the street. Happy Easter.

We drove on in stunned silence until I asked her rather belligerently why she had flipped him off.

"Because he was being an asshole!" she said. "He was beeping because the person five cars in front of us wasn't moving fast enough."

"You shouldn't have done that. How do you know what someone is going to do?" I countered. I knew I was blaming the victim but was too upset to care. "What if he had a gun?"

"So I'm just supposed to let some fucking moron honk like a maniac or nearly hit us and not defend myself?"

"Just don't do it when I'm in the car with you."

"Fine."

We didn't speak until we pulled into the parking spot in front of my house. "That was really scary," I said, finally admitting to fear.

"Shit like that happens to me a lot. I just don't want to be taken advantage of anymore."

We sat staring at each other. She was letting me know she could handle herself but also that we live in two different worlds. She's butch, I'm femme. And although I've never doubted the difference in our experiences, I've never been confronted with it so directly.

The week after the "fucking faggot" incident she came home and said someone else had called her a faggot. Again I wonder why "faggot" is used. This incident didn't hold the same charm as the "bull dyke" one. I think the harassment was beginning to wear us both down.

Lately I envision my lover as a open target driving down the road in her red pickup and short hair—motorists driving her off the road before they let her cut in front of them in traffic. At the wheel of my four-door sedan, with red nails and long hair, no one even looks my way. I'd like to think our experiences are different because I'm a considerate driver, but I know better.

My lover enrages people easily. She is neither a feminine woman nor a polite, androgynous lesbian. There's nothing subtle about her dykeness, and her mere presence pisses people off. Her walk, her clothes, her truck—they all flaunt her orientation in a loud, authoritative cry. She is routinely mistaken for a man. Once some drunken girls tried to pick her up. There are plenty of nervous stares when she enters the ladies' room. Everywhere we go, people stare. Whenever I am out with her, I watch as people try to figure her out.

When I'm brave I taunt them by saying, "They must think you're cute, honey." When I'm not brave I pray that the young, muscular white boys on the porch with beers in hand aren't paying attention to the lesbians stopped at the light in front of frat row.

What's it like to walk around in her shoes day in and day out? Are my high heels any safer? I know she worries about me too. As I go in to get us coffee, she waits in the car making a mental note of how many men are in the parking lot and which of them is looking at me. It's times like these that being a woman overwhelms me, and I think neither one of us has a chance.

Even for the odd moments of fear, I love to be out with her. She makes me visible in my own community, and it thrills me. When I walk down the street with my lover, I am guilty by association. She makes our presence known with her swagger and muscles, and I am so grateful and turned on by her energy that I can't keep my hands off her.

A week after the traffic incident, I told her I was sorry about my reaction. I told her she could do whatever she needed to defend herself, and if flipping that guy off felt right, then so be it.

"He deserved it," she said.

"I know."

Would I Dare?
Toni Amato

Toni Amato is a 31-year-old working-class butch living in Boston. S/he has been writing since s/he was knee-high to a grasshopper, and hir work has appeared in Leather Women II *as well as* Best Lesbian Erotica 1998 *and* 1999, Turn Magazine, *and* Fish Tank. *Hir two passions are writing and making femmes happy in any way s/he can.*

"Where the women come and go, speaking of Michelangelo." I don't know what old T.S. meant, but I know what those lines, like clarion bells, mean to me. The floors covered over with crushed oyster shells, the pearls and pulsating life long gone. What does he say? Do I dare?

I read it as young dyke without a name yet. Gay, lesbian, dyke, queer—none had found a footing. Ah, but those women. Always older, better-dressed, more erudite. And always so much, so indisputably women in that intimidating way Eliot caught for me.

It feels that way each time my pulse quickens. Each time my tongue feels larger than my mouth, heavy like a sleeping, inarticulate thing. Would I dare? Would I have the courage—me—to speak a word or toss a gesture into her flow. To try to stop her long enough to see me, to settle gently on those immaculate crushed shells, to speak with me of whether pigs have wings?

Now the women are gathering in smoke-filled rooms, now the women are gathering, and I almost feel like an intruder, like when I use a roadside rest stop and someone asks, "Do you think it's a boy or a girl?"

It's a girl, Mrs. Robinson, a girl. Sitting at a corner table, with perhaps a drink in front of her, adding silently and ceaselessly to the smoke hovering like tossed veils. It's a girl, full of awe and wonder and amazement and desire thicker than the air or the shattered mollusks beneath her feet.

Or it could be a boy, if that's what you want. It could, really, be a 17-year-old boy, at the mercy of hormones, full of romance and quivering lust, full of flowers and chocolates and bad poetry for the giving. It's a girl. Or a boy, if you want it. However you want it, following with smoke filled, teary eyes, the rustle of a skirt, the curve of a shoulder, the line of a jaw. Would you want it, boy or girl? Would I dare?

Would I dare to stand and touch your hand, gently lay palm to elbow, cupping the fine joint in a callused embrace? Would I dare to disturb the softly sifting smoke, make waves that would eddy around you, around us?

The women come and go, speaking of Michelangelo, and I have measured out my life in coffee spoons. Sometimes at my small table, an empty chair, and would I dare? Would I dare?

There

Not really a locker room, as in athletes suiting up for the big game while their families wait on the sidelines, wait to go wild on the long shot or the final run into the end zone. A changing room with small cubicles for folded shirts, skirts, trousers, and underwear. Shoes left in the hallway. One neat row of loafers, sneakers, high heels, and boots under a long wooden bench.

She doesn't know it, my lover, but being here at this bathhouse, doing these ablutions, is the most difficult thing I have ever done. Harder than all the childhood horror shows. Harder than boot camp. More trying, even, than leaving those little black pills behind, slowing down enough to feel.

Because what I feel now, what I am, is naked, and exposed is a difficult thing to be. Showing breast and belly and ass in contradiction to my self-imaginations is excruciating, humiliating.

Well, used to be. It's better now. Mostly. I still avoid full-length mirrors. Still place those little black censor's triangles over some of her favorite places. Just so long as she doesn't go and tell me about it. She's found a way to them, though. Found a way to melt the stone.

It's awkward here in this fluorescent room that smells of girl sweat and sometimes girl blood; this room that smells of powdery deodorant and hair spray and even lipstick. In here where a big part of me—or maybe a small part of me (I don't want to brag)—knows it does not belong.

It's hard, because I know I'm not supposed to stare. Because I don't want to make anyone so much as one fraction as uncomfortable as I am as I strip down to boxers, white T-shirt. As I strip to nothing but the tattoo on my thigh.

Even then, even when the boxers are gone, carefully folded, into the cubicle; even then, some woman will look at me and see the thing that isn't there, mostly, but kind of is there, only not really, and she'll scream, "There's a man in here. Goddamn it! A man."

This has happened. It could happen again. What is most awful is that for a split second my discomfort will go away. For the most fleeting of moments, what I feel like and what she sees match up. Even naked.

Then, as I watch the contempt on her face, I'm just a freak again. And everybody, all these gorgeous women I've been trying so very hard not to offend, will be upset and angry. There will be no possibility of an exit stage left, no rock to crawl beneath.

I couldn't do this alone, just the way I cannot use a public restroom alone. I can no longer stand the whispers, the sideways looks—even once a slap in the face. She doesn't know, my lover, what a difference her angry responses make to me. "Yes, it's a girl. And it has ears." She doesn't know, my lover, what she has saved me from by her seeing and wanting what isn't there, not really, except for sometimes, when it's really, really there. Doesn't know what she's saved me from by her seeing and loving and gently not acknowledging—mostly—what's always, really there.

What she does know is that I need her hand on my thigh when the stewardess calls me "Sir." That I need her hand even more when the stewardess calls me "Ma'am." What my lover does know is that I didn't know a thing about the deep, slow release of a sauna or so many other undressed things. That now when the cop does a double take over my

ID, when the cashier is hesitant to accept my credit card signature, when some lady pulls a face as I shut the stall door—when these things happen, I laugh, and think that they are jealous because they can't walk between the worlds, because they don't know the half of it, and because they better watch out, better be careful, better step lightly, because I'll have my girlfriend beat them up.

Penis Envy

Penis envy. That's what they call it when a little girl wants to be a little boy, right? Except I never thought that shrinky, exposed, bouncy little frog thing was anything to envy. Didn't want one. Nope.

What I did want was a yellow Tonka Truck, a silver pistol with a box of red paper caps, boots with spurs. And a girl. A girl to hold my arm like I was holding up her world. A girl to rest her cheek on the lapel of my leather jacket, to cup her fingers around the back of my head where short hairs would grow if only I could have the cut I wanted.

Forty, no 30, no maybe only 25 years ago, I could have gone to jail for impersonating a member of the opposite sex. Three articles of clothing for your biological gender, or off you go. Off you go to where the nice man in the blue uniform is more than happy to remind you of just exactly how you are built. Let's see: muscle shirt instead of a bra, boxer shorts. I'm in trouble. Since the queens and butches pelted the cops with pocket change at Stonewall, I can dress any way I want. Mostly. But, hey, where do you stick the wings of a sanitary pad in boxers?

Penis envy. Someone said, "Sure, if it would get me a decent job, you bet I'd want one." I want a suit, though. And a girl in a tight red dress beside me. Or maybe swim trunks to show off stomach muscles like a washboard, which I don't have now but I did in the Army. I got kicked out for being queer. That's a good one. Twenty women in khaki and leather boots, communal showers, no men, and you gotta go home if you're queer. Military intelligence.

Penis envy. Like when the no-neck monsters leaning against their pickups, waiting to harass the women leaving the bar, yelled, "What you need is a real dick," and my girlfriend answered, "What, like you?" and I thought, *Help me, Jesus. I sure as shit can't fight these guys,* but planted my engineer boots square on the asphalt anyway. A real man dies with his boots on.

Penis Envy

Halloween in the Castro. Mardi Gras. I'm walking down the street in my old uniform—the best I could do for a costume—watching a beautiful boy in gossamer float and flutter. Once more, the no-necks. They grow and spread like fungus, like mildew in a damp, dark place. And they, all of them, such brave men, start in on this reed-thin apparition. So I mouth off, ask them why they come to the Castro if they don't like queers. After all, I don't live in the Bible Belt.

"Shut up, dyke. What you need is a real dick."

I plant my feet. "I've got one, right here," and reach for the bulge of a rolled-up sock, remembering how being loved made the Straw Horse real. Remembering my girlfriend who cuts my hair, folds my T-shirts and boxers, and every now and then bleaches the bloodstains out of my button-downs when my mouth goes into gear before my brain does. Then I remember it's me against this pack. Bad odds.

They start toward me, and I regret, for a moment, that my muscle mass doesn't match my attitude. And then another pack of men turns. These with full beards, high heels, and gorgeous gowns. They step between me and the no-necks.

"That's right, honeys. She's got one that stays hard all night."

Penis envy. Ha. Because, see, me and my people, we've got balls.

Wanting Men
Lionhart

Lionhart is a feminist therapist who specializes in working with queer and trans families. It is with great sadness that she uses a pseudonym; there are, however, many people who think it inappropriate for a therapist to be public about desire. She is a longtime femme activist, a dyke mom, and a womon whose passion is not easily contained, despite the dangers (just ask her guy).

I find myself looking at men on the streets. What a strange thing for a lesbian to do. Where did these desires come from? I'm on the verge of an orgasm thinking about her wonderful, thickly hairy legs and thighs and how they meet her wet, woolly pussy, and suddenly there it is—wanting a penis where? In my mouth—then I come. Very strange.

I have never denied my fantasies. I have fantasized about men and never once felt guilty. This is a new kind of desire. Wanting a man for real, in my bed, in my mouth. In my mouth.

I ask a womon lover, who is bisexual, if she likes sucking cock. Her mouth is on my breast, her cunt grinding into my thigh; I already know the answer. She nods, brushing her finger on my clitoris.

This is not just a dildo fantasy. I have loved many a butch womon who's worn a strap-on in public and loved the idea of getting me pregnant. I have sucked my womon lover's cock and was relieved we could remove it when the scene was done. This desire cannot be removed when the scene is done.

I am not the first lesbian to desire a man. To be honest, half of the womyn in my life have been fucking men for a decade (though not the same half who pack in public). I've never considered fucking men to be lesbian behavior. I have demanded that the lesbians in my life who do fuck men call themselves bisexual. It seems only fair. Sometimes they argued that they weren't bisexual and insisted they were lesbians. I thought they were just afraid of rejection from the lesbian community. Oh, yeah, like I'm feeling right now.

I've heard Holly Near has said she feels like a lesbian when fucking womyn and feels like a lesbian when fucking men. How can you feel like a lesbian when fucking men?

I assume she means that she feels sexually empowered in her body and in charge of her sexuality. I assume she enjoys it. But does that make it lesbian? Can't sex be considered empowered and enjoyable when it's not lesbian?

When I first came out at 21, after 10 years of bisexuality, actively making love to both womyn and men, a male ex-lover said, "Everyone knows you'll go back to fucking men. You like it too much." The truth was that I rarely liked it; it hurt and made me feel bad. This was 1979, and in the crowd I hung out with, his comment was bad politics—even among straight people. I lie in womyn's arms laughing at his misplaced arrogance. I am still wanting to prove him wrong.

For over 15 years, I slept only with womyn. When I told four different friends that I had taken a new lover they each asked, "A man or a woman?" This is before I had openly acknowledged that men were even an option, before I had even admitted to myself that fucking men was an option. When I started to tell lesbian friends I was thinking of fucking men, they said, "I'm not surprised." Why were they not surprised? How could they see something in me that I couldn't yet recognize?

I felt exposed. A friend said I should feel "visible," that dykes are seeing me and accepting me (very unusual lesbian behavior). I do not feel visible; I feel transparent. Mostly though, I hear the voice of my male ex-lover, with a dyke tone: *We always knew you'd go back to men. We knew you were never really one of us.*

Suddenly my long hair and long skirts and lipstick fantasies are suspect again. For 25 years I've been fucking, kissing, loving, and hurting over womyn; for 15 years I have been sexual only with womyn. And now my whole life revolves around a relentless desire for dick.

I have always denied the stereotype, but it does seem true that the more femme the lesbian, the more likely she's not a lesbian.

I know what those lesbians are thinking, because I know what this lesbian thinks when womyn start to fuck men again. Traitor. They are not the old angry voices of the '70s; they do not accuse me of wanting heterosexual privilege or of sleeping with the enemy. They support my finding pleasure and love, and they want me to move with my heart. It is, however, my heart that makes me a traitor. I am no longer one of them. I am different—a half-breed. A womon with strange desires.

My bisexual friends listen quietly. They just nod and smile. They know this process intimately, so it is not particularly interesting to them. They have heard this coming-out story over and over again. Though bored, they are not judgmental. They will let me talk late into the night...

I say, "I'm turned on to some men, but can't imagine being close to a man." I say, "I'm close to some men, but can't imagine fucking them." I say, "Men feel so alien—sometimes it is this very alienness that attracts me." I say, "I love womyn, am moved by them, love them, feel romantic toward them, want them to take me, want to take them—I do not feel any of these feelings toward men." I say, "I want to feel a man on top of me, inside me. I don't think I want more."

They nod and smile.

I say, "I may not want to act on this." I say, "There is no one in particular whom I am attracted to." They nod and smile. I feel at home among bisexuals. They are open and diverse and honestly in their sexual bodies.

I feel at home among lesbians. They are strong and clear and virgin. My bisexual lover told me she liked that I was lesbian. Later she told me that when she listened to me talk about coming out, it sounded like I'd compromised a lot of myself to fit in. Ouch!

I had been saying the same thing for years, but hearing her say it freezes my heart. Wasn't coming out all about coming home?

Another friend says, "When I first found the lesbian community, it was the closest place to home I'd ever found, but...not quite."

I find myself angry again. Angry that I'd cut my hair off and left my sweet male lover—the first man who'd ever pleasured me with pene-tration. Angry that there had been no space for me to talk about my femme fantasies or my S/M fantasies. Angry that I wore flannel shirts and hiking boots because they'd shamed me when I wore pretty dress-es. Angry that I, who had always insisted on being *me*, compromised so much of myself—for what?

Oh, yeah, because I loved womyn. You see, womyn wouldn't love me if I kept loving men. It was the times; it was the rules. No fence-sitting allowed. I did the only thing a lesbian-feminist could do. I threw my male lover out, cut off my hair, and made gagging sounds when anyone discussed penises.

A friend asks, "Are you sorry you did it?" and I suddenly realize there was nothing else I could've done. I loved womyn. I love how womyn have moved me. They move me to anger and tears. Her breasts fill my memory. I hunger to smell her hair. My heart jumps when I hear her voice on the phone.

A dyke friend sighs, "I know I'm a lesbian because womyn just kill me." A bisexual friend says, "I don't get it." Womyn kill me. I get it.

Men were always easy. Easy to please, fun to be with, rarely chal-lenging. I did not experience my male lovers as abusive or angry or dom-inant. I sometimes experienced them as lazy, dull, foolish, or removed. I left them because they didn't do the dishes, didn't have brilliant thoughts, and didn't have breasts.

Womyn have always killed me. They never love me enough and won't sit still long enough to get dull. They have beaten and raped me. They have put their hands into my heart cave and, with tender looks on their faces, mangled my heart into unrecognizable shapes.

Still, my heart soars when she kisses me. I remember her weight on my body and I want to be...filled? A friend says, "You want a woman with a penis." A male lover in the '70s once said I wanted a man with breasts.

This is not simply about desire, although maybe it should be, for lov-ing womyn has always been full of unmanageable feelings. Wanting my butch girlfriend to kiss me at age 11 was scary. Knowing I was in love with my best friend at 15 was overwhelming. Joining a lesbian support group at 19 was invigorating. Leaving my male lover and naming myself lesbian at 21 was terrifying. Having my womon lover tie my hands down on the bed, gag my mouth, and force her whole hand inside me was intense and expansive and exhilarating.

Yet one of the most transformative moments in this lesbian life took place alone reading Jan Clausen's article in *Outlook* magazine in 1990. I read Jan's account of her choice to walk outside the parameters of the lesbian community to love a man, and wondered if I wouldn't have the courage to do the same.

Is this then the question? Do I have the courage to risk fucking a man—an unknown man, an abstract "man"—for no better reason than I simply feel like it? Why does wanting a man demand more courage than any other desire that has rocked my world?

Does having this desire change my identity? If I desire men for another 20 years but never sleep with one, do I remain a lesbian? If I sleep with a man, do I automatically become bisexual? If I never sleep with a man again, do I avoid being bisexual?

A lesbian friend once met a man on an airplane and felt more connected to him than she'd ever felt to anyone in her whole life. He asked for her phone number, and she said, "No. You don't fit into my life."

Now I ask, "What kind of life are we living when our deepest human connections simply don't fit into our lives?"

A lover tells a sweet story: She was a young lesbian when she met her male lover. They were close, loving friends, and people kept asking, "Hey, what's going on between the two of you?" They'd laugh because they knew she was a lesbian and that they were just close friends. Then they became closer. They called themselves cuddle friends, and then sensual friends. She says, "When we started having orgasms we had to admit we were lovers." Indeed.

Long before we became lovers, I asked her if she ever missed being with womyn. She said no. I was her first womon lover in 10 years. When we became lovers I asked her again—while her face was between my legs. She again said no. She was satisfied then, and she is satisfied now.

This is a different kind of bisexuality than whatever my body knows. I always craved womyn, even when I was partnered with men. I have never not wanted womyn lovers. It has taken 15 years to miss male lovers. The reverse could never have been true.

Is that what my lesbian friends who fucked men meant years ago? Is this the difference between lesbians who fuck men, bisexual lesbians, and bisexuals—the degree and insistence of queer desire?

There seem to be as many forms of desire as people in my life: My ex-lover's male lover has a male lover but identifies as heterosexual. He explains, "It's just not that important; it doesn't feel like a core issue in my sexuality, although I'm glad to be open to a man in this way." Is this denial, internalized homophobia, or is he simply telling his own truth?

The first great love of my life has been in heterosexual primary relationships for the past two decades. She often lusts after womyn, and has had herself one or two. But men move her, womyn titillate her. I have never not wanted her, but for 20 years she's rebuffed me. Lately she seems interested. Does my new desire for men make my lesbian world feel less like a vortex that will engulf her?

One womon I know identifies as a dyke but has only male lovers. She explains that dyke identity is essential in a heteropatriarchal world. Aren't false identities the hallmark of the heteropatriarchal world?

Another friend (who died recently) called herself lesbian but loved fucking men. She was a lesbian, she said, and swore me to secrecy. And now I wonder: Would loving a man make her love me less? I cannot imagine loving a man as easily, as deeply as I have loved womyn, but then I guess some of us have had more practice.

Another friend who loves, actively loves, both men and womyn, resists the word *bisexual* because she says the word *bisexual* is not inclusive enough. She says she is not "gender-erotic"—that gender is not what she notices in a sexual partner. She says, "If women who sleep with women threaten the structures of patriarchy, then women who sleep with whomever they please are outright anarchists." She defines her sexual identity as Sovereign.

I am beginning to understand that many of us with many different sexualities have lived, hidden, and passed in the lesbian community not only because it was the best show in town, but because it was the only live girl show in town. If you loved womyn enough to let it move your life, the lesbian-feminist community had to be home; there was nowhere else to go. A radical dyke friend who always talks about the old days and still calls men mutants and dogs, gently confesses, "I've always been more physically attracted to men than womyn."

Too many of us have chosen to live in sexually ambiguous, sexually boring, sexually dead lesbian relationships because it wasn't safe to talk about desire—desire for cock, desire for pussy, desire for leather, desire for diversity. Exploring my desire for men has led me in an interesting circle—back to my incredible passion for womyn. My queer world will have to stretch (again) to make room for my fantasies, and perhaps even an affair or two. It will have to stretch to make room for whatever I desire.

Finally I realize what I am so afraid of. I am afraid that men and penises have so much power in this heteropatriarchal world that simply desiring one can invalidate 25 years of deep womon-loving. I'm afraid that lesbianism is so fragile it needs to be protected by an iron fence. I am afraid that by desiring a cock, I will be excommunicated, torn away from the world of womyn. I am afraid that if I allow myself to open, perhaps I will want more. This is why a lesbian wanting a man demands so much courage. Courage to stand outside of identity politics, to insist that our community grow to accept all of us.

My lesbianism is as sure and solid as the Himalayas, as predictable as the seasons and the phases of the moon, as familiar as a womon in my arms ("Wherever I go, there's one thing I know, I'm sure to have a womon around me"). My desire for men is as fleeting as good chocolate and ripe strawberries—not always available, sometimes bitter and disappointing, often intoxicating as nectar, somewhat allergic, and extremely tempting.

I can live with all these desires. I will not compromise myself again. Fitting in is less important than filling out. There is a revolution afoot, and it is stretching the parameters of the old gay life. The hundredth monkey. A friend says, "Oy, I'm not ready for this century." But she is. She is.

Just when I thought I'd made some sense of these desires for men and had come to peace with them, my ex-lover called. The butch who couldn't communicate and who could never fuck me right. She has something to share, something important, something very personal. She has decided to come out as a transgendered person—bi-gendered, s/he calls it. S/he has come to realize that s/he has both a male body and a female body. Hir language may be new, but the experience is familiar.

It was hir male body I always wanted. I'd called it butch. S/he says that when s/he is in hir male body s/he desires men; when s/he is in hir female body s/he desires womyn. In other words, s/he's as queer as a $3 bill.

Suddenly, a fog begins to clear. If I desired hir male body, and hir male body desires men, and when she is in hir female body she desires womyn, then s/he must've wanted me womon to womon (or man to man?), while I wanted hir butch to femme (Dare I say, male to female?). Suddenly our sex problems become very clear.

I always felt hir switch. As I filled with desire, wanting hir hardness, hir maleness, s/he would become soft, almost girly, and it was like someone pulled the plug on the bathtub, the desire leaked out of me, leaving me—us—empty.

This starts me thinking about the lover before hir. The one with the sweet curls in her hair, the big round belly, and the soft eyes. The kinky one, where anything goes. She loves my femme self, calls me bitch, and desires to fell me with hardness, to force me into submission.

Somehow though, it never quite worked. I am beginning to see what went wrong. This one wanted butch/femme, boy/girl sex, and I wanted lezzie sex. I loved hir female body and wanted to touch her. S/he wanted to give me hir male body. When I tried to touch hir breasts, I was reminding hir that she was a womon and was therefore rejecting her power. The lover s/he picked after me identified as a heterosexual woman (although she too used to be a radical dyke). When my ex-lover told me this new lover wouldn't touch her (after all she did identify as straight), I thought, how terrible, such internalized homophobia. Now I am beginning to understand how, by ignoring the girl body, the boy could feel his power. It got old fast, but for a while it worked, fed the rejected boy place inside.

I began this piece saying I hadn't had a man in 15 years. I am beginning to suspect that I've had many men. They'd called themselves butches.

I suppose none of this makes sense if you just think about biological bodies. These girls definitely had female bodies, tits and ass, and oh, so lovely to touch. But there is no doubt that these womyn have also had dicks. I've never said this out loud before, because dick is a dirty lesbian word. But I have been filled by womyn's dicks, and no, they are not "just" dildoes.

A bisexual womon and I were watching a lesbian porn movie (boring). She says, "I don't understand what pleasure a womon would get from sucking a silicone dildo; her partner can't feel it." What she doesn't say, but I suspect she thinks, is, "If you want to suck a cock, why not go for the real thing?" After all, that's what she does. How can I explain how sucking my butch's silicone dick (*Shhh, don't tell her it's not flesh.*) is way hotter than any "real" dick I've ever had?

In 1980 I was at a lesbian committee meeting at a womyn's health collective. Someone passed around a picture taken from a het porn magazine of two womyn—one wearing a dildo and harness and the other on her knees sucking her off. The dykes all laughed at the picture: How foolish men were for thinking lesbians did such things. I remember thinking the picture looked hot. I remember feeling very dirty and sick.

Years later: I am at a lesbian S/M party. A womon in a prom dress, with high heels and red lipstick, hikes up her dress and out pops a large penis—is it real or Memorex? Another womon crawls over to suck her off. The room roars with laughter. Massive genderfuck. Great turn on. The fantasy is better than the reality.

Years later still: I come home from work tired. My lover is visiting; she is propped up in bed reading a lesbian novel. I put down my knapsack, go over to the bed, kiss her hello, curl into her arms, melt into her body, roll over on top of her and…pushing into my body is her—dick! Hard and grinding. I gasp as never before, pull her close to me…have I ever been so hot, wanting her dick? I pull off her clothes, my clothes, sit on the lavender cock that is as much hers as her cunt has always been, and I am fucking her. She is inside me, rocking and rolling. I am alone in my ecstasy. She is withdrawn, sullen, sad. "What is it, honey?" I ask, gasping for breath.

She looks at me, frightened, "I can't feel it," she says. "I can't feel it."

"Did you expect to?" I ignorantly ask.

"Yes," she nods, "I did."

Another lover says s/he can feel hir cock in a womon. S/he can feel it.

I have not yet told my bisexual ex-lover this, but I suspect it's true. Sucking a silicon dildo is hot, in part because it is taboo. Bad lesbian behavior. Within the context of the lesbian feminist community, putting my lover's cock in my mouth, in my pussy, whether or not she can feel it, is the radical edge of consciousness. We are doing what the hets think we do, what the dykes know we don't. We are doing what the hets do and the dykes can't. We have transcended the limits of the bodies we wear. We are being boy and girl dykes.

Some lesbians I know have gay male sex. I know this is what they do. I don't quite know how they do it because I don't really have a cock—not in any of my bodies. I am all girl. I like being a girl.

I like being a girl fucking girls and a girl fucking boys and a girl fucking boy-girls. I like being a girl fucking butches and a girl fucking femmes. I like being a girl being fucked by boys and girls in all kinds of bodies and costumes. I sometimes even feel a little butch, but I don't have a cock of my own. I do have two dildoes in my drawer, and sometimes I want to fill a womon with my whole hand, but I am always a girl.

Years ago I thought that since I was such a girly-girl I couldn't be a lesbian, because lesbians were so much more masculine than I was. But then I figured out there was a name for me, that I was a femme. This was incredibly liberating, and I loved being a femme, and I loved loving butch womyn. What I didn't know was that some of the womyn I was loving were not womyn. Or not "just" womyn, not only womyn. I didn't know womyn could be men. I thought male was a dirty word. I thought wanting men meant I wasn't lesbian anymore. How could I have known how many lesbians were really men?

Indeed, I have been wanting men. I am beginning to understand how a lesbian can really want men. I am beginning to understand how much bodies with breasts *and* dicks really do turn me on. Is this bisexuality? How do I label my sexual identity?

One friend identifies as a female-bodied butch. He says he is neither a womon nor a lesbian, and he takes only womyn lovers. Another friend says that s/he is a lesbian but is also a man. Yet another says s/he is a masculine womon. I know two people who identify as transgendered womyn—one is a biological man and the other a biological woman. The bioman dresses and lives as a womon; the biowoman dresses and lives as a man. Both call themselves lesbian.

I have come to understand that, although there is not yet a name for my desires, I am a womon, a lesbian womon, and a femme, who deeply desires male presence in female bodies. I love men on top of me and inside me. This is my kind of lesbianism.

Twenty Passings
Stacey Montgomery

Stacey Montgomery is a Tryke who lives in Somerville, Mass. She designs computer games for a living and is generally seen with the Lesbian Avengers of Boston or other troublemakers.

1. We are in the bathroom. "You can pee standing up," my sister says.

"I can?" She is five years older than I am, and she knows everything. Adults are often incomprehensible, so I rely on her.

"Yes, because you're a boy and I'm a girl."

"Oh," I say. I am thinking that I am in trouble; and suddenly I'm afraid. I know somehow that I should not discuss this. Ever. I am 5.

2. It is Halloween, but the air feels warm for autumn. My father takes my sister and me around the neighborhood. I am wearing a costume my mother made from a pattern in a magazine with a strawberry cake on the cover. It is made of long, shiny fabric that flashes silver.

We go from house to house. I know these houses, and this neighborhood, though I do not know all of these people. One nice man gives us candy and speaks to my father. "Is she dressed as a princess?" he asks.

"No," my father says, his voice light. "He's a space alien." He laughs.

My gut clenches for a moment, but it's OK, nothing to be afraid of. I look up. The moon glows the color of parchment. I know I am still safe.

3. We are naked. The afternoon sun tattoos us with longitudes of venetian blinds. Our hearts beat in separate rhythms, but our skin runs together in the heat. I am beyond my boundaries. I look up at her. Sunbeams dance in the droplets of sweat that roll down her face. "I'm a girl," I blurt out. She looks down at me for a moment, her dark eyes shining. Suddenly I remember what I have risked. Then she nods.

"What's your name?" she asks.

4. "I'm sorry," she says, "I just can't do this anymore." Neither of us speaks. It seems to me suddenly that if I never speak again, time will stop and I'll never have to deal with what comes after this moment. I can't possibly face what comes after this moment. It stretches until we can't bear it anymore. She speaks, and the moment is broken. Time starts up again.

"I think that you are a very special man. I love you. But you're not a woman. I'm gay, and I need to deal with that."

This has been coming for a long time, but I have no idea what to do. My throat is lined with razors—it is not safe to talk. *If she doesn't see it,* I think, *it isn't there.*

Later, looking in a mirror, a boy looks back at me. I don't see it either.

5. The dusk breeze is cool after the heat of the afternoon. The harborside is swarming with young women, and the tent still echoes with the sound of the concert. The place is emptying out slowly, and we wait in our chairs for the crowd to thin. She sits next to me. I'm wearing her wedding ring on a chain around my neck.

A guard walks by. "OK, ladies, the show is over. Let's go," he says to us. I am shocked. I passed as a woman.

"Oh, no," she says to our companion. "I bet he'll be talking about this for days." Her voice seems hard but when I turn to look, her face softens with a smile.

6. I am surrounded by transexuals. They are all well into transition. I am trying to listen and learn. I feel like an outsider among them, which is disappointing. They seem older than I am and very serious. The support group

meets in a small dining room. The woman who runs the group and I have the same therapist. It was my therapist who suggested this group to me.

They talk about passing. "I don't really pass," I say, and I notice a wry smile making the rounds. I know what they're thinking—I don't pass at all, and I'm not trying. Do they doubt my sincerity? My gender?

I feel my spine stiffen. Why am I suddenly stubborn? Like so much of what is bubbling up inside my body, it is a mystery to me.

7. The march unfolds under a bright, hot sky. I watch the parade form and begin. From the sidelines, I watch a few hundred queer women start down the street. It is a wonderful sight.

Even in my Transexual Menace T-shirt, I seem invisible here, perhaps just a gay boy who has come to support his queer sisters. I watch them go by. A few women notice me and call for me to join the parade. Suddenly exposed and less comfortable, I swallow something and step off the curb. We all march together in the clean summer heat.

At first I'm marching by myself, alone with hundreds of women. Eventually I see some faces I know—Lesbian Avengers. I march with them the rest of the way. After the march we mill about and talk. I feel distinctly out of place. I mention an idea for tryke T-shirts. "They'd say 'Trykes Like Dykes' on the front," I explain, "and 'Dykes Like Trykes' on the back. I wonder if anyone would wear them?"

One of the Avengers looks at me. She is very pretty. I feel something pass between us. "I would wear it," she says. I wonder what she sees, what I've passed as.

8. It is the Fourth of July, and I am an Avenger. We have gathered near the Boston Esplanade, where the holiday crowd comes for music and fireworks.

We hand out fliers demanding better access to health care for women. The air is thick and sticky on my skin. I stand near one of the subway exits and, as people emerge, offer them our flyer. My new Lesbian Avenger T-shirt is snug against my body, revealing the shape of my new breasts.

People give the other Avengers double takes as they walk by. The first one is *Who are you?* and the second seems to be *Hey, you're a dyke!*

When they take their fliers from me, they do triple takes. What is the third question they are asking? And what would the correct answer be?

9. It is late, and I'm in my own neighborhood, just grabbing some essentials at the convenience store. The area has always seemed safe to me. I often walk here at night without concern. After all, I was raised a male.

I turn a corner, and a group of young men is on the sidewalk ahead of me, just sort of milling about waiting for some evening plan to get started. I would rather not walk by them, but it is too late. If I cross the street now, it will be obvious and attract their attention. I am unshaven and casual, so I know they will read me as a boy. If I want to be safe then, I should act like a boy. I straighten my spine and walk as if I don't care.

As I approach, one of them looks my way. "Hey, young lady!" He would say more, but I am suddenly under a streetlight, and he sees me more clearly. He is suddenly silent. My stomach turns icy, but I keep walking.

I can hear some small commotion as I pass. His mates know they missed something, and they ask him, but he is slow to respond. I can hear the tone of this voice, though—he is angry. As I stride away, I realize he is in no hurry to draw their attention to his mistake.

A minute later, I am home and safe. I wonder how close I just came to being in real trouble. I look in the mirror and see only a boy—receding hairline, stubble, and all. What did he see in the darkness? Later I start to shake.

10. I am at a conference for female-to-male transexuals. I listen sagely as the boys—men—teach each other how to bind breasts or use public urinals. The guy in the seat next to me is friendly, boyish, and takes pictures of everything.

"I live in a rural area. I need to teach my therapist about this stuff."

"That really sucks," I say, suddenly feeling new privilege, one I hadn't noticed. I had no trouble finding an experienced gender therapist.

"Yeah," he says. He leans forward, studying my face. "Say, you look pretty good. How long have you been on testosterone?"

"Since puberty," I say. I can see that he doesn't get it. I've passed for something new. I start to laugh.

11. The art show is in a small room, and the air-conditioning has been bad throughout the conference. A lean young man drifts over to me

while I pretend to look at the sepia portraits. We know each other vaguely, through mutual friends.

His body is limned with ink, his face glistens with steel. He walks with a bounce. I don't see any sign that he was born a girl. There is a kind of energy inside him; you can see it in the way people are drawn to him; he has charisma. I'm not sure if I like him. Yet.

"Are you enjoying the conference?"

"Yes," I answer. "I've never seen so many cute guys. I'll have to wear my Lesbian Avenger T-shirt tomorrow, just to keep my allegiances clear."

His mouth fills up with white teeth then he puts one arm around me. I consider protesting but instead let myself lean against him.

"You make me feel like a butch again," he says, much later.

12. The conference is ending, and the hardy remnants are drawing together in the lobby.

"Well, you got me in trouble," he says.

"I did?" I run my hand gently over the stubble on his scalp.

"I'm supposed to be the poster boy for gay tranny-boys, remember? I'm not supposed to be seen with girls!" He laughs as he says it.

I laugh too and wonder—do I count as a girl? The boys do seem to treat me differently than they did at the start of the conference. They are more polite, more respectful. What has changed? Who am I now?

13. The wind rattles my windows. It is a very cold night. I am hunched unladylike over my keyboard as I type.

I need something to wear. In two weeks I am going to the New England Tiffany Club's "First Event." There will be transgender folks there of all genders. There will be lots of straight, upper-class, white male cross-dressers in dresses.

I have no idea what to wear. Formal clothes have always been a problem for me; the gender signals are so confusing. I hated dressing formally as a boy, and I have never dressed formally as a girl. I live rather androgynously, claiming as much of my femme identity as seems safe and…proper.

I want to have something lovely, something that says "femme" to the world, or perhaps even "desirable." I deserve it. I've paid for it with blood and chunks of my soul.

After all I have done, why does this scare me so much? I have told my friends and family, and I have dared to begin transitioning. Why can't I allow myself the simple luxury of looking good? Will I always hide behind my gentle androgyny?

Riki was right after all. I am not transgressing gender; it is gender that transgresses me. I want my body back. I want my pride back, my identity, my childhood. I was not a little boy. I was not a little girl. I was a little femme tranny freak. I thought I was making choices, but they were all being made for me.

Who would have believed that, of all people, I would find a problem only shopping could solve and yet be unable to proceed? Maybe there are problems I can't solve by shopping. Maybe I just need to find better stores. Stacey Radical Femme Tryke—vulnerable, but with talons. Do not approach!

I hit a button and send my thoughts to my favorite computer bulletin board, where they mostly discuss butch and femme identities. Eventually, a lot of friends—mostly people I have never really met— post their support. I wonder, as I read their responses, what they see when they imagine my face.

14. He is young and more than a bit James Dean. We are underground waiting for a subway train. Our friends stand nearby. I've been told I should be his role model, but the fact is, he has been living the life as long as I have. I think we are friends instead.

"I like the coat," he says.

"Thanks. I was lucky to find it. And it works—I got ma'amed today, which doesn't happen all that often."

"I thought you didn't care about passing," he says with a sly smile.

"Well, I don't try very hard to pass—it's true. I don't wear a wig or makeup, or anything like that. I'm skipping the whole drag thing. But it is nice when people say 'ma'am' or 'young lady.'"

He restrains a grin and nods, and I know he has seen right through me. I am the only one who calls him by the male pronoun.

15. Harvard Square is warm for a winter evening, and the sky is black and starless. She and I are shopping. As we approach the bookshop, a man hails us. I have seen him before. He seems to inhabit this stretch of sidewalk where he makes his sales pitch for some sort of

time-share plan in a private school or something equally inexplicable.

"Excuse me, ladies," he says with a bright smile. I sort of nod at him but she and I continue our own conversation. I am aware of having passed, and that makes me happy.

"Wait a minute," he says as I go by him. "Are you a man or a woman?" I look up at him, caught off-guard. He leans close to me, and he suddenly seems very large and aggressive. I think I hear anger sliding into his voice. "No, really, I want to know!"

"I'm a woman!" I spit out at him. Fear curdles quickly into anger in my belly. We go into the store. I don't hear his final comment. I don't want to.

16. We sit next to each other on the train. He is taller than I am and good-looking. His life story is as complex as mine, but he passes easily as male. He has come from the other side of the country to see me. I envy him the calm assurance of his gender. We are sitting close, our bodies gently touching in a dozen places.

"Did you see that guy?" he asks with a lopsided grin.

"What guy?"

"The gay guy who was just sitting across from us? He gave me this big smile. When I took your hand."

"Ah—he read us as a gay couple."

"I'm sure he did."

"Gay guys usually don't read me as a gay man, actually."

"Of course they don't," he says shaking his head. "But you're sitting with me, Princess." I start to answer, but I realize I have no idea what I expect from people anymore. When I look in the mirror, I have no idea what I see.

17. I have known her and her husband for over a decade. We have worked and had fun together. Coming out to them takes all day. They ask a lot of questions—hard ones.

"So," she asks lightly, "does this mean you'll be dressed differently tomorrow?"

"Not much," I say. "I don't live a double life. I dress androgynously. I suppose I don't need to hide my breasts from you anymore, but it won't change things very much.

The whole subject of dress and appearance is politically loaded for me."

She nods. "Well, I can see why a transexual would want to look…what did you call it?"

"We say 'pass' as a woman. And if you don't pass, you've been 'read.'"

"'Pass' and 'read?'" she says, her eyes lighting up. "That's so interesting. Those are the same terms black people used to use in the south—'pass' as white or be 'read' as black."

I nod to her. "Exactly."

She looks back at me, and I can see she is starting to get it. By the end of the day, she is calling me by my real name and getting the pronouns right. She is one of those people who seem to accept my new gender more easily than I do. I wonder how they do it.

18. "You're really pissed, aren't you?" I ask over the phone. "What's wrong?"

We're both at work. This is our third conversation today.

"It's one of the women I work with," she answers. "The one you met last night."

"I remember her. She seemed very nice."

"We were talking about you. She kept calling you 'he' and said she couldn't understand how I could date a man. I told her you weren't a man, and she absolutely refused to hear it. She said it was sad that you couldn't just accept yourself. I thought I was going to kill her."

I am quiet. I have heard this sort of thing plenty of times before. "I don't understand," she says. "I guess I expect lesbians to be more enlightened than that."

I swallow. "It's just that she's met me now. If she read me as male last night, then that's how she's going to think of me. For a lot of people, that's all there is to it. When you have a tranny in your life, you have to get used to things like this, you know."

"No, I don't," she replies.

I wonder, suddenly, why I have.

19. We're looking at expensive dresses. I need a dress for a wedding. I've been a best man and even a groom, but I've never been the maid of honor.

"No," my companion says, "I'm looking for something formal for my girlfriend here." She gestures toward me vaguely as she examines the dresses on the rack. The saleswoman glances at me and sort of stumbles over her next sentence. Then she drifts away.

"Now where did she go?" my companion asks.

"Maybe she didn't like you referring to me as your girlfriend," I answer.

"The poor dear." She smiles sideways at me.

Tonight, at least, we're above worrying about such things. What do I care what other people think?

20. The morning is bright and clear, but I shuffle across Harvard Square without enthusiasm. It is one of those mornings where the world seems unbearably optimistic, and I wish it would just shut up.

I'm off to work. I brace myself slightly as I pass by the obligatory panhandler in front of the ATMs. "Good morning, young lady!" he says with a big smile.

My heart is suddenly light. As I give him a handful of quarters, I happen to glance at my reflection in a store window behind him. Yes!

Courage From Necessity
Mr. Barb Greve

Mr. Barb Greve is a lifelong Unitarian Universalist. He is a New Englander, godparent, classical bassist, and home brewer. He enjoys watching Babylon 5, *meditating, doing cross-stitch, and experiencing the sunrise on Cape Cod. He and his spouse live in Marlborough, Mass.*

"Are you going to change your name?" he asked.

"No," I responded.

"I admire your courage."

I knew he meant it as a compliment, but I had a hard time accepting it as such until a friend of mine reminded me that sometimes courage is born of necessity. That is certainly the case here. "Courage" is the last word I would have used to describe my actions.

My decision to ask people to use masculine pronouns in reference to me comes from a feeling of need. I need to be honest about my whole self and am not willing to put part of me aside to make others feel comfortable. I realize this will challenge and scare a lot of people and that it already has.

As a friend so aptly wrote after I told hir about my pronoun change, "I have to admit, I felt kind of unsettled by this news when I was thinking about it last night. I thought about it a lot, actually. I came to the conclusion that it feels this way because it's kind of scary. I mean, before, your transgenderism seemed like a totally internal thing. Now you're challenging the rest of us to completely change our mind-sets, to step outside our safe boxes and see the world completely different from what is as ingrained in us as responding to our own names. And that's scary…you bet it's scary."

I think the most frustrating part for me and probably the scariest for you is that I can't clearly explain the "why." I can tell you this change feels right, and for me, this is enough. But I fear that by my using masculine pronouns and keeping the name Barb, I will confuse the issue for you and make life harder for others who identify as transgendered. I know human instinct is to try to group like people together, but like so much of life, two people who appear to be alike on the outside may be entirely different. For this reason I want to say clearly that I am speaking only about my experience and no one else's. I've found the most comfortable combination I can imagine for myself but there are many people, transgendered and not, who will make other choices.

I choose to keep the name Barb because it has great significance to me. I was named Barbara because my adoptive mother always wanted the name for herself. The meaning used in our family is "stranger in a foreign land." As an adoptee, I can't think of any name with a more appropriate meaning. While I have tailored the original name to fit my personality, I still consider it a precious gift from my parents.

My father asked me if I was intentionally trying to confuse people by keeping my name. The simple answer is no. But I've come to the realization that in order for me to be comfortable with myself, I may need to confuse others.

Many people have asked me why I can't just identify as a butch woman since that is what I am…really. But they fail to realize I don't understand myself to be a woman. When I was younger, I thought I was really a boy and some mistake had been made with my body. Ever since kindergarten I've understood that I would grow up to be a guy.

When I hit puberty in junior high, I discovered I was attracted to girls. One day a girl in my class called me a lesbian. I went home from school that day and looked up the word in the dictionary to discover it meant "women who love women." I decided this must be who I am. After all, I had the same type of body the other girls in my class had, so I must have just gotten confused somewhere along the line.

I came out publicly as a lesbian in college. My friends encouraged me to join women-only meetings. They thought I would enjoy being in women-only spaces more than hanging out with the guys. I tried hard to find my place during those years. I surrounded myself with all types of women, many who were working to redefine women's roles in the world. Yet the more I hung out with them, the less I felt I belonged. Other than our attraction to women, we had very little in common.

I've since learned that gender is not as simple as biological sex (which can be altered); nor can we simplify and limit gender's definition to social constructs. I believe gender to be a combination between biology and social roles. We all choose to express our gender in different ways—our styles of dress, how we show emotions, what hobbies we enjoy, and who we hang out with are just some of them. For some people, this means limiting how they are in the world; for others, it means challenging stereotypes.

I struggled with my gender for years. I wanted more than anything to blend in and fit a stereotype. My only problem was, I couldn't find one. I looked to the men in my life to be my role models. I accepted their standards of behavior as my own. As I grew older, I discovered some of the limitations I had put on my behavior were uncomfortable. I then began to look to the women in my life for help. But I ran into the same types of problems. I realized I wasn't comfortable expressing my gender as either one.

Most people think gender expression is the same as gender identity, but for me, it isn't. My understanding of my gender identity is the same today as it was 20 years ago. The differences between then and now are (1) the words I use to describe myself and (2) the way they express my identity. As a child I never heard the word *transgender*. No one ever told me it was OK to identify as something other than male or female. Alone, I struggled with how to describe what I knew inside was a truth: I was not going to grow up to be either a man or a woman. I had already spent many years trying to make myself into one or the other and had been unsuccessful.

Society's need to make gender one or the other sacrifices the life experiences of people like me. We are forced to choose between a man and a woman. For me, this would mean denying a large part of who I am. My journey is not about transitioning into one of the two acceptable genders. It is not about making a political statement. My journey is about becoming a whole person. It is about being the best person I can be: a transgendered guy named Barb.

Whose Body Is This Anyway?
C. Jacob Hale

C. Jacob Hale teaches philosophy at California State University, Northridge, where he transitioned and received tenure (1995–96). Active in trans community work, Hale also enjoys doing drag as Miss Angelika and hanging with genderqueer sex radical friends.

There was the doctor who told me that if I wanted testosterone, I should be looking for a surgeon to cut on my genitals.

There was the passport agency official who told me that if I want an M on my passport, I should have already had a surgeon cut on my genitals.

There was the human relations employee who told me that if I wanted a faculty ID card with a current picture and a name matching the one on my driver's license, I should have already had a surgeon cut on my genitals.

There are FTMs who tell me that if I want to go to their meetings, if I am a real/true/genuine transexual, if I am one of them, I should be looking for a surgeon to cut on my genitals.

There are FTMs who tell me that if I want to be one of them, I should be delighted and congratulatory when one of them finds a surgeon to cut on his genitals.

There are FTMs who tell me that if I want to be one of them, I should be filled with pity or disdain when another FTM finds a surgeon to cut on his genitals.

There are FTMs who tell me that I should want to look at the results when one of them has had a surgeon cut on his genitals.

There was the psychiatrist who told me that if I want to have sex, I should get a surgeon to cut on my genitals first.

There was the nontransexual butch leatherman who told me that if I want to suck his cock, I should have plans to find a surgeon to cut on my genitals.

There was the MTF who shoved her tits in my face and told me that I should give her a call after I had gotten a surgeon to cut on my genitals because I'm just so cute.

There is Donald Laub, who says that if I am to have sex that isn't lesbian sex, I should have him cut on my genitals—but only if I quit my job first.

There are the leathermen of Hellfire who say that if I want to be one of them, I must have had a surgeon cut on my genitals because Inferno is for people without vaginas.

There is David Gilbert, who says that if he cuts on my genitals, he will remove my vagina no matter what I want because otherwise he would be making a chick with a dick, and no one wants that.

There was the nontransexual gay man who told a group of FTMs how glad he is that not all of us have surgeons cut on our genitals because he likes fucking our hot sexy wetness.

There was the nontransexual bi-guy who told a group of FTMs how glad he is that not all of us have surgeons cut on our genitals because we are the best of both worlds—male psyches in female bodies.

There are MTFs who tell me that if I am really transexual, I should define myself according to whether or not I have, or intend to have, a surgeon cut on my genitals. "Pre-op or post-op or non-op?"

Which op?

There was the social service agency director who shook my hand—the first FTM hand he had knowingly shaken—after a political meeting and asked if I'd had a surgeon cut on my genitals.

There are people in the audiences at the academic trans theory talks I give who don't ask about the content of my work but do ask about whether or not I've had a surgeon cut on my genitals.

There are shrinks who tell me that if I want testosterone, I should get myself diagnosed with a mental disorder and seek a surgeon to cut on my genitals when the shrinks tell me I am ready to have a surgeon cut on my genitals.

There are all those nontranssexuals who tell me that if I get some surgeon to cut on my genitals, I will be mutilating myself or sinning or making myself into a monster or a freak.

There is Sheila Jeffreys, who says that Janice Raymond didn't go far enough and that surgeons should be prohibited from cutting on transsexuals' genitals because it is mutilation.

There are all those transsexuals who tell me that if I want to have a surgeon cut on my genitals, I must believe myself to be mentally disordered or disabled or suffering from a birth defect.

There are some nontransgendered academic theorists who tell me that if I am a transsexual rather than a cross-dresser or a transvestite or a butch lesbian, this must mean I want a surgeon to cut on my genitals. And they tell me that if I get a surgeon to cut on my genitals, this will show my internalized misogyny or my internalized homophobia or my lack of agency or my complicity with the medical regime, consumer capitalism, or the bipolar gender system.

There are all those transsexuals who tell me that if I get a surgeon to cut on my genitals, I will no longer be a transsexual but a complete man who blends into society, pays his taxes, and lives a normal life.

I'm tired of listening to other people talking about whether or not I should have a surgeon cut on my genitals. And I'm also tired of people talking about whether or not my trans sisters should have some surgeon cut on their genitals. Whose genitals are these anyway?

Performing Translesbian
Nancy Nangeroni and Gordene MacKenzie

Nancy Nangeroni is host of GenderTalk Radio *in Cambridge, Mass., a weekly radio program that challenges traditional views of gender and sexuality (at www.gendertalk.com). She is an outspoken transgender community activist, writer, musician, and media producer.*

Gordene MacKenzie is author of Transgender Nation. *She is a writer, lecturer, and gender activist who teachers transgender politics, identity, and representation at the University of New Mexico.*

"There is an erotic and identity dimension I longed to travel to with my partners that I have only recently begun to explore. The erotic vehicle to those experiences I only dreamed about is gender..."

I love women. I love living as a woman, but I did not grow up as one. I spent many long years living with the unfulfilled need to live as a woman and with the desire that arose in me whenever I met a woman I found attractive. Lesbians, it seemed to me, had it best: They were women, and they loved women. What could be better?

It was not wrong that I was born male, but simply one more piece of evidence that I was ill-fated, destined to suffer a life tainted by what seemed a fetishistic compulsion that would surely prevent me from attaining my true potential—let alone the happiness of a fulfilling partnership. While I mourned my lot, I nonetheless accepted it. It never occurred to me that my desire to experience life from the perspective of a girl or woman might be an expression of a healthy interest in exploration and learning.

At some point during my youth, I heard about Christine Jorgensen, the first widely publicized transexual. I felt a kinship to her and secretly harbored a desire to be like her. But I couldn't see how to get there from where I was.

As I grew older and found myself strongly attracted to women, I despaired. I thought I could never be a real lesbian. I was born male, and even if I changed my sex I knew this wouldn't make me a "real" woman. I could pretend to be one and get my body surgically altered to look like one. If I kept my mouth shut, I might even pass as one.

But I would always know that I had lived my youth as male, except, of course, for those few precious moments of liberation when I gave rein to my transgender desires. Not growing up female, I was not privy to the formative experiences—positive and negative—that I presumed to be common to women. My desires were buried so deeply I never spoke to anyone about them. Because of this, nobody told me that all women do not feel the same and that lesbian desire is not uniform but highly diverse.

So I struggled with the question: If I lived as a woman, then what would that make me? And, more important, who would love me? Lesbians (I presumed) wouldn't, because I would not be the kind of woman they wanted. I had lots of male experience and thought I was moving in the opposite direction—away from masculinity (and all that it implied) toward femininity. I was trying to escape from a life that was overly mechanical and isolated. I was seeking connection with my sensuality and escape from conditioned gender roles. I refused relationships with women who would depend on me to care for them without being willing to care for me in return. I was a holdout for true partnership.

I recall a period when I listened to an audio tape to give myself hope that I could attain whatever I wanted in life. As I listened daily during my lunch hour, burning the lessons into my mind, I repeated to myself, "I want to live as a woman." And I heard and accepted the admonition to have faith that for each desire created within us by the forces at play in our lives, its fulfillment is created by the balance of those forces.

So I came to trust that someone must exist who would find me attractive. Whether they might be lesbian or not, man or woman (or something else), I couldn't begin to imagine. I simply trusted that they were out there somewhere. I needed merely to be prepared to recognize them when we met.

I have never succeeded when looking for love; what real successes I've enjoyed have always developed by chance. At one point, some years before my transition to living as a woman, I had a conversation about love with my very Italian and Catholic aunt who is also my godmother. She asked me about my love life, and I told her it was not going so great. She advised me, "You've got to merchandise yourself." Coming from her experience, she meant for me to put myself forward, out front. And so I set about to do just that, to present myself to the widest possible audience in the hope that somewhere out there, a person with whom I might form a real partnership—a meeting of mind, spirit, and body—would take notice.

The truth is, I've been a show-off my whole life. First on violin, then at sports. I've always reveled in whatever attention was available for the doing of something others could not do. In my mind, performance was key. I thought it was the means by which I would finally achieve my happiness.

Strangely, not until I decided to take the most intense risk I could imagine—ultimate humiliation—and "out" myself as transgendered did I gain some insight into my personal performance as a misdirected means of acquiring loving attention. When I finally accepted gender as a performance in which I was free to act according to my own direction, I somehow acquired the perspective to recognize that my struggle to perform in other areas of life was misdirected.

What I really wanted in this life was loving attention and connection with others. Those stunts might indeed win me some passing recognition, but they would never bring me the intimate connection I desperately needed. Moreover, my dependence on performance as a means of acquiring attention was probably doing more to keep me from having what I wanted than anything else.

With this recognition, I resolved to seek loving attention and connection more directly. I still enjoy performing in a variety of ways, as a writer and activist, radio talk-show host, and musician. But recognizing that my need for loving attention and connection is best fulfilled by giving loving attention has proven far more effective and satisfying than any amount of performance.

In the area of intimacy, as I've moved out of performance and into conscious sharing, I find it takes careful consciousness on my part not to fall into the initiator role. Years of training—or simply hormones—ingrained a habit of responding to my excitement with action. I tend to think of this as masculine, though others may feel differently. When I am with a lover and begin to feel excitement, I feel a tendency to assert myself—and my needs. I want to grab my partner and make things happen. It is so easy for me and guaranteed to keep me from being intimately loved and cared for by another. When I am the initiator, I make things happen, my partner responds to me, and together we embark on a sensual journey of my direction. But my greatest joy is in discovery, which comes more abundantly when I share with or follow the lead of another. I am learning to quell my urge to surge and instead let my partner drive.

I am learning to remain present in each moment, to let go of control and even knowledge of our direction, to encourage my partner's explorations and participation, which, added to mine, set our course. I am learning to replace my fear of nonperformance with the acceptance of nonpredetermined outcome that will not always result in crashing orgasms.

In the absence of fear, I am more genuinely present, and the connection I experience with my partner is more intensely intimate than sex ever used to be. When there is no precedent, every act must be creative. The demand to be present and aware is unrelenting, but the rewards are the joy of discovery and the fulfillment of cooperative creation.

We are standing, staring into each other's eyes, the tip of your breast pressing into my breast. Our nipples find each other on our bodies that have become beautiful quicksilver mirror maps of pleasure. Your tongue traveling in the circle of my mouth. I don't think I have ever kissed anyone so long or so differently... My face and tongue do not travel all over your face and tongue only in search of my own pleasure but move through you as you move through me in a symphony of constant communication... My tongue probes yours and the cavern of your lips and mouth as our bodies merge together. We hold each other so tight...lost in the pleasure of each other. Our bodies transcend gender, yet gender is our launch pad.

And yet I feel greater uncertainty on approaching intimacy—especially with a new lover—than ever before. Where do we go when there are no roles, no pathways, no norms? How can we connect physically, when neither of us knows what we will do together? How we will please each other? If my new lover is a lesbian, what will she expect of me, and how will she relate to the fact that my genitals are unmistakably male in appearance?

As you move your long honey-spun fingers down the slope of my back you are my first lover to remark that I have a guy's ass. You quickly spin to every gender-ambiguous site on my body—where the hair grows proudly across my small breasts and where long, giant hairs sprout from the mole in the middle of my right arm. As we lick each other's ears, we find it all. Your body is beautiful. Small breasts standing up in the moonlight. Your whole body a lunar surface with two navels. The second one made from the terrible tubes they put in you after your near-fatal motorcycle accident that left you split open, hanging between life and death, man and woman. I see your two navels as a sign that you are twice born.

To be a lesbian can mean erotic desire, sex acts, and political identity. However, I flounder at what this or any other identity means when applied to myself. Identity seems to be a guide to performance, the very thing I have at long last escaped—at least for a time—in my relationships. "Lesbian," which cannot hope to define all the complexities of my identity, nonetheless may serve as a type of shorthand to represent an aspect of my public performance of self.

As I enter into a relationship with a new woman friend, I begin to experience what it means to be a lesbian—not because I am a lesbian, but because I am performing what passes for lesbian. I am a woman being with another woman in an intimate relationship. As I walk down the street in Albuquerque with my lover, I begin to feel the heat of public scorn, I begin to fear the consequences of simply walking down the street with an arm around my lover. I begin to experience what it is to be a lesbian. I begin to know the real risk of imminent danger to myself and my lover. I begin to know the oppression of presumed immorality, of a hostility that poisons casual encounters for no reason, with no warning.

I could walk down that same street, the one that brought me fear yesterday, by myself, and escape the oppression. The difference is not in who or what I am but in my performance. Yesterday I performed a lesbian act, and for it I am damned. Today my lover and I are less publicly demonstrative, and we are presumed to be simply two women. There is no hostility in sight. The lesson of identity as performance is vivid.

At the same time, calling myself lesbian is a decision I make—a political decision—about how I will associate with others. It's about what role I choose to play. Will I assert my belonging with others who call themselves lesbian? Will I expect admission to spaces closed to all but those calling themselves lesbian? Will I expect to be treated in the same manner as those who call themselves lesbian? Will I defend this identity against all who challenge my right to claim it for myself? And will I present myself as an object of attraction to lesbians, and will we love, touch, play, sleep with, suck, and fuck each other?

Moving across the ocean of your shoulders with my kisses, I am carried to the shore of your mouth by a wave of gender blowing like a warm breeze through us… Trying to excavate the intensity and complexity of my feelings for you as I hunger for your presence, I anticipate the exact moment your body will arrive in my universe. The orbit of my desire surrounds you like we surround each other in a sea of arms and hands circling our bodies.

Looking back, I can see that I grew up resentful of being denied access to experiences freely enjoyed by the women around me. It was clear to me then that my penis was the reason used to justify this exclusion. Had I grown up a woman, I would surely have felt just as resentful of the limitations placed on me for my *lack* of a penis and may have eventually found buried beneath years of denial and repression an overwhelming need to live as a man. I doubt I would be any better off than I am today. I am a product not just of my place within the gender belief system of the culture but of the whole system and the way it hurts us all.

As I move into tomorrow and consider my politics and where to place my activist effort, I have to remember that oppression is based not on what I am but rather on what I am presumed to be. Oppression does not ask how you wish to be identified. It takes one look, nails a label to you, and proceeds to dispense perverse justice upon your body. I don't have to feel like a lesbian to suffer the consequences of being presumed one. I just have to look like one.

Identity serves a crucial role in the emergence of any liberatory movement. It provides a haven for those seeking liberation along the dimension being challenged. By claiming a new, transgressive identity, those challenging the status quo can identify with one another for collaborative effort and mutual support. In claiming the identity, there is a presumption of some shared oppression and some common desire to stand against the imposed suffering. The new identity can be a rallying point for the formation of new alliances and coalitions.

Within a more established movement, identity too often becomes a limiting factor used to exclude others and assert control over the movement's agenda. For years now, some within the gay liberation movement have used the term *sexual orientation* as an identity-defining litmus test to exclude genderqueers and narrow the scope of queer activism.

Because this is such a repressed society, we find liberation through liberated identities. Once we're free, we're able to really grow and develop politically, and then we can learn to appreciate the pitfalls of identity and to surf identity. Identity-based movements need to grow beyond the identities that established them, because basing a movement on an identity always privileges those who sit in judgment of who gets to be included and fails to liberate those at the margins.

I am entering your soul through the long lashes surrounding your eyes, lost in the sequined slopes of our bodies where there are no rules. We are making love on the borders of sex and gender, blissfully exploring the peaks of our desires... Loving you there are no road maps, only wild fractals where chaos is the only map for our desire... Traveling beyond the linear, we become stems and flowers all at once. Pushing past the front and the back doorways, opening all the windows to our bodies, capturing the cross-dressed negative imprints of our souls on all the mirrors, the house of our love rattles from attic to basement. We are creating new doorways. Our genitals touch in a new and open Universe.

Moving into the new millennium, my trans sisters and I can finally rejoice in our increasing acceptance as women and lesbians. The Michigan Womyn's Music Festival notwithstanding, I find myself routinely accepted in (and often invited into) women's and lesbian spaces these days. For this acceptance and inclusion, I am grateful. But I join with all who challenge us to be impatient with the politics of identity and insist upon a focus on the mechanisms of oppression. To dismantle these with minimal destructive impact on surrounding wildlife, our vision will need to be sharp and clear.

Disorderly Fashion
Wally Baird

Wally Baird is a bicoastal boy-dyke who believes the "standards of care" and emphasis on "transitioning" will only further the oppressive binary-gendered regime. Her writing has appeared in queer and mainstream publications across the country.

"Hey, pretty lady, don't you look nice today."

It's a surprisingly sweltering day in San Francisco, and I, in all my boyhood, am crossing an intersection under construction. The hormones are pumping through my newfound muscles, and I smell about as good as the men in the manholes before me. Yet to them, I am "beautiful" and "baby"—among other names I haven't heard since I started wearing boxers.

I kind of love it.

In my typical full-time lesbian existence I have a lot of explaining to do. Why taking testosterone does not mean I want to be a man. Why a boy dyke is not necessarily a butch. Why "transitioning" is not in the vocabulary of those who live between the binary lines.

In the outside world there are no such nuances to fumble through. I am simply a woman who presents herself differently, and that's good enough for the sexist men on the corner. Ignorant and predictable but strangely refreshing after another disappointing day with the "queer-positive" company I keep.

This morning I had an appointment with a gender-savvy lesbian therapist so that I can obtain permission to cut off my tumor-ridden breasts in an aesthetically pleasing manner. My mother, her sister, and their grandmother all developed breast cancer before menopause, a strong indication that there is a hereditary link. A few months ago I fought my way into an underage mammogram to confirm what I already knew: I had a solid mass in my right breast, which immediately increased my chance of developing disease. A prophylactic mastectomy would decrease my breast cancer risk by 90%, according to my cancer surgeon. It's a no-brainer, particularly for a boy who has longed for the flatness of her yesteryear: Take 'em off.

I've seen what can happen to women who decline new breasts after a mastectomy. They are left barren, scarred, and sometimes uneven, as if the moment they say no to fake boobs they become unworthy of cosmetic attention. So the local transgender surgeon agreed to step in to do my reconstruction in the likeness of a male. He just needs a note from a therapist stating that I am able to make this decision.

It seems reasonable enough. But a woman who wants a flat chest is dangerous territory in a queer therapy session.

"I cannot sign off on your surgery until one year has passed," said the lesbian therapist, who wore a permanent scowl throughout the entire expensive hour. "You need to live with your breasts bound for a while, to see what it's like to pass as a man."

"But I don't want to pass as a man," I protested. "And I have clearance from my cancer surgeon, who is willing to do this right now. I just want the transgender surgeon to make it look nice."

"Your attitude is part of what I am trained to watch out for," she answered. "Being indignant about wanting immediate surgery is expected from every patient."

It would probably be easier to ask for and receive seven D-cup breasts all over my body. Nevertheless, I stayed past my appointment to observe the gender support group she runs, where an FTM described how his transition includes interrupting people when they speak and swearing off female chores like laundry and dishes.

"It is important that you seek and receive male affirmation for your behavior," concluded the therapist upon whom I depend to label me sane.

I left that office in a hurry.

If it weren't for the all the distance between myself and the mainstream, I may not have come as far as I have, I realize as I flirt with the workers at the intersection. To them, the world is narrow enough to both ignore and allow my multifaceted existence.

Just a few more steps until I reach the women's health clinic, where I am greeted with smiles and kisses by the staff. To straight women, I am mischievous yet darling. I wear oxfords, a cowlick. I'm the little brother they never had. And most of all, I am so far removed from what they know that I am not a threat to their own identities.

"She'll be right with you," the receptionist grins, referring to the practitioner who is almost singlehandedly changing the face of gender in San Francisco. I happen to have found one of the few physicians who sees no problem with administering hormones to anyone who wants them, so long as each patient is monitored.

"Tell me if I'm right," the busy doctor says to me as she pulls back the needle and draws in the powerful shot suspended in deceptively tranquil oil. "I think there are women who definitely want to be men, and that's their goal when they do stuff like this. And then I think there are lesbians who are transgender but want to remain women."

She has come closer to the truth in these few seconds than anyone I've listened to all day. And with that I am stuck through the ass with her dart of yellow vigor.

"It's a whole different generation," she says, plunging the tenor and sharp angles into my body, shaking her head in wonder while injecting a revolution.

This Butch Body
Kristen Walker

Kristen Walker is an Australian working in the area of law and sexuality. She is a campaigner for queer rights in Australia and internationally.

No one expects this body to bear a child. This butch lesbian body. Maybe even I don't. It's funny how many people say, "I can't imagine you pregnant." My own mother said it to me the other day. Or "I would like to see you pregnant," as if it were something weird, something they could not imagine. Or they assume that M., my partner, will bear our child(ren)—after all, she is more femme than I am. Never mind that I have more curves, more hips and thighs, bigger breasts than she does. She is the one they expect to have a child. Butch lesbian bodies do not have children.

When you have been trying for a while, everything about the process becomes magnified. Every little change in me is a sign—a sign of pregnancy, if we have been trying. Or a sign of infertility, if it is just an ordinary month. And, of course, in our initial enthusiasm, we told lots of friends about our plans. So now, after two years, people are still asking us how our plans for a baby are going. It is impossible to share with them what we have been going through: the emotional roller coaster, the legal obstacles, the infertility issues, the geographical problems. Now I just say "Oh, you know, it is going." Every time you tell someone you have news, they you are about to announce that you are pregnant. If only.

When other lesbian friends announce that they are pregnant, it is hard to be happy for them. Of course I am, but part of me is simply sick with envy. The most recent friends to announce became pregnant the first time they tried. They were not really ready for it; it was just supposed to be a practice run. We smiled and talked about it over coffee, and then I had to come home and cry. Why couldn't it be so easy for us? We thought we would have a baby by now. He or she should be about 1½ years old by now. At every turn, though, we seem to simply face more obstacles, especially legal ones. This would be much easier if society, both Australian and American, were not bent on making it hard, if not impossible, for lesbians and gay men to have children.

We have two gorgeous gay men who will be dads for our children. They provide sperm for us, so it should have been easy. But it was not. First there were the restrictions on gay men donating sperm to sperm banks in the United States where we started this process. Our friends flew in when necessary. Imagine—a 20-hour international flight just to donate sperm. But it did not work. When we returned to Australia, we thought it would be easier. Oh, we knew we would have to go interstate, to Sydney, as it is a crime for a clinic or doctor to provide donor insemination to lesbians (or single women—which is how the law sees us) in Victoria, our home state. We carefully planned our Sydney meeting, only to discover that clinics in New South Wales will not use sperm from gay men. There went our months of planning.

Miraculously, it seemed, the legal rules in Victoria changed over night. The federal court ruled that excluding single women and lesbians from direct insemination and in vitro fertilization was unlawful discrimination on the basis of "marital status." Hooray! We could dispense with the interstate clinic and try in Victoria. We would still have the six-month quarantine to make sure the sperm was safe, but we could do it without the need for regular, expensive, difficult interstate travel. Then, in another twist, the Infertility Treatment Authority (so Orwellian) received legal advice that restricted access to women who are "clinically infertile," whatever that means (unless you are in a heterosexual relationship, in which case the woman does not need to be infertile.) More discrimination. Well, we thought, we have been trying for ages and we are not pregnant—it would seem I am infertile. But if

I am, then the only treatment the doctor will provide is IVF, an invasive and difficult procedure. I don't want IVF; I want to keep trying the "natural" way—with a syringe. The doctor will not, cannot, provide donor insemination, though, as that is not an appropriate treatment for infertility. If I am fertile, I cannot get treatment at all, and if I am infertile, I cannot get donor insemination. Catch-22. And we do not even know if they will agree to use gay sperm. After all, it is a health concern. Never mind that I have had regular doses of the stuff inside me already through all our tries and that if I use a clinic, it screens and quarantines the sperm donation.

Sometimes it feels like the world is out to get us—to stop lesbians and gay men from bearing children, and I now think this is true. The Australian federal government is trying to change the law to permit discrimination, and the Australian Catholic Church, with the government's support, has rushed off to the highest court in the land to stop lesbians and single women getting access to assisted reproductive services. After all, perhaps it is genetic, we might produce more perverts. And who knows what we will do to the kids—effeminate boys, masculine girls, all kinds of gender differences. Not to mention the threat they see of child abuse by pedophile gay dads. Never mind that we truly want children, that we have thought it through very carefully, that we have planned financially, that they will have parents who will love and care for them—none of this seems to matter. All that seems to count is for the children to have one male parent and one female parent. There is much expressed social concern about boys being brought up without a father, that they will not learn to be a man without a masculine role model. No one has suggested that a butch dyke might be able to model masculinity for a boy child. Somehow I think that might be too confrontational. I would like to challenge the idea that boys and men have to be "masculine," as we have come to know this term. Nothing wrong with sissies and boys who like dolls.

Sometimes I wonder about how pregnancy fits with being butch. It almost seems like a contradiction in terms. How would that large, distended belly fit with my body image? Would people perceive me differently—more femme, more of a "real" woman? Would I perceive myself myself differently? And how would I deal with giving birth? These questions always seemed too hard. I think I simply went into denial about them. Once I was pregnant, then I would have to address them, I would be forced to, but until then, I would just leave them alone. I still do not have any answers, but I know that many butch women have had babies and will continue to do so.

After a long while, I finally gave up trying to become pregnant. I had flown overseas to try; our donors had flown here. It all seemed too hard. I needed a break from the roller coaster of attempt, hope, and disappointment. My partner took up the journey, using an interstate clinic. We had sperm stored all over the country, ready to use depending on the changing legal developments. While we were waiting to see if she was still menstruating, I tried to imagine how I would feel if what had not happened for me worked with her. Would I be upset, sad, disappointed? But whenever I thought of the possibility that she might be pregnant, I just smiled. Then on her second try, we saw the pink line on the stick, the positive result. I had one moment of sadness, but we are going to have a baby and it is not possible to be sad about that. We have beaten the system; we will bring a child into the world with a different kind of family: two mums, two dads, eight grandparents. This is an exciting event, bringing great joy to our friends who have witnessed this long difficult process. This butch body can still be a mother. Maybe the second child will be from my butch body.

Be a Man
Susan Wright

Susan Wright writes science fiction novels and books on art and popular culture. She is the policy director of the National Coalition for Sexual Freedom, an advocacy organization that protects freedom of sexual expression among consenting adults.

I've cross-dressed several times in the past few years, and I have discovered my alter ego, Steve. I started cross-dressing because I wanted to see what life was like as a man. I still don't know what life is like for a man, not really. But I do know that cross-dressing has shown me things I never knew about myself as a woman. I am so much a product of our gender-determined world that until I tried to become a man, I couldn't see how many aspects of myself have been dictated by culture.

The first time I cross-dressed it was such an intense experience, I could hardly absorb everything. As I transformed myself physically into a man, I wrestled with my ambivalence. Can I act like a man? Won't it be embarrassing when people recognize that I'm a woman? What if someone gets mad?

But I did it. I got dressed in baggy jeans and bound my breasts under a loose T-shirt. I applied a mustache using snips of my own hair adhered over my lip with spirit gum. Then I darkened my cheeks and jaw with eyebrow pencil, giving my skin a shadowy look. I also used the pencil to darken and thicken my eyebrows, removing the arch and almost joining them in the center. That and a baseball cap pulled low, with my long hair tucked under the collar of a black leather jacket, and I looked as good as I could get.

But I didn't look like a man. I looked like a woman in drag. I caught a glimpse of Steve only when I glanced at the mirror out of the corner of my eye. To my surprise, he was a young Latino guy, trying to act older and tougher than he was. I was a little disappointed at my obvious youth, and I'd been wistfully hoping for some white male privilege so I could see how it felt. But that obviously wasn't in store for the kid in the mirror.

"Stay in the shadows," my partner, Kelly, suggested doubtfully.

I figured I didn't look like a real man because I was still missing something—my cock. I don't feel like a man unless I'm packing. Putting something as simple as a rolled-up sock in my jeans serves to focus all my attention on my crotch. I'm aware of it like no other part of my body because it's out there and vulnerable like my breasts usually are. It's the first thing that walks into a room. Packing helps me understand why some men are so focused on their penis.

The first time I tried packing, my stride was completely thrown off. I found myself spreading my legs and leaning my shoulders back to balance my cock. It felt like a real man's swagger. I wanted to go straight to the subway and sit down with my legs spread wide apart, to revel in taking up more space. With heavy cowboy boots finishing off the outfit, I felt darn proud of myself.

Until I left the apartment.

It turns out that Steve is barely legal—18 at most—and deeply insecure about his manhood. Steve has trouble in crowds and one-on-one. He's not comfortable with men or women. He mumbles and doesn't know what to do with his hands.

Eye contact is the trickiest part of cross-dressing. I constantly wonder, *Do they see through me? Do they think I'm crazy? Do I look scared to death?*

In my panic, I turned to Kelly for advice. He explained to me that most guys don't look at each other. Instead they look *through* each other while they're passing by or checking out the room.

"If you want to cruise a guy, hold his eyes for just a beat longer, then drop them down his body," Kelly helpfully warned. "Don't look right at a guy because that's challenging him."

"Why didn't you tell me that?" I demanded. "I could have gotten into trouble. What else is a big brother for?"

"Brothers don't have to tell you. It's something you pick up along the way."

I was worried that there were other things I should have picked up on my way to manhood, things that would keep me from getting my ass kicked. I tried to get more information out of Kelly, but nothing coherent emerged.

OK, I can be maddeningly vague and inarticulate. But I felt so inadequate and puny next to Kelly, who is tall and strong.

Even now, the issue of whether I pass as a man is a big one for me. As it turns out, Kelly was right: Most people don't really look at men. Women avoid men's eyes to be sure not to encourage them, while men are careful not to challenge each other. Yet I can't believe that everyone doesn't see right through me. I always expect pointing fingers and questioning looks as people wonder, *Why is that woman wearing a mustache?* But when I'm on the city streets, cab drivers and pedestrians don't give me a second glance.

The real test with passing came when I cross-dressed to go to an S/M play club, Hellfire, where Kelly and I have known people for years. He introduced me to our friends as Steve, claiming, "Susan is on her way."

With each person, I grunted a greeting, then quickly began to survey the room. It must have been convincingly doggish enough to not raise any suspicions. Even though I was with my partner, for some reason my friends couldn't recognize me. I wore the trappings of a man and was introduced as a man, therefore I was a man.

That was a delicious moment. People I had known for years looked me right in the eye without seeing me. Since they weren't reacting as my friend, exchanging the usual banter, I could see them from a startlingly objective point of view. I became something new, something completely different.

I was surprised to see how little attention is paid to a strange guy. Gone was all the flattering regard I usually get as a long-haired, flirtatious woman. At first I was strangely upset at having to do without the attention. I never realized how much I relied on that attention to define myself as a person.

In the midst of my confusion, I also began to feel relief at being invisible, at being able to watch people instead of resisting the pressure of dozens of eyes. I was left alone, a blank slate, and I could make Steve anything I wanted him to be. It gave me the freedom to start enjoying myself as a man.

But in talking to people, inevitably my voice gave me away. Or my laugh—which is far too loud and unmistakable. So gradually my friends realized I was Susan, not some strange guy named Steve.

Every time it happened, the realization was written on their face. My friends looked so alive and young at that moment. They laughed with their eyes wide open in pure amazement. It must have been like a 3-D picture; only with the glasses could they see the image among the wavering lines.

After they got over their astonishment, I got all kinds of reactions. One friend of mine, a heterosexual man, had trouble talking to me after he realized who I was. It clearly freaked him out to feel attracted to me when I looked like a man. Most of my friends thought it was fascinating, and they didn't spoil it for the others. Some of them joined in the game to see who would be the next to discover me.

Everyone who found out continued to give me sidelong looks, as if they couldn't get over the mirage. I continued to be Steve, complete with my somber male expression. Their reactions toward me changed, even after they had seen through my male persona and knew it was me. They treated me differently, not like they did when I was female, as if they weren't quite sure who I was anymore.

It was a priceless experience.

I also enjoy cross-dressing among strangers. Once I cross-dressed to go to a lap-dance joint with Kelly. But I didn't feel comfortable. I didn't want the women to touch me, and I was far more interested in the men than in the women.

I was surprised because I tend to focus more on women when I'm in public. I've been to that lap dance place before, and I was much more interested in the women than the men. As Steve, all I could stare at were the men. I wanted to see exactly what they were doing and what they were looking at.

I guess I'm not a bisexual male, even though I am a bisexual female. When I'm Steve, women frighten me because I don't know how to act with them. I'm not sure why. It's one of the strange ways my personality reacts to my change in gender. Maybe as I continue to cross-dress and get older that will change.

Since lap dancing didn't work out quite like I had planned, I decided to explore my gay male side. The first time I cross-dressed and went to the Lure, a leatherman's bar in New York City, I was nervous. Going into a male-for-male defined space upped the consequences if I was discovered to be a woman. I remember shaking as I approached the front door, wondering if they would card me or simply stop me with an incredulous, "Where do you think you're going, lady?"

But nobody stopped me. I paid for myself and breathed a sigh of relief as Kelly and I entered the bar. We were early, and I got a prime cruising spot in the shadows near the bathroom.

I was happy and flustered the few times I got cruised. I found out Steve is shy, and he's definitely a bottom.

It looked as if most of the guys at the Lure that night were bottoms too. I could understand why a lot of them were cruising Kelly, who is most definitely a top. As the place got more crowded, I enjoyed watching the attention he got. Even though nobody knew it, I felt proud to be his "boy."

I was so comfortable in the Lure that I finally realized something important about why I wanted to pass as a man. When I cross-dress, it's not just my appearance that changes. Wearing the mustache and the cock reminds me every second that I must *be* different. I feel bound by the constraints our society puts on all men to act a certain way.

I suppose that's why I feel so young when I'm Steve. I'm hardly yet a man, because I'm confused about how to behave. I want to be cool so the other guys will like me.

Part of learning how to be a man is in the talking. Keeping my voice low is nothing compared to changing the way I convey information. As a woman I speak very fast, tossing off comments while I gesture a lot. But aren't men expected to be more straightforward? Aren't they expected to keep their hands and hips still when they talk? So I usually stand there stiffly, unsure of my words and afraid to laugh for sounding like a schoolgirl. It's hard to think when I'm trying to talk in a different way. And that tension carries over into everything I do.

But that first night at the Lure I finally relaxed in the midst of men and felt like Steve more fully than ever before. I wandered around on my own, cruising the other men and feeling desirable. I wasn't just acting like Steve; I was thinking as Steve and experiencing the night as Steve.

When Kelly found me again, he gave me a deep kiss. He said he liked the feel of the bristles of my mustache against his freshly shaven skin.

Then he pulled me over to the benches along one wall. There were two tiers, so he sat on the top one and I sat on the bottom between his legs. He surveyed the place from his spot while I leaned my head against his thigh, feeling safe. We slowly sipped our beers without talking.

Then Kel leaned over to whisper, "Look at that couple."

It was an older couple, with the elder man in his 60s and the younger in his late 40s, the quintessential leather daddy and his boy. They were seated in the same way as Kel and I were, with the boy between his daddy's knees. They looked like they could have been part-ners for 20 years.

The couple beamed at us with fond approval, clearly pleased to see a next-generation couple enjoying the bar together. It made me feel like part of something much bigger than a cruising scene. I was accepted and treasured by members of my community.

I know how precious this ephemeral contact is because I've seen the anger and sorrow among my friends as one leather bar after another has closed down in the increasingly antisex environment of New York City. I felt then that as long as we can continue to come together in places where we accept one another, our community will survive no matter what orientation or identity we are.

I experienced being a part of something greater, and I owe it all to learning how to be a man.

At the end of that perfect night Kel and I got in a yellow cab and the driver asked, "Drop you at the same address?"

We both said yes, and I snuggled next to Kelly in the seat, happy to be a gay man in the eyes of the driver. Happy to be Steve for a few more min-utes longer, knowing I'd have to wait the whole summer, until the weath-er cooled, before I could wear my leather jacket and become a man again.

I started cross-dressing to learn more about men, but I ended up learning more about myself. I didn't realize I'd discover how much of my personality and ways of interacting have been patterned by outside forces. Does the clay need to know how it is molded? Maybe not, but I think we can all benefit from looking at life from outside the gender traps we've grown up in. I certainly did.

The A Train
Carrie Davis

Carrie Davis lives in New York City and identifies as a woman of transexual experience. She works as a counselor and outreach organizer for the Gender Identity Project at the New York Lesbian, Gay, Bisexual, and Transgender Community Center.

It is 7:30 P.M., late into the rush hour at the end of a wonderful, warm Friday in New York City. I am feeling pretty, happy, and calm on the A train from West Fourth Street in Manhattan to the last stop on Lefferts in the Richmond Hill section of Queens. The subway car is crowded, but I manage to get a seat. Across from me sit a woman and her male friend.

The woman points her finger at me and turns to her friend. "That's not a woman, that's a man." He looks away, as if embarrassed, or possibly bored, by her gesture. She will not be deterred. She turns to her left. "Who's he trying to fool? Those breasts aren't real. He's a man. That's a man."

The subway car around me is filled with young men and women, some seated, some standing, all acting as if I can't hear them. A festive atmosphere of loud jokes and rude comments at my expense fills the car. One man even breaks into an impromptu rap about my obvious maleness. Soon the entire group is laughing and joining in with his song. The invective is relentless, the sound deafening.

The train moves through Manhattan into Brooklyn. In Bed-Sty and East New York, the new friends trickle off the train to go on their way. As the train moves into the last stop in Queens, I am left in the nearly empty car with the woman who started everything. She is quiet now. She seems anxious and will not meet my eyes.

Until now, I have had my head bowed and eyes tightly closed. Like a small child, I'd tried to pretend that as long as I couldn't see my tormentors, they couldn't see me. I'd tried to imagine that this was not really happening. Now I try not to cry. I want to die.

The train eventually stops, and I wait until I am the last person on it. Then, as I get up to leave, I stagger a little, feeling almost drunk with sadness and depression. The woman who started this small episode is gone, and her part in my life is over. I will not forget what has happened. In my short life, living as a woman, I have been attacked, bashed, and raped; I have endured worse moments, but this seems different. I am losing my sense of hope.

Rules
Carrie Davis

I occupy a shadow world where the politics of attraction can be difficult to clearly understand. To simplify this, I try to follow my heart regarding affection, attraction, and intimacy. Since transexual women like myself exist, it is logical to think that there are individuals who prefer and are attracted to us. The identity police have yet to create a label for these folks, but I can personally attest that large numbers of them exist.

I identify as a queer girl who is openly attracted to male, female, and trans-identified people. Given this vision of myself, on any given day I am called upon to present and self-identify as a sex worker (I use the name Faith) or an activist and social worker (Carrie).

The men I see are mainly those who seek out transexual women. We know these men as tranny chasers, trans fans, or simply chasers. Almost all these men identify as straight.

For some, possibly most, their attraction to me is born of erotic desire. They are captivated by a sexual longing and fantasy involving preoperative transexual women. They seek out intimate interludes but are rarely interested in long-term relationships. Many of these men feel that their sexual identity may be questioned if they publicly date me, and they are frightened of this. Some are consumed by guilt and cannot accept me as a true partner. Others know better but still feel unable to escape the closet. The desire of men who seek me out based solely on their visions of sexual fantasy often collides with my need for intimacy.

My instinctive reaction is to protect myself. For my emotional safety I have always restricted business interactions to Faith—a sex worker. As Carrie, I have sought out and developed relationships with men and women who are open and out about their affectional and gender preferences. Coincidentally, many of these folk live outside the world of privilege. They aren't ashamed to be seen with me in daylight, in public, and proudly introduce me to their families and friends.

Over the last half dozen years I have slowly and consciously crafted a defined but overlapping set of rules for both Faith and Carrie. Rules are necessary because there are times when I do not feel safe, physically or emotionally, and it helps to have a default setting to rely on when I am less than lucid. Here they are:

* *If I do not feel safe, I am not safe.* I believe in my intuition.
* *No means no.* I don't change my mind once I've decided, no.
* *I never bargain my rates.* My rates are fair, and I am worth every penny.
* *No drugs.* Many clients want to do cocaine or crack during a session and share it with me. I'm not puritanical, but I have no interest in social drugs. Drugs make a session more difficult because they tend to make a client's behavior erratic. Although I don't smoke, I don't think of smoking pot as substance abuse any more than I consider social drinking alcoholism.
* *I never discuss money with a man in a club until he touches my genitals.* Undercover cops dislike touching a pre-op's genitals. Since most chasers are eager to do so, it becomes a litmus test of sorts.
* *I never touch or directly handle money for sex work in view of the client.* I have him place the money on the table or dresser and pick it up when he goes to the bathroom or is otherwise occupied.
* *No same-day sessions.* I require at least 24 hours' notice to schedule a session with a client. Men who say they want to come right over usually haven't clearly thought through the implications of their desire or will masturbate immediately after hanging up. Four out of five last-minute dates never show up.
* *I move completely through a bar when I first arrive.* I scout the territory and people. I want to show myself off to everyone quickly. I also seek out the best places to display myself and see if I have allies or enemies in the house.

Rules

* *I maintain an appropriate distance from my grrrl friends when working a bar.* A meaningful distance varies from a few inches to a couple of feet. This distance signals my availability to potential suitors. If my grrrl friends and I are both obviously working the bar (as demonstrated by our clothing or mannerisms), this separation is less important.

* *I never buy alcoholic drinks.* When I am at a sex-focused club or bar, I'll buy a Diet Coke.

* *I never drink more than a single drink (approximately) when working.* I'm a very light drinker; 1½ is my limit if I want to remain coherent and not lie there giggling, waiting for him to do me. Few men pay a hooker to just lie there.

* *If a man wants a long-term relationship, I will not have sex with him until we have dated at least three times.* And these dates will be public "getting to know you" outings. By taking the physical element out of the way, we can get to know each other and see if something lasting might be there for us. I get seriously propositioned by men daily. Most of them seek nothing more than casual sex. Since most will treat me like a prostitute, I forthrightly ask for and receive payment in cash. I'm not choosy. And I fall in love too quickly. To protect myself from myself, I insist that men who desire a more serious, long-term relationship prove it with time and attention, not their cash.

* *No casual sex with men.* This is a mantra I repeat constantly and fail to heed. I get plenty of physical and emotional attention as an escort and from my long-term relationships, so why am I always seeking it out? It's either "sex equals money" or "sex equals love." I've had lots of sex with tranny grrrls, but that feels different. It's comforting and creates a safe haven for our emotions.

* *I do not travel to meet new clients.* I often get offers to travel out of Manhattan, but I insist that men who are interested in sharing more than an evening with me first visit me and decide if I am their kind of girl. The wrong time to discover that I'm not their type is just after I've stepped off an airplane in their town.

* *I don't say more than is needed to a client.* It is best to listen to whatever fantasy or illusion they have and try to give it to them. Clients have no interest in who I am or what I think.

* *I am not online to engage in cybersex or pen-pal chat.* I want my cyber relationships to evolve toward the physical; otherwise, I have no interest.

* The subways are not an option. A working tranny grrrl displays herself in an unambiguous, flashy way. It is unsafe for me to make that sort of statement within the confined and unsympathetic spaces of the New York City subway system. The same applies if I am not working but it's after midnight.

* I never acknowledge hecklers. It can only get worse.

* I never acknowledge compliments from strangers on the street. When they realize they're talking to a transexual, it can get nasty.

* I never carry ID if I'm planning to engage in illegal activities.

* I always carry ID if I'm planning to engage in legal activities.

* I always carry safe-sex materials and enough makeup items in my purse to spend the night out. Be prepared.

* Prostitution is work and doesn't count as cheating in a monogamous relationship. Business is not romance and should not be compared to it. My boyfriends and I do not agree about this.

* Opposites attract. As a white, 30-something, educated, Wasp tranny grrrl, I am often instantly turned on by taller (rarely found, alas), younger, stronger, working-class men of color—especially from the Caribbean.

* Uniforms are sexy. What can I say? Fire-boys are *always* sexy. Police officers are often sexy. But this may just be my love for doughnuts. UPS drivers are sexy and—surprise!—approachable. I don't understand why so many UPS drivers are hot for transwomen.

* I love beard stubble on a tranny grrrl. I especially enjoy the way drag queens change as morning approaches and their beards push through the makeup. A turn-on every time.

* Boyfriends of trannies get special privileges. I lose emotional control with a man who is proud to publicly date trannies. Unfortunately, most of these men occupy a less than desirable place in society. Many are unemployed; some are pimps, dealers, and addicts who can be possessive and abusive.

* Rules can be broken.

Transy House
Rusty Mae Moore

Rusty Mae Moore is a woman of transexual experience who has been on the faculty of Hofstra University for many years. Writer, folksinger, cyclist, woodworker, and mother of Transy House, she lives in Brooklyn, N.Y., with her lover, Chelsea Goodwin.

Transy House is the name by which our loose collective of transpeople living in the Park Slope section of Brooklyn is known. The actual house where we live is a funky 100-year-old town house on the "ghetto" fringe of the "South Slope." I bought the house in 1994 and moved in during August with two other transwomen, Chelsea Goodwin and Julia Murray. The three of us had been sharing an apartment for several years in North Bellmore on Long Island (spanning the period during which Julia and I came out full-time). We were all living as women 24/7 when we moved to Brooklyn.

I wanted to live in Park Slope because I wanted to be near my children who were living there with their other parent. The real estate agent told the neighbors the house had been sold to "a doctor," so the first neighborhood reaction to us was some disappointment that I was only a Ph.D. They thought they were in line for some free medical advice. When we moved in, there was no perceptible reaction to us aside from normal interest in new neighbors. As our friends came to visit and as more transpeople came to live at the house, we became notorious throughout the immediate neighborhood as "that house with all the queens." It seemed to be a surprise to some people that the house was owned by a transperson.

Our house shares a common wall with another house that is the mirror image of ours. This space was occupied by the grandchildren of an elderly Italian couple who had lived there for 40 years and then moved to Staten Island. From the first we had a lot of contact with one of the cousins, Annette. She was 21, living in the two downstairs floors with her three children and their father. The father was from the local street culture and had reputedly been involved in unsavory business at one point. He had many young male friends who sat on the front stoop or stood in the street talking and smoking pot. The macho men in this coterie had a hard time with the transpeople going in and out of the house. At first some would scream "That's a man, that's a man in a dress" as one of us walked by. The children up the street learned from them to hurl epithets at us as we went about our business. We turned a deaf ear to this abuse and by ignoring it maintained the upper hand in this tense relationship.

The majority of the people in the neighborhood said nothing. After a few years people began to come to us for help—from small loans to advice about dealing with various bureaucracies.

Annette took us to her heart and made friends with everyone in the house. She is a woman who seems to love being a part of trans culture. Since she was the granddaughter of one of the oldest families in the neighborhood and was a key opinion leader among the young people on the block, the general attitude toward us was positive in spite of the bashing from her husband's friends.

In the fall of the first year, Kristiana Th'mas, a tall African-American transwoman who was a photographer at the Workers' World Party, came to live with us. All of the people in the house have political orientations to the left of center in some aspects, but Kristiana tended to have a rigid Marxist approach that often clashed with Chelsea's intellectual approaches and led to bitter arguments.

In January a young transwoman named Antonia "Marilyn" Cambareri came to live with us at Chelsea's invitation. She "came out" as she walked through our front door. She had been living in the closet in a leftist collective in Michigan that was not supportive of her trans-gendered nature. Marilyn took a lot of heat on the street around Transy House because she was young and sexy and too insecure about her appearance to be able to ignore the harassment of the young men on the street or turn it back on them. She was sexually open to any man who showed an interest in her. This proved to be a pattern for many of the young people who passed through Transy House over the years, and has made relationships with the neighborhood more difficult.

Everyone in the house frequented a Times Square drag club named Sallie's II during this period. Chelsea and Julia and I were already known in the club. As Transy House people began to appear at balls and shows as a recognizable group, we gained presence in the club and street scenes as a kind of "house." The difference was that we were known to focus on political and social change rather than the demi-monde of the balls. We developed a unique reputation as living openly, in our own house, with mainstream jobs such as legal secretary, tele-marketer, photographer, and college professor. We were among the few activists at that time in New York who pushed for the political involve-ment of the girls in the clubs and on the street.

Another aspect of the Transy House subculture is that residents are always involved in intellectual debate and making music and art. Chelsea has a wonderful library of European and American 20th-century literature and politics and a big collection of key works in queer history. As our life at Transy House has evolved, we have adopted the goal of accumulating and cataloging as much information on trans culture as we can. When Dr. Leo Wollman passed away in 1998, his widow asked us to take all of his professional papers and other material on transexuals. Dr. Wollman was a colleague of Harry Benjamin.

Inspired by our friend Joan Nestle, the founder of the Lesbian Herstory Archives, we established the Wollman Archives of Transgender History and Culture. In 1999 we were given the extensive transgender library of Lew Brewster, one of the key early leaders of the queer rights movement in New York and for 30 years the proprietor of his famous Lee Brewster's Mardi Gras Boutique in New York City.

The house is bursting with books, which are piled about precariously in the midst of antiques, the belongings of eight to 12 people, Santaria candles, several litters of kittens, and two or three dogs. Many leaders of the trans community visit the house when they pass through New York from the U.S. hinterlands or other parts of the world. The house has been the subject of four video documentaries, and one master's thesis (by a Norwegian student of social anthropology).

In 1996 Chelsea reestablished contact with Sylvia Rivera, who at that time was homeless and living on the Christopher Street piers with a group of homeless queers. Chelsea brought Sylvia to the Metropolitan Gender Network as a speaker. We were all taken by her spirit and shocked by her worn appearance. Chelsea and I agreed that if there was one thing we could do for the community, it would be to provide a living space for Sylvia Rivera. We felt as if we had a living relic of our queer history with us, our queen in exile.

Chelsea had regaled me with stories of Sylvia Rivera and STAR House for years. I had been impressed with the idea of trans people taking care of their own, and this was part of our inspiration for making Transy House into a collective living arrangement for transpeople. After Sylvia came to stay with us she came to see Transy House as a kind of successor to STAR House and became a great supporter of the concept of transpeople helping transpeople learn the skills needed to survive in society. Sylvia and her coconspirator Marsha P. Johnson led the way for us.

Without a doubt, the single greatest positive influence of Transy House has been to provide a space in which Sylvia could get her feet under her again and return to her work as a political activist. Sylvia was the most charismatic political leader we had in the trans community, the one best able to bridge the gaps between people of color, sex workers, and the broader queer community.

By the end of 2001, with seven years of experience living collectively with trans people at Transy House, I am often exhausted, despairing, frustrated, and angry. It is hard to live in an overcrowded space, with everyone wanting to play their music and have their friends over and not everyone willing to wash dishes or clean the hallways. Even though everyone pays rent in cash or in kind, there is still a steady drain on my resources to cover the cost of broken furniture, smashed walls, burned-out appliances, broken dishes, and stolen tools. Overriding these problems is the sense of satisfaction we get when a young person comes in and marvels that this is the first time in their life they have been in a social environment where they can be themselves as a transperson.

The house has an open and accepting culture. Not everyone knows how to behave within this openness. Some people have substance abuse problems. Some people have psychological problems. We try to deal with these issues from the perspective of a supportive family. I am the final decision-maker in the house, but Chelsea takes on the brunt of day-to-day management. Before Sylvia's death this year, I relied a great deal on her counsel, especially with respect to relational problems that developed. Kristiana is a big help in keeping food and cleaning supplies stocked and in shouldering a lot of responsibility for cleaning and maintenance.

Transy House is just one of other collective experiences of its type, from STAR House in the early 1970s to Tiffany House in the 1980s to the others today across the country. Trans people are often rejected by their families, left without resources, and thrown into the street to survive as best they can. For the young and poorly educated, sex work is often the only option. Social services agencies are not accepting of transgendered people. The homeless shelter system forces beautiful young women to sleep and shower with men. The police tend to arrest many transwomen on the charge of "suspicion of loitering with the intent to commit prostitution." The demand for help in New York is overwhelming. Day after day we receive telephone calls from agencies and social workers asking if we can provide shelter for transwomen or transmen. The house is always overwhelmed by people, and we simply have to say no 95% of the time.

I believe that collective houses based on the family approach like Transy House may offer an option for dealing with the practical issues of living that face trans people. It is an approach we can adopt in the trans community to take care of our own in a caring and supportive manner.

The Gender Cops Work Overtime
Gina Reiss

*Gina Reiss is managing director of GenderPAC. She has served
as executive director of the New Jersey Lesbian and Gay Coalition,
cochair of the Federation of Statewide LGBT Advocacy Organizations,
and action vice president of the New Jersey chapter of the National
Organization for Women.*

The Gender Cops work overtime, form unions, walk beats. The Gender
Cops have big strong arms, hard hands, harder stares. *Whatthe
fuckareyou?*

The Gender Cops make no arrests, just hand out sentences, to genderqueers like Fran and me.

Fran's bangs, large hips, round breasts, my face. My twin and me
and the cops. They're out tonight, walking the beat, watching for crime.
My twin and me, we're on the run.

Fran has my face, gets the same stares from the same men. She has
the girl body, girl clothes. Long hair, soft dresses, softer eyes, heeled
shoes. I look at her, see me/not me.

I'm the boy: boy clothes, boy body. Narrow hips, short hair, muscled
arms. Shined loafers, oxford shirts, boxer shorts.

We always have one mind, Fran and me, a twin thing. We're two
equal halves of one full gender.

The Gender Cops hate us both. Hate Fran and want to fuck her. Hate me and want to fuck me up.

We keep on walking. The Gender Cops watch us pass. They weigh the odds, then let us go. This time we walk.

We cross the street. Another block, another squad. They pick us up. Light turns green; we start to walk.

Alex is my brother. Soft hair, cute smile. "There's no Santa," he tells Mom.

She has a friend call. "Ho, ho, ho," he says. "I'm Santa. You don't believe in me," delighting Alex, scared half to death.

"Good little boy?" Santa asks.

"Oh, yes," swears Alex.

"What is your wish for Christmas?" Santa asks.

"A hundred Barbie dolls!" screams Alex at the phone.

Santa takes his time with that one.

"Well, you be a good boy. Santa will see you at Christmas."

Next day Mom asks, "Who called?"

Alex screams, "Santa called!"

"What'd you ask for?" Mama asks.

"A hundred G.I. Joes," Alex answers.

True story; Alex knew. The Gender Cops are out. They work overtime, form unions, watch little boys.

We pass the next corner, turn left. One squad hands us off. Another picks us up, walks patrol, stands a post. The Garden is in sight.

My other brother, Peter, hates soccer, plays with girls. At practice he starts to cry, leaves the field. Boys follow, calling names, making faces.

Mom reaches down, holds him close, wipes his face. Petey's tears leave long, wet tracks, cross his cheeks, leave his chin. His face is a window in the rain. I look through, see his pain.

Mom looks at me. "I have to toughen him up," she says.

"Don't you dare," I say, then shout.

But no sound comes. My mouth won't work. Mom looks away. Pete looks at me.

I'm on my porch, our new house. I'm just 12—the "new kid." A girl from next door walks by, wants to kiss, thinks I'm a boy.

A year later my first kiss, feels strange, something wrong. I let go, get mushy. Then pushy and on top. He's shy, pushes off, rolls away, swipes his hair. "You're the girl. I'm the boy. I control."

One of the boys, I beat them up, spit better, jump farther, run faster. The class joker. Girls laugh, boys glare. My twin, always watching my back.

After school, I kiss a girl. Feels right. I'm not a boy. Not a girl. A boy/girl, that's me.

Madison Garden. We round the corner. Go inside, find our seats. Settle in. I get up.

"Gotta pee," and then I'm off. Stand in line, ignore more stares.

I walk inside, get yanked back. A large white woman, rosy cheeks. My collar's in her hand.

"It says 'Women's Room,'" she yells.

I lift my shirt, walk back in.

The Gender Cops work overtime, form unions, walk beats. Gender Cops carry large arms, hard hands, and harder stares. *Whatthefuckareyou?* Gender Cops make no arrests, just hand down sentences, to queers like me.

Epilogue

Gender Rights Are Human Rights
Riki Wilchins

The following is based on a speech originally presented September 2000 at OutGiving—an annual donor retreat hosted by the Gill Foundation, the country's largest LGBT funding group.

Someone has just been kind enough to remind me that Tim Gill is sitting right here and that I'd better be good. So I just want you to know I'm not intimidated—much. And since I'm not, I want to tell you about the last time I *was* intimidated.

Patricia Ireland had invited me to address NOW's National Board on transgender inclusion.

For reasons which now escape me, I thought it would be in good taste to remind them of NOW's purges of lesbian and bisexual women in 1969 and their resulting confrontation with the Lavender Menace.

So I wore my black Transexual Menace T-shirt with its blood-dripping red letters. Patricia introduced me and then sat down, looking politely and encouragingly up.

Now, there are only two ways to do this.

Way 1 relies largely upon guilt coupled with earnest appeals to good old-fashioned liberal values like tolerance and acceptance.

To wit: You should include us poor trannies because it's the right thing to do, there are all kinds of women, after surgery we're physically pretty much like you, etc., etc., etc.

Way 1 depends on your audience's goodwill and well-honed con-sciences, and it often works.

But it's no fun—not to do and not to be on the receiving end of. I mean, who enjoys feeling guilty? Between you and me, I'd much rather be bitchy.

So I chose Way 2.

Now, Way 2 consists of building a postmodern argument so hope-lessly perverse and downright insubordinate it undermines the very par-adigm that created the issue of trans inclusion and made my presence there to address it necessary in the first place.

Way 2 is a lot more fun.

So I looked around the room at all these powerful, very serious, and intimidating women, and said, "Many of you are no doubt wondering why a man with a vagina is standing here lecturing you on where femi-nism should go…" I look down at Patricia here and notice she is now searching vigorously in her wrist for a good vein to open. "But consider for a moment that men with vaginas are what gender looks like when it's deregulated, and so my presence here today is a sign of your success and not your failure."

And they got it. I was not going to plead for their acceptance or tol-erance or ask them to validate my poor white postoperative body as female.

Instead I was going to recruit them to take a step with me out of the old paradigm that had created these boundaries between us, these boundaries we were now so busily engaged in surmounting.

I was going to invite them to have a different kind of dialogue, one whose origins lie in a totally difference place, one where our task was not to surmount our separateness but rather to explore the strengths of our already being together.

And that's what I'd like to do with you this evening.

If you hoped to hear a lot about how we're all basically bisexual or about how it feels to be a "man trapped in a woman's body," this is going to be a bit disappointing. I've never been trapped in anyone else's body, and I hope you haven't either, although I was once trapped in Manhattan for almost 18 years and suspect it feels pretty much the same. And if you want someone to tell you why you should expand your charitable giving to include bi and trans, I'm none too good at that either.

And as far as my gender is concerned, I admit I do still occasionally awake quivering in the night with the conviction that I am trapped in the wrong culture.

But we're not going to do Way 1 tonight.

I'm not going to tell you about Kinsey sexuality scales from 1 to 6 or tell you that debating bi and transpeople in the gay movement is like debating gays in the military: They've always been here, they always will be, and they've always given and served with courage and distinction.

I'm not going to tell you that as far as our apparently endless public debate over whether gender belongs in a gay movement, the boys we beat up after school, the girls we humiliated for looking just like the gym teacher, and all those people from Liberace on down your mom and mine "just knew" were "homosexuals"—all that was about gender.

Because the gays and lesbians picked out for harassment or assault are almost always targeted because of their gender; because they aren't "just like everyone else"; because they are "visibly queer."

So if you want to know what it's *really* like to transcend narrow gender stereotypes and what it costs, please don't come up afterward and ask me. Just look into your own childhood or turn to that nice person sitting on your right or your left. Because chances are, they've been there.

And so it's not so much a question of including transgender as of recognizing that gender has always been a part of a gay agenda and always will be.

I'm not going to make these and a dozen other telling points we both know I could make. First, because if you're here today, you're probably smart enough to know most of this. And second, because I don't think our work as activists should come from a place of guilt or tolerance or even from wanting people to feel included.

Giving is activism. And I believe we do activism because we have no other choice. Because in our guts we have those three impractical and totally inconvenient things: a passion to make the world a better place, a spiritual faith that it is possible, and a personal vision of what it should look like.

For the next 15 minutes I'd like to recruit you on a ride into another paradigm, another discussion of our bodies, identities, and desires.

So fasten your genders. It's going to be a bumpy night.

I know this ride's going to be bumpy, because I've been on it myself. Twenty years ago I was telling anyone who would listen that I *was* "trapped in a man's body." My FTM friends were telling everyone they were "men trapped in women's bodies." And collectively we sounded like a bunch of internal organs plotting a prison break.

That's how it was for me in 1980.

But then last month I was at Camp Trans outside the Michigan Womyn's Music Festival where they'd just kicked us out again. I was throwing football with a boy-identified dyke named Ellen who prefers being called Jesse.

Jesse was leaving the Lesbian Avengers, and I asked him why. He replied that it was because of that tired old lesbian pecking order.

I told him I knew *exactly* what he meant. The cutest lesbians are always at the top, the least attractive at the bottom, and so on and so forth.

Jesse looked at me pityingly and said, "Well, dude...actually it's more like the fags and tranny boyz are at the top; FTMs, boychicks, andros, and faggot-identified dykes are in the middle; and the butches and femmes are at the bottom."

I looked at him and said, "Obviously. *I* knew that. I just wanted to see if *you* knew that."

For Jesse, the dyke community he knows is mostly "boys." As he told me, the right word might be "fags," "hets," "bi's," or something else related to sexual orientation, but among bio grrrls, T-boyz, andros, and tranny girls, that doesn't make sense "because it requires silly things like gender."

The identities you and I spent such time coming to grips with, coming out about, and defending at such great cost are not even an issue for these kids. They are beyond the boxes in which we have made our lives.

For many of them it's not about the right to be gay or lesbian, bi, trans, or even straight, but something they hold more dear: the right to be who and what they are, whole and complete and without omission, even if that means they don't fit any of the preexisting categories and have to make up whole new names for themselves on the spot.

I am reminded here that Audre Lorde taught us the Master's tools will never dismantle the Master's house.

Is it too much to say that the notion of the homosexual—and perhaps even gay identity itself—is not in some way an invention of heterosexuality? Perhaps even a reaffirmation—if only unconsciously—that the most important thing about us should be where we stand in relation to reproduction?

Would it be overreaching to say that just as light requires dark and male an opposing female, so gayness actually requires an antecedent and opposing straightness? So that instead of struggling against a heterocentric culture, gayness actually demands and solidifies it?

Is it possible these kids are on to something? That with these prefabricated identities of gay, lesbian, bisexual, and transgender we are so quick to occupy, we are still living in the Master's house? And so that when it comes to inclusion, we are less interested in tearing down the house than in building a small yet tastefully furnished addition out back? One that will hold Jesse and all these troubling new identities?

So I am very interested when my good friends at the Log Cabin Republicans say that they don't think gender belongs in a gay movement because it's not sexual orientation. Or when some activists denounce the "diluting" of gay rights with bi and trans issues. Because I take it as axiomatic that if what we want is a civil rights movement for gays and lesbians, then these voices are right: We should keep the walls around our movement intact and get on with our business.

But there's a funny thing about walls: They not only keep others out; they also keep us in.

We are on the verge of creating a movement that says to its own young: Be all you can be, go wherever your heart and mind and talent can take you. Just don't find out you're straight. Don't become too bisexual. Don't change your body or gender too much, and don't find out your struggle is too complicated by issues like age or race or class. Because if you do, we're not sure you'll still qualify to be represented in a gay and lesbian movement.

Such a movement, which sets out to free gay people, actually ends up erecting yet another set of barriers and constraints to keep them in.

It is beyond dispute that gay rights today, like feminism before it, is going from strength to strength.

Yet just as young women in droves are refusing to identify as feminists, so I routinely speak before groups of young queers like Jesse who refuse to identify as gay or straight because they don't want to leave any of their friends behind, because they don't want to be known by something as simplistic as who they sleep with, or because they don't even select their partners by sex.

They want not only their freedom *as* gay people but, paradoxically, also their freedom *not to be* gay—to have their primary social identities determined by something greater than whom they sleep with or even whom they love.

They are not seeking submersion into large, impersonal preexisting categories, but instead searching for newer, smaller ways to be and understand who they are. They are asking themselves a new sort of question: Who might I be, who would I see in the mirror each morning if I didn't have to be gay? What other "me's" could I be?

In fact, for 20-somethings with buzz-cut purple hair, bull-rings in their noses, and androgynous hip-hop clothes, the harassment they get at school, at work, and on the street is not just about orientation or even sex, but about gender.

And this is where I'd like to talk about my own organization, the Gender Public Advocacy Coalition. GenderPAC is the national advocacy organization working to end the violence and discrimination caused by gender stereotypes.

And here I mean gender in its widest sense—including sexual orientation, because I take it as self-evident that the mainspring of homophobia is gender: the notion that gay men are insufficiently masculine or lesbian women somehow necessarily inadequately feminine.

And I include sex, because I take it as obvious that what is behind misogyny and sexism is our society's astonishing fear and loathing around issues of vulnerability or femininity.

GenderPAC's work focuses on public education, legislative advocacy, and legal action, so we can all enjoy safer communities, fairer workplaces, and schools where each child is valued and respected.

To get an idea of how important, and moreover how urgent, that work is, consider this year:

• The partially decomposed body of a gay and two-spirit Navajo youth, Fred Martinez, was unearthed in Cortez, Colo.

• Incidents of school bullying surged, now accounting for one of the most common forms of school violence.

• Male-on-male gender harassment is now the source of one out of every seven new claims filed with the Equal Employment Opportunity Commission.

• Willie Houston, an African-American Nashville bus driver, was killed while celebrating his engagement by a man who became enraged at seeing him hold his fiancée's purse while she used the restroom. According to witnesses, his last words were, "Just remember, I'll always love you."

From the classroom to the boardroom, from reservations to city streets, transcending narrow gender stereotypes can get you—or your child—harassed, fired, bashed, or even killed.

Change won't come quickly. The struggle to end gender stereotypes has just begun. But with each step, we get closer to a society where all Americans can be all that they are, without fear, without omission. Because gender is too basic to be confined to any one group and too fundamental to leave anyone behind. Gender rights are human rights, and they are for all of us.

So perhaps the question here isn't so much a matter of you accepting us or of expanding your work to better include us but of possibly coming out to join us.

And all these confusing, even threatening, new identities are not barbarians at the gate but a doorway out. Their messiness is not the problem; it's the solution: a tactic, even an essential political goal.

Because success looks less like bi and trans inclusion than my friend Jesse, the football-throwing ex–Lesbian Avenger who personally identifies as a queer tranny boy but politically identifies as a dyke and who says someday he may want to take testosterone.

Success looks like messy new identities we don't like and can't name that create possibilities and freedoms we never intended.

So if by now some of you are wondering why a man with a vagina who lives with her lesbian lover is standing here lecturing you about where gay activism should go, consider that lesbian men with vaginas are what gay liberation looks like when desire is deregulated, and so my being here today is a sign of your success and not your failure.

I hope you will leave thinking less about how to refine the noun list (so no one feels excluded from our gay, lesbian, bisexual, transgender, intersex, leather queer, questioning, straight sympathetic, youth movement) and more about how to begin thinking of new foundations for our politics. Foundations as rich and rude and messy and complex as the lives we lead, the challenges we face, and the scars we bear. Foundations demanding that we build bridges to one another instead of burn them, that we stress our commonalities instead of our differences. Foundations reminding us that discrimination is like my new cable-knit sweater—I pull it here and it also tugs somewhere else. So that it's never just about gender, and always about gender and sexual orientation or gender and race or gender and age or gender and class. So that whenever there's a wall, we should be with those outside of it. And whenever there's a vote on inclusion, you and I should be standing among those voted on.

No matter who is included, we should always be left behind because, as Alice Walker says, "Never be the only one in the room." And so I take it to be our responsibility as activists to always stand with those smaller voices forgotten at the margins. Just as I take it to be our responsibility to see which faces are alone or unrepresented in the room.

Because, in the final analysis, the moral center of a movement is not defined by how well and how long we fight for our own rights. Important as that is, it's also enlightened self-interest: We all want our own rights. The moral center of a movement is defined by how well and how long we fight for those who are not us, for those more easily left behind.

And so for me, the whole point of a gender movement is that it's not only about those familiar specimens inevitably corralled in the Binary Zoo: the stone butches and diesel dykes, drag kings and queens, leather dykes and dyke daddies, radical fairies and nelly fags, the transexuals, transgendered, cross-dressers, and intersexed. It's also about the 17-year-old Midwestern cheerleader who ruins her health with anorexia because "real women" are supposed to be unnaturally thin. It's about the 46-year-old Joe Six-Pack who hits a crowded school bus on his way home from the bar because "real men" are supposed to be heavy drinkers. It's about an aging lesbian who suffers through a wholly unnecessary hysterectomy because certain kinds of gendered bodies simply don't matter as much. And it's about an artistic, shy, and entirely straight little boy who is taunted and assaulted in school each day because within that environment he is perceived as genderqueer, gender-different, or simply gender-vulnerable.

In short, ensuring full equality for all Americans regardless of gender is not only about Matthew Shepard, Brandon Teena, Freddie Martinez, and Willie Houston—people who lost their lives, who were picked out and picked on because they were slight or gay or blond or black or visibly queer—but about working until each and every one of us is freed from this most pernicious, divisive, and destructive insanity called gender-based stereotypes.

Thank you.